Lectures
on Godmanhood

VLADIMIR SOLOVYOV

Lectures on Godmanhood

With an Introduction by Peter Peter Zouboff

Semantron

San Rafael, Ca

Second, facsimile edition
Semantron, 2007
First edition, Dennis Dobson Limited, 1948

For information, address:
Semantron, P.O. Box 151011
San Rafael, California 94915, USA

Library of Congress Cataloging-in-Publication Data

Solovyov, Vladimir Sergeyevich, 1853–1900.
[Chteniia o Bogochelovechestve. English]
Lectures on Godmanhood / Vladimir Solovyev ; with an intro
by Peter Peter Zouboff. — Reprint ed.
p. cm.
Originally published: London : D. Dobson, 1948.
Includes bibliographical references (p.).
ISBN 978-1-59731-250-9 (pbk.: alk. paper)
ISBN 978-1-59731-275-2 (hardback: alk. paper)
1. Religion—Philosophy. 2. Wisdom—Religious aspects.
I. Zouboff, Peter Peter, 1893–1964. II. Title.
BL51.S61813 2007
200—dc22   2007027056

CONTENTS

ACKNOWLEDGMENTS

In publishing this work I wish to express my profound gratitude to Professor Clarence A. Manning, of the Department of Eastern European Languages, Columbia University, for his untiring interest in it and in all my studies; and to pay deep respect to the former Head of the same Department, Professor John Dyneley Prince.

My very warm appreciation is also due to Professors Herbert W. Schneider, Irwin Edman, and Horace L. Friess, of the Philosophy Department, for their invaluable advice and guidance. I must not neglect thanking Dr. Arthur P. Coleman, Department of Eastern European Languages, and the staffs of the Libraries of Columbia University, the Union Theological Seminary, and the New York Public Library. Nor can I leave out the praise due to the painstaking labours of my wife in the preparation of the manuscript and publication.

PETER ZOUBOFF

NOVEMBER 19, 1943
NEW YORK

FOREWORD

VLADIMIR Solovyev holds an important rôle in the history of Russian religious and philosophical thought. Yet it is very difficult to define that rôle with full and sufficient clarity. The study of Solovyev has just commenced, and the present dissertation and translation of the Lectures on Godmanhood is far from an attempt to solve all the problems that are involved.

First of all what is Godmanhood? It has long been recognized that the differences between the Orthodox and Roman Catholic Churches are not to be found in their differences as to the great dogmas of the Church and the articles of the Creed. The Orthodox, Roman Catholic, Anglican and many of the Protestant Churches definitely accept the doctrine of the Incarnation and in the same way they accept the doctrine of the Atonement. So far it may be said that these doctrines are universal and it is easy to find sources here and there to prove the various points which are made.

It is remarkable that Solovyev, in accepting the doctrine of the Incarnation, devotes little space to any discussion of the person of Christ, the God-man. We are all familiar with what is called the extension of the Incarnation in the Liturgy or the Mass. Solovyev, and with him many of the later Russian thinkers, is interested rather in that phrase of the Epistle to the Romans (viii. 22), 'For we know that the whole creation groaneth and travaileth in pain together until now'. Godmanhood is the problem of restoring all mankind, and indeed the whole of the universe to its proper position according to the plan and providence of God as foreordained before the beginning of the world. As Donald Lowrie says in his introduction to the translation of Bulgakov's *The Orthodox Church*, 'The Orthodox concepts of conciliarity (the best word for the quite untranslatable "sobornost"), of salvation as a process of becoming divine, not only for men but for the whole created world, will open vistas as new as the proposal here made of a basis for reunion rarely suggested in Western Christianity'.

It is still too early to trace all the highways and byways by which the Eastern Church maintained its attitude through the centuries. Some instinct made it draw back, even in its darkest hours, from the full acceptance of that Westernizing process which was ever present as the political power of the West grew and that of the Byzantine Empire and Eastern Christianity declined. There has been a steady shift of emphasis in Orthodox thought ever since those days when the promised help to save Constantinople, as a return for the recognition of the Papacy

7

ended in despair and the great Church of Agia Sophia, the Divine Wisdom, was turned into a mosque.

The Russian thinkers of the nineteenth century played an important rôle in that process. Of course many of them knew Western and Germanic philosophy, but some of them, like Kireyevsky, found, surprisingly, many of the same ideas in the writings of their own Fathers. Very few modern scholars are familiar with all the authors of the Eastern Church. Solovyev, with all his faults, acquired an enormous grasp of theological and mystical literature. He, like his predecessors and followers 'was extremely sensitive' to such problems as the religious meaning of history, of creativity, of culture (Bolgakov, *The Wisdom of God*, p. 21). In connection with the doctrine of Sophia, Bulgakov says: 'Solovyev's doctrine of Sophia is undoubtedly syncretistic; side by side with ancient Orthodox tradition we can detect elements derived from the ancient gnostic systems, together with the obvious influence of Western sophiology in the writings of Boehme and others. All this is further complicated by his own poetic mysticism. In his poetry Solovyev is indeed very far from the Orthodox conception of Sophia. . . It is very important to emphasize this general link between Solovyev and all the preceding currents of Russian thought, for his Christian philosophy in a certain sense embraces them all' (save for his 'Romanizing' recognition of the primacy of the Pope—op. cit. p. 23ff).

For this reason it has seemed wise to present in the introduction to this translation an introduction which expresses a sort of summary of the Russian attitude to Vladimir Solovyev and not to attempt to separate from his vast reading the direct sources of each of his ideas. To do this adequately there would be needed volumes of research in all the literatures of the world and even then the separate specialist would be able to pick flaws and point out where Solovyev or his critics had erred in his interpretation of the vast mass of material involved.

There can be no doubt that Solovyev, if not an original thinker, was an unusually sensitive thinker (Florovsky, *Puti Russkago Bogosloviya*, p. 318). He was a source of inspiration, even when he was not followed, and in these Lectures on Godmanhood he reached at the start of his career his greatest success. His influence is still continuing, and a comparison of his *Three Conversations* with Monsignor Robert Hugh Benson's *The Lord of the World*, will show how far he was from ordinary Western thought. He came from a rich and still not fully understood tradition, and this translation with the introduction by Dr. Zouboff, should be of the greatest value to Western scholarship.

CLARENCE A. MANNING

COLUMBIA UNIVERSITY,
NEW YORK

INTRODUCTION

1. Solovyev: Philosopher, Mystic and Poet

VLADIMIR Sergeyevich Solovyev was born in Moscow, January 16, 1853. His father, the eminent historian Sergey Mikhailovich Solovyev, was an erudite man of broad vision, deeply interested in religion as well as in science and in politics. His mother, Poliksena Vladimirovna (née Romanova), belonged to an old noble family which included among its members the Ukrainian philosopher Gregory Skovoroda (1722-94). An itinerant wise man who wandered throughout Ukraine and called on everyone to lead a more upright life, Skovoroda found that happiness rests on inner peace, knowledge of one's self, and self sacrifice; his life and example were of greater importance than his written work. The traditions about him preserved in the Solovyev family are said to have had a considerable influence in the development of the young Vladimir.

His grandfather, the Reverend Michael Solovyev, had perhaps an even greater influence upon the boy. A God-fearing child, Vladimir was quite convinced that his grandfather was in direct communication with God. And one day not long before his death, the Reverend Michael took his little grandson to the Sanctuary and blessed him for the service of the Church.

Solovyev's early childhood was spent in most favourable surroundings, in the home of his parents, in Moscow. His primary education he received at home. Later on he attended the Fifth Moscow Gymnasium, a school rated the best in the city, many of the students of which in subsequent years attained great prominence. Here Solovyev manifested an ardent love of reading and excellent scholastic aptitude, graduating with a gold medal.

At the age of fifteen, Solovyev entered the University of Moscow. During the first two years he studied in the department of Physics and Mathematics, and in 1870 was accepted as a third-year student by the Faculty of History and Philosophy; he also took a course at the Moscow Theological Academy at the same time.

His studies in philosophy began shortly after he entered the University. Spinoza soon became his favourite philosopher, especially because in his writings Solovyev found a philosophical basis for the spiritual unity of the world-view which he sought. During this period Solovyev was fluctuating between extremes, changing from faith and

piety to atheism, from nihilism to religious philosophy. He passed
through socialism, and even communism, with a fervent belief that
socialism would 'restore mankind' and 'redeem history'. His close
friend, L. M. Lopatin, writes that he had never met anyone as firmly
convinced—for a time—of the final triumph of the truth among men
as the result of a socialist reorganization of society.[1] But then Solovyev
took an interest in John Stuart Mill's criticism of materialism, and came
to the conclusion that the substance of matter is as incomprehensible
as the essence of spirit, and that materialism (and hence socialism also)
has no real foundation.

Kant's theory of knowledge convinced Solovyev that (the empirical)
knowledge does not contradict faith, and that religion and science may
be reconciled. But although it did justify a search for God, Kant's
philosophy did not satisfy Solovyev; for in Kant's presentation, God
was not the living God of Christianity, but a mere postulate of practical
reason.

Schopenhauer gave him greater comfort. In his philosophy Solovyev
saw a religious understanding of life, and a spiritual foundation for
Darwin's theory of biological evolution as well as for Spencer's theory
of social progress. In the light gained from the study of Schopenhauer,
Solovyev came to regard the life of the whole universe as a process of
its moral purification.

Under the influence of Schopenhauer's philosophy Solovyev became much interested in Buddhism, and proceeded to study other religions of the East. He was disillusioned, however, and then undertook
an earnest study of the German idealists: Fichte, Schelling, and Hegel.

In the positive romanticism of Schelling, Solovyev found a reconciliation of the widely divergent views of Schopenhauer and Hegel.
Schelling's ideas dominated the Russian mind at that time almost as
universally as had Hegel's philosophy a while before. In Germany,
'during the last period of his work, Schelling lost his influence because
of his change from rationalism to the "philosophy of revelation", but
in Russia his work came to be reflected in a quite different manner':
Schelling became 'the teacher of the Russian religious philosophy'.[2]

August Comte's positivism brought Solovyev to the conclusion that
empirical knowledge is limited to the phenomenal reality only.

Solovyev's interest in religion revived, and by 1872 he became again
a zealous Christian.

Solovyev studied now the Fathers of the Church and the early
Christian philosophers, and read the recent mystics. Among the influences in this new development should be noted that of St. Augustine

[1] L. M. Lopatin, 'The Philosophical Solovyev', in *Put* (The pathway), 1911;
    p. 55.

[2] Prince E. Troubetskoy, *The World-View of V. S. Solovyev*, II, p. 52.

(especially in regard to the doctrine of the freedom of the will); also of Swedenborg and Boehme, Paracelsus and Baeder.

Plato meant so much to Solovyev that he made a translation of his works.

This evolution of Solovyev's interests and development in philosophy may be traced in his correspondence with his friends; his letters to E. V. Romanov, in particular, may be regarded as his philosophical diary.

In the year 1873 Solovyev graduated from the University and published his first article, *The Mythological Process in Ancient Paganism*. *The Crisis of Western Philosophy*, his next work, was presented as his Master's thesis; the defence of it was so successful that he was appointed a Fellow of the University of Moscow in the Faculty of Philosophy (1874). Shortly afterwards he was sent to England for research in the Indian and Gnostic philosophies at the British Museum.

He arrived in England in 1875. As the subject of his studies might suggest, his work was marked by a decided emphasis upon mysticism. Solovyev had shown an interest in mysticism in earlier years, especially in his poetry. In the poem entitled the 'Three Meetings', he described three mystical visions of what he called the 'Eternal Feminine'. Once, he writes in that poem, when he was nine years of age, he was stirred with a feeling of jealousy while at Church on a Sunday; during the singing of the Cherubic hymn in the course of the Liturgy, he perceived, suddenly, the blue of the sky all around him, and in his own soul; and through this blue he saw the 'Eternal Womanhood', woven as it were of blue ether, and holding in her hand a blossom from unearthly countries. She nodded in his direction, smiling at him with a radiant smile, and then disappeared in the mist. His soul became blind to all mundane things, and the childish love which caused his jealousy became repugnant to him. A devotion to this 'Eternal Feminine' grew within him; with time, it developed into a cult—the more so because he identified that 'Eternal Womanhood' with the Sophia, or Wisdom, of the Scriptures. And now, in his work in London, he again busied himself with this problem, the mystery of the Sophia.

While at work in the museum, he addressed this mysterious being on one occasion with a prayer asking her to show him her face, which he had not seen since childhood, although he had felt her presence on several occasions. At once everything around him was covered with a sky-blue colour, with a golden shade about it, and the face of 'Sophia' shone before him. On another occasion he asked his mysterious visitor if he might not see her in full, but was told in reply, 'be in Egypt'. Solovyev sailed for Cairo, and there awaited the desired meeting. At length an inner voice said to him, 'I am in the desert; go, seek me there'. He went to the desert, was seized by a band of Bedouins, and when they freed him, lay down in the dark of the night. After a long while he heard a voice saying to him, 'Sleep, my poor friend'. He went to sleep. When he awoke, he saw 'the earth and the circumference of the sky as if breathing with roses, and amidst the roses and the purple of a heavenly radiance, with the eyes full of a flame sky-blue, "Thou lookedst out, as at the first radiance of the first day of creation".' It was the Eternal Feminine. The vision lasted but a moment but in that instant Solovyev caught a glimpse of the 'imperishable purple', and felt 'the radiation of Divinity'.

The following excerpts from his 'prayer for a revelation of the supreme mystery', found in Solovyev's note-book, bear out a further development of his notions concerning Sophia:

In the name of the Father and of the Son and of the Holy Ghost. An-Soph, (J) Yah, Soph-(J) Yah. . .[3]
O Thou, the most Holy Divine Sophia, the substantial image of beauty and the delight of the transcendentally extant God, the bright body of Eternity, the soul of the worlds and the queen-soul of all souls, by the fathomless blessedness of Thy first Son and beloved Jesus Christ, I implore Thee to descend into the prison of [the] soul, fill this darkness of ours with Thy radiancy, melt away the fetters on our spirit with the fire of love, grant us freedom and light, appear to us in a visible and substantial manner, become Thyself incarnate in us and in the world, restoring the fullness of the eons, so that the deep may be covered with a limit and God may become all in all.[4]

The Biblical and cabalistic, Gnostic and Christian elements mixed together in this invocation illustrate Solovyev's interest in spiritualism which he manifested in his subsequent sojourn in Cairo; he is said to have spent whole nights there in discussions of spiritualism with his friend, D. N. Zertelev, who was also a poet, a spiritualist, and a philosopher. In his later life, Solovyev was fully disillusioned in regard to spiritualism and considered spiritualist seances sinful.

In the year 1876 Solovyev returned to Moscow and resigned his position at the University. Appointed a member of the Committee on Education in the Ministry of Public Education, he established his residence in St. Petersburg, and started a series of public lectures at the University of St. Petersburg and at the (Institute of the) Higher Courses of Studies for Women. It was at this time that the 'Twelve Lectures Concerning Godmanhood' were delivered. They were so popular that the large hall where they were given was always crowded. All the leaders of the intellectual world—Dostoyevsky and Leo

[3]The English letter J, in 'Jah', or Jahve, Jehova, is read here as Y in 'Yah'; this is the way Solovyev connects Wisdom (Soph) and God (Jah) into 'Sophyah', for Sophia or Wisdom. *Sophya* (as well as Sophia) is a feminine Christian name, not uncommon in Russia.

[4]Quoted by K. Mochulsky in his book, *Vladimir Solovyev, His Life and Teaching;* p. 71.

Tolstoy among them—were present at these lectures. While Solovyev's charm and a gift of fiery eloquence added much to his popularity, the depth and originality of his thought began to attract the attention of the learned world.[5]

This was a very fruitful period of his life. He published during these years three of his major works: *The Philosophical Foundations of Integral Knowledge* (1877), the *Lectures Concerning Godmanhood* (1878), and the *Criticism of Abstract Principles* (1880). The last work was presented as his dissertation for the doctorate in Philosophy, which he brilliantly defended at the University of St. Petersburg on the sixth of April, 1880.[6]

On the 28th of March 1881, shortly after the assassination of Alexander II, Solovyev made a speech on capital punishment at the auditorium of the Credit Society; much to the surprise of the listeners, the speech ended with a plea for clemency for the assassins. Solovyev's argument was that evil cannot be overcome with evil; that Alexander III, as the Emperor anointed of God and a bearer of the highest conception of the truth, should pardon the murderers of his father.

The speech evoked an unusual excitement. In view of the reactions to it, Solovyev found it necessary to write to the Emperor directly:

Your Imperial Majesty and Most Gracious Sovereign: Undoubtedly Your Majesty was informed of the speech which I delivered on March 28th, [but] probably in a perverted, or at least exaggerated, manner. I deem it to be my duty, therefore, to report the matter to your Majesty as it actually occurred. Trusting that only the spiritual might of the truth of Christ can overcome the forces of evil and destruction, which in our days are manifesting themselves in such unprecedented dimensions; trusting also that the healthful organism of the Russian Nation lives and is moved by the Spirit of Christ; believing finally, that the Tzar of Russia is the supreme representative and the herald of the national spirit, the bearer of all the best in the Nation: I dared to profess this faith of mine from a public platform.

At the conclusion of my speech I said that the painful contemporary conditions present an unprecedented opportunity to the Russian Tzar to show the might of the Christian principle of supreme mercy, and that this act would constitute a great moral exploit which would exalt his power to an inaccessible height, and would establish his authority upon an unshakable foundation.

By granting pardon to the enemies of his own power, contrary to all the calculations of mundane wisdom, the Tzar would rise to a superhuman height and would demonstrate by that act the divine nature of his imperial authority,

---

[5]K. Mochulsky, op. cit. p. 71.

[6]A letter from P. Tchaikovsky, the well-known Russian composer, to Mrs. N. F. Meckk, (Oct. 19, 1879), may be cited as an example of the admiration and enthusiasm which the 'Criticism of Abstract Principles' had evoked at the time.

proving that within him resides the supreme spiritual might of the whole Russian Nation, by virtue of the fact that in the whole Nation there would be no one else capable of so sublime an act.

This is the essence of my speech which, to my great sorrow, was interpreted in a manner quite contrary to my intentions.

Your Imperial Majesty's faithful subject,

Vladimir Solovyev.

This letter is very characteristic of Solovyev. It shows the reality of his Christian convictions, as well as his courage in professing them.

When he submitted his resignation to the Minister of Public Education, the latter, Baron Nicholay, remarked, 'I did not ask you to do that'; for, indeed, no pressure was brought upon Solovyev to resign his governmental position. He decided to do so, however, in order to have complete freedom for the expression of his ideas in the future.

The remaining nineteen years of his life may be divided, from one point of view, into three periods.

From 1882 to 1889 Solovyev was concerned primarily with religious and ecclesiastical problems, and wrote the following works: *The Religious Foundations of Life* (1882); *The History and the Future of Theocracy* (Zagreb, 1886); and *La Russie et l'Eglise Universelle* (Paris, 1889).

From 1889 to 1895 he was preoccupied with problems of national and political interest, revealing himself a brilliant publicist.

Finally, from 1895 to 1900, the year of his death, he was once more engaged in religious and philosophical subjects. He set forth his system of ethics in the *Justification of the Good*, wrote the *Three Conversations* (which includes the 'Narration About the Antichrist', a striking conception of the end of the world) and started working out an analysis of gnosticism, but did not complete it.

Solovyev's works were collected by his friends and followers, and have been published in one complete edition. There are nine volumes of his philosophic and religious writings, three volumes of his correspondence[7], and one volume of poetry.

The latter was devoted mainly to the presentation of his mystical experiences, and to his ideas concerning the 'world-soul' and the 'eternal womanhood'. The poems show an absorbing interest in the 'eternal beauty', with an almost religious expectancy of its realization—and his own feeling that, somehow, there was a major discord in his own soul.

Solovyev was very kind. Everything he had went to the poor—not only money, but, literally, whatever he had. In private life he was helpless and impractical; with others, there was always an abundant spiritual vitality radiating from him: and with all that, an easily perceptible dualism in his whole personality—it seemed he lived in two different worlds at the same time.

[7] A fourth volume of his letters has recently been published.

He was aware of it, yet continued to be in private life quite rigid with himself, trying to conceal his ascetic tendencies by entertaining friends with an extravagant generosity.

There are no records of any serious or lasting attachment to any woman of flesh and blood, although he was in love more than once. (These romantic experiences may be found in his article, 'At the Dawn of a Misty Youth', published in the third volume of his letters). His romance with Mrs Hitrovo was mysterious and tragic.

He made several pilgrimages to the Optina Hermitage, and kept up a correspondence with its 'elders', or senior monks.

In 1900 Solovyev made his last public appearance, when he read his novel on the Antichrist. The passionate intensity of his mental work shattered his health. On the thirty-first of July, in 'Uzkoye', the country residence of Prince P. N. Troubetskoy, near Moscow, he passed away in the arms of his close friend, Prince S. N. Troubetskoy.

Just before his death, Solovyev received the last rites from the hands of a Russian Orthodox Priest, Father S. Belyayev. The funeral took place in the Chapel of Moscow University, where he had seen his first mystical vision during the Liturgy. His remains were buried at the cemetery of the Novodevitchy Convent in Moscow.

Solovyev's work was essentially a philosophy of Christian pragmatism.[8]

If the empirical Pragmatists fought against the divorce of the ideal from the practical, Solovyev fought with as much force and with a greater enthusiasm against the separation of the practical from the ideal —from the *Christian* ideal—which in itself means the integration of that polarity, first in the God-man Christ, and then in the man-godhood of Christianized humanity.

Thus the deification of mankind, for him, is the purpose of history; in the gradual penetration of the created world by the divine beginning, the changes and variations in the forms of social organization—as well as the evolution and variations in religious conceptions—represent but different stages of the nascent man-Godhood preparatory to the final realization of the universal God-manhood.

The dualism of the divine and the human, the spiritual and the natural, is thus a datum of experience, originally inevitable; but the final purpose of creation is the overcoming of that dualism, according to Solovyev—and his great pathos lies in his quest for a progressive unification of the practical with the ideal. The task of his whole life was the preaching of the marriage of humanity to Divinity, and not in a mere subjugation of one to the other, but through an integration of the evolving man-Godhood in the God-manhood of Christ.

In the long process of the gradual penetration of natural existence

[8]As a philosophy of Christianity, it was, of course, pure Idealism.

by—and with—the life and light of God, the latter could at first act upon man only externally, either restraining his natural being with an external discipline or enlightening his mind with the divine idea (which is the ideal). But at neither of these two—preparatory—stages had Divinity acquired any *real* hold on man. In order that the divine beginning could really *take possession* of him, man had to be first freed from the domination of the natural elements, in himself as well as around him. If the anthropological development (including industrialism) aimed at his external liberation, the evolution of religious thought constituted the liberation of his consciousness from the domination of the natural elements.

But, freed from the material content of experience, and at the same time conscious that in itself it is nothing, the soul had either to abnegate its being or seek a new non-material content. The first solution was chosen, in principle, by the Hindu consciousness and the Oriental thought generally; the second path was taken by classical humanity.[9]

Buddhism expressed the last word of the Hindu consciousness: all that exists as well as all that does not exist is alike but an illusion and dream. That point of view . . . [represented] the awareness of the soul of itself, within itself; for in itself, as pure potentiality, separated from the active divine beginning (which gives the soul its content and actuality) the soul is, of course, nothing. . .
In the Greco-Roman world the human soul appears free not only from the external, cosmic forces, but also from itself—from its inner, purely subjective contemplation of itself, in which it was absorbed in the Hindu [type of religious thought]. Now the soul again receives the action of the divine Logos, no longer as an external cosmic or demiurgic force but as a force purely ideal . . . in the objective creations which realize beauty and reason—in pure art, in scientific philosophy, and in the state founded upon law.[10]

'The creation of this ideal sphere . . . was a great triumph of the supreme Reason, an actual beginning of the true unification of humanity and the universe. But it is a unification in idea only . . . In knowledge, in art, in pure law the soul contemplates the ideal cosmos, and in that contemplation egotism and strife vanish, the power of the classic material beginning disappears. *But the soul cannot eternally remain in contemplation, it lives in practical reality, and this [practical] life of it remains outside the ideal sphere. . .*[11] With the unfolding of the ideal world, two orders of being appear before man—the factual material existence (in Greek, *Genesis*), that which ought not to be, or evil, the

[9]V. Solovyev, *Lectures Concerning Godmanhood;* Works, III, p. 156. (Second Edition, S. M. Solovyev and E. L. Radlov, Editors. St. Petersburg). All quotations in this work are from that edition.

[10]Ibid. p. 156.

[11]Italics are mine.

root of which is the wicked personal will; and the impersonal world of pure ideas (in Greek, *to ontos on*), the domain of the true and perfect. *But these two spheres so remain opposed to each other, find no reconciliation in the classical world-view.'*[12]

At the root of the problem of that dualism is the mean will of the natural man—and,

This wicked and suffering will is the basic fact which cannot be done away with either by the Hindu idea that it is but an illusion . . . or by an escape from it into the sphere of the ideal contemplation; for man will have to return from that luminous domain back to the evil experience.[13]

The main task, thus, is the redemption of human *experience* through the *regeneration* of man himself.

In order that the divine beginning could actually overcome the evil will and [evil] life of man, it is necessary that it [Divinity] would itself appear in the soul of man, as a force which could penetrate into the soul and take possession of it; it is necessary that the divine Logos would not merely influence the soul from the outside but would be born inside it, not limiting or enlightening but *regenerating* it.[14]

It was the function of Judaism to prepare man for the revelation of Divinity as the 'living, personal force' *in* his soul, as 'ego', effecting, thus, the last stage in the long chain of theogonies and theophanies which preceded the *incarnation* of God in the Child-Jesus.

The incarnation of the divine Logos in the person of Jesus Christ is the appearance of the new, spiritual man, the second Adam. . . The evil spirit of discord and strife, eternally powerless against God, had at the beginning of time overcome man, but in the middle of time was overpowered by the Son of God and the Son of Man—as the First-born of all creation—in order to be driven out of the whole created world at the end of time: this is the essential meaning of the Incarnation.[15]

And the whole history subsequent to the Incarnation is the spread of the power of Christ throughout the world, in all mankind—the internal regeneration of humanity by the God-man Jesus, who from within, transforms it into men-Godhood or 'Sophia', according to Solovyev: the body taken on by the Logos, the deified humanity.

This body of Christ, which appeared at first as a small sprout in the figure of the community of the first Christians, little by little grew and developed so as to embrace at the end of time all mankind and all nature in one universal organism of Godmanhood; for nature also, by the word of the Apostle, is awaiting, with hope, the manifestation of the sons of God. . .

[12]Ibid. pp. 156, 157.

[13]Ibid. p. 157.

[14]Ibid. p. 159.

[15]Ibid. p. 163.

This manifestation and glory of the sons of God . . . is the full realization of the free divine human bond *in all mankind, in all the spheres of its life and activity; all those spheres are to be brought into one divine-human concordant unity,* are to enter into the composition of the free theocracy, in which the Universal Church will reach the fullness of the stature of Christ.[16]

This thesis of Godmanhood, with its aspiration for the sociological as well as the religious realization of the Universal Theocracy as the purpose of history, was changed by Solovyev later on in the light of his perception of the biblical truth that the kingdom of God cannot be fully actualized in the conditions of this material world—an ideal Kingdom, it will become possible only after the apocalyptic transfiguration of humanity and the universe. The new point of view was presented by Solovyev in his late work, the *Three Conversations,* which included the 'Narration About the Antichrist'.

In the latter, the ideal of the Universal Theocracy was replaced with the vision of a spiritual aristocracy, or a minority of true Christians, who alone remain faithful at the end of the world. That minority, says Solovyev, will attain the final victory, but not in this world; for the Antichrist will usurp the power of government in all lands, and a false Christianity will temporarily reign upon the whole earth. With this prospect before the Church, the development of the powers of theocracy as a direct aim of the Christian policy had to be abandoned. His own interest in mobilizing the great ecclesiastical power of the See of Rome for the practical realization of his ideal of the Universal Theocracy, as well as his earlier enthusiastic belief in the great Christian mission of the Orthodox Tsardom, faded away.

Three apostolic mediators are portrayed by Solovyev in the 'Narration About the Antichrist', as they are understood by the Russian Orthodox theologians generally: the Elderly John, who personified the highest ideal of Orthodoxy, namely, the witness-ship of Christ (for the *spirit* of Christ, the incarnate Word, has been the central religious idea of the Eastern Church); the 'Pope' Peter, whom Solovyev presents as the summit of the Roman Catholic spiritual development, the unshakable rock of the Christian Confession, and the utmost expression of the energy of the human will fully established in God; and the Confessor Paul, the symbol of Protestantism. The Beloved Disciple manifests Christ; Pope Peter consolidates John's profession of faith into the solidarity of a rock; and Paul the Confessor represents the spirit of a free analysis, of an unceasing search for the truth.

It is in the figure of these three men that the whole Christian world is said to be ripe for the harvest and ready to meet Christ 'coming amid clouds, clad with great might and glory'.

Thus, liberated from the sociological terms of his earlier aspirations, freed from his excessive idealization of the external forms of the Church

[16]Ibid. pp. 171, 172.

and State organization, and cleared of the pantheistic mysticism of his metaphysics, the utopia of a Christian Theocracy—the vision of which set afire the youthful philosopher even more than the vision of the Eternal Feminine inspired the mystic-poet—gave place in the matured mind of Solovyev to a calm expectation of the Second Advent.

Solovyev led Russian thought out of the temptations of socialism, through the allurements of German Romanticism and Idealism, to the primary problem of Christianity—the tragedy of the Church schism, of the Body of Christ rent in two—and called Christendom back to unity, for the joint and earnest work of the Christianization of the world as the major purpose of history.

Had he not, thus, fulfilled—in a circuitous and unconventional manner, and in a different, perhaps in a wider, sense—the grandfather's dedication of the little boy Vladimir to the service of the Church?

In the estimation of Nicholas Berdyaev, Solovyev's analysis of the mystical differences between Catholicism and Orthodoxy was not deep enough; and it is in the mystical differences, Berdyaev maintains, not in the differences of the Latin and Greek dogmas or of the Roman and Byzantine Church administration, that lie the causes of dissention which prevent the reconciliation of the two great Sees.

Be that as it may, Solovyev's appeal to Orthodoxy to forget the historical offences and to take a brotherly attitude towards the Roman Catholic world, will always sound as a friendly church-bell from the belfry of the Russian religious-philosophic thought for all future generations.

Nor did Solovyev ignore Protestantism. He regarded Orthodoxy, Roman Catholicism, and Protestantism as different levels through which man has to pass on his divergent ways towards the evolvement of the spiritually reborn mankind.

The complete, universal regeneration of mankind requires not only the combined efforts of all the branches of Christianity, Solovyev believed, but also, finally, the participation of Judaism.

'The Jewish problem is the Christian problem', he boldly asserted,[17] and always prayed for 'Israel'. Besides his high appreciation of the significance of the Old Testament in the evolution of the religious ideals of mankind, regarded by him as the progressive self-revelation of the Deity, Solovyev elaborated in a separate article, 'The Jewish Problem', certain historical values of Judaism a mention of which appears particularly pertinent in these days of world crisis. 'One can say that the whole religious history of the Jews was directed towards the preparation for the God of Israel not only of holy souls but also of

---

[17]V. Solovyev, *Judaism and the Christian Problem;* Works, IV, p. 134
This point of view was maintained also by the great Russian Church authority, Archbishop Nikanor of Cherson, and by other Russian theologians.

holy bodies':[18] with the peculiar accentuation of the material element in their historical-religious traditions, they had also—thereby—emphasized the problem of the purification of matter as a necessary prerequisite to sanctity, although the human body and all things created by God in general are in themselves not evil but 'good'.[19]

The Jewish people were preparing, historically, for the greatest function of all creation—the reception of its Creator, the Incarnation of God, who is the 'all-consuming fire' of holiness:

Reason and piety require us to acknowledge the fact that besides a holy and virginal soul, it was also a holy and pure body which was to serve in the realization of that mystery.[20]

Christianity, according to Solovyev, ought to be gratefully mindful of the great historical function of the Old Israel, chosen to prepare—at the climax of its national history—a body meet to be the Vessel of God.

Anti-Semitism has no possible grounds, Solovyev maintained. For if Christ is not God but was merely a man, then the Jews are not more guilty of crucifying Him than the Greeks of poisoning Socrates; but if Christ is God, then they are the nation which was chosen and prepared not only to receive Him in their midst, but also to evolve a human being of such sanctity and perfection that it was deemed worthy to be the human mother of the divine Son of God.

Behold, a virgin shall conceive, and bear a son, and shall call his name Emmanuel[21] (which means, God with us.[22])

The historical merging of the Hebrew religious burden and racial nationalism had been so complete that their segregation has been unfailingly disastrous, whenever it occurred. Then the national self-consciousness of the Jews, collectively as well as individually, 'degenerated into a sort of national egotism, into an unlimited self-adoration coupled with disdain and enmity towards the rest of mankind; and the realism of the Jewish spirit degenerated into the exclusively "business", selfish, and unscrupulous character',[23] which causes the best traits of the true Judaism to vanish, wrote Solovyev. The belief in One God and the expectation of the Messiah, not only historically but almost ontologically, have been the life, the *raison d'être*, the very soul of the Jewish people; and Solovyev confidently expected them to enter, and become a part of, the universal Theocracy.

[18]Ibid.

[19]Genesis, i, 31.

[20]V. Solovyev, op. cit. p. 134.

[21]Isaiah, vii. 14.

[22]St. Matthew, i. 23.

[23]V. Solovyev, op. cit. p. 135.

Like many of his contemporaries, Solovyev was disillusioned by the political and social disturbances of the time. Since his death, Russia has had an especially large share in the efforts at accomplishing the socialist ideal of ascending from the realm of 'necessity' to the realm of 'freedom', to use the Marxist-Hegelian terminology. But long before Lenin and Stalin, Russia had given birth to a thinker, Hertsen, also a Socialist, who left a prophetic warning that 'Socialism in all its phases will develop to extreme limits, to absurdities. It is then that, once more, out of the titanic breast of the revolutionary minority will come an outcry of negation, and once more a mortal struggle will take place, when socialism will be in the position of a new conservatism, and will be overcome by an oncoming revolution of a nature as yet unknown to us'.[24]

And it is the same Russia which has given the world also Dostoyevsky and Solovyev: one, a student of the Christian souls, the other, of Christianity. It may well be that now, in the world aflame with the greatest crisis in history, Solovyev's ideal of the Universal Theocracy as the means for the pragmatic realization of Christ's Godmanhood— with its corollary ideal of a Christ-like humanity—may yet supplant the proud absurdities of the 'super-race' theories as well as the all-too-grossly human theories of material satisfaction.

And in Russia itself, with its thousand-year-old background of a deeply Christian tradition and culture, men may yet come to try the way, not of illusory political liberty or economic equality, but of true freedom in Christ. Then the thought which Solovyev fondly preached that regardless of one's wanderings in the course of a search for the truer ways (is it also a search for one's truer self?), he who seeks the Truth will surely find it, may yet reconcile the lost wanderers to their Father in Heaven.

The all-one divine Wisdom can say to all the false beginnings, which were all her offsprings, only in their rebellion became her enemies—she can say to them with assuredness: Follow your ways straight forward until you will see in front of you a precipice; then you will give up your enmity and will all return, enriched with the experience and understanding, into the fatherland common to all of you, where there is for each of you a throne and a crown, and where there is room enough for every one, for 'in My Father's house there are many mansions'.[25]

Some Roman Catholics regard Solovyev as the Russian Newman,[26] and claim that he died in the fold of their Church; the Russians, on the other hand, maintain that he always remained Orthodox and died in

[24]Hertsen, *Works*, V. p. 137. (Geneva, 1879 Edition).

[25]V. Solovyev, *Criticism of Abstract Principles;* Works, II, p. XI.

[26]M. D'Herbigny, *Vladimir Soloviev; a Russian Newman.* (London, Washbourne, 1918).

full communion with the Russian Orthodox Church. It is only right, therefore, that both of these claims should be analysed in this sketch of his life.

The Catholic contention is based on a statement, signed by the Reverend Nicholas Alekseyevich Tolstoy, Princess Olga Vasilyevna Dolgorukova, and Dmitry Sergeyevich Nevsky, which attested the fact that at a Uniat Liturgy, on 18th February, 1896, Solovyev sacramentally joined the Roman Catholic Church; a facsimile of the statement was published in the magazine *Kitezh*, No. 8, of 12th December, 1927, in Warsaw. The testimony reads as follows:

After his confession heard by Father Tolstoy, Vladimir Sergeyevich in our presence read the Profession of Faith of the Tridentine Council in the Church-Slavonic language and then during the liturgy which was performed by Father Tolstoy according to the Greek, or Eastern, rite but with the mention of His Holiness, our Father the Pope, he, Solovyev, received the Blessed Sacrament.

Besides ourselves, at the memorable event there was present only a young Russian girl who was helping about the house in Father Tolstoy's family; unfortunately it has not been possible to ascertain her name.

We believe that the publication of this testimony will eliminate all doubts concerning the facts brought forth in the above statement.

On the Russian side of the argument, the available data are as follows: The Reverend S. Belyayev, the Orthodox priest summoned to Solovyev's death-bed, described the visit to a Mrs. Yeltsova, and the latter published an account of it, on the occasion of the twenty-fifth anniversary of Solovyev's death, in the magazine *Contemporary Annals*, volume XXVIII, 1926, Paris, under the title 'Dreams of Another World'.

The Reverend Sergey Belyayev related, she writes, that 'It was with a true Christian humility that Vladimir Sergeyevich made his confession. It lasted half an hour, at least. Among other things, he said that he did not go to confession for a period of three years, because at his last previous confession (I cannot remember with any certainty whether it was in Moscow or St. Petersburg) he had a dispute with his confessor over a certain dogmatic problem (Vladimir Sergeyevich did not mention specifically what it was) and that therefore he was not allowed to receive the Holy Sacrament'—of Communion, it is here implied (the prohibition might have implied the withholding of the absolution as well, pending the penitent's compliance with the request of the confessor). ' "The priest was right", said Vladimir Sergeyevich, "I disputed with him because of my passionate disposition. Afterwards we kept up correspondence on that subject, but I was not willing to give in although I was well aware that I was wrong; now I fully realize my error and repent with an open heart". After that Father Sergey Belyayev administered to him the Sacrament of the Holy Communion'.

According to Mrs K. Yeltsova, in 1897 Solovyev became ill and de-cided to receive Communion. He invited his former teacher from the Theological Academy, the learned theologian, the Rev. A. M. Ivant-sov-Platonov to hear his confession. Evidently Ivantsov-Platonov, having learned from Solovyev about the act of 18th February, 1896, told him that from the canonical viewpoint, he had to be considered as an Uniate, and had to invite an Uniat priest, or a Catholic priest of the Latin rite. Solovyev very obstinately maintained his 'one Universal Church' point of view and did not receive Communion. He continued the discussion of the subject in his subsequent correspondence but re-mained outside of Church life until he was on his death-bed.

Mr Lopatin, Solovyev's friend since childhood, writes in another magazine that Solovyev persistently denied that he changed his Church allegiance; and, he adds, 'Solovyev was a truthful person'.[27]

Solovyev's sister, Mrs M. S. Bezobrazova, also presented her con-siderations in regard to his alleged conversion to Catholicism in an article published in 1915 in *Russkaya Mysl* vol. XI pp. 39-53. 'Could a person such as my brother was, secretly embrace Catholicism and con-ceal the fact with a lie?' she asks indignantly. Had he done so, and had he remained a Catholic, could he 'who on his death-bed prayed con-tinually until he lost consciousness, could such a man receive Com-munion from an Orthodox priest and give permission to be buried ac-cording to the Orthodox rite? No, he could not'.

Mrs Bezobrazova states that Solovyev throughout his life had a burning desire to see the reunion of Churches, that he considered their separation to have been a painful misunderstanding, and professed a single Church. Consequently, in her judgment he could not have changed to Catholicism without incurring the guilt of a logical falsity. 'What would have such an act meant? The pre-eminence of Roman Catholicism over Orthodoxy. Solovyev considered that both of them had equal rights. It would have meant also that for the sake of the Universal Christianity, not a union of the Churches was needed but a complete extinction of the Eastern Church and the universal establish-ment of Roman Catholicism.' And she points out that not only the Orthodox and the Catholics but even the Protestants were regarded by Solovyev as representative of Christ at the last Universal Council of Churches which was to be convoked by Antichrist according to Solov-yev's thesis in the 'Narration About the Antichrist'.

The hard facts of Solovyev's biography, however, indicate plainly and definitely that while Solovyev never did openly acknowledge the fact that he sacramentally joined the Roman Communion, his writings, his utterances, his activities for fifteen years were wholly given to a

[27]L. Lopatin, 'To the Memory of V. Solovyev', in *The Problems of Philosophy*, 1910. (Vol. CXCV).

militant profession of Roman Catholicism, by an ardent conviction, although he remained a member of the Orthodox Church, by inclination and choice. Those who speak of his integrity and courage in the expression of his beliefs are quite right: once Solovyev came to the conclusion that, because of its historical function,[28] the Roman Church was to embrace others in one, federated, Universal Church, he did not, in the slightest measure, hide his conversion—a philosophical conversion, in public profession of his broadened views, not a change in denominational allegiance—but, on the contrary, with the entire fervour of his passionate nature threw himself, headlong, into a one-man crusade for the realization of his idea of the Universal Theocracy with the Bishop of Rome as its High Priest and the Tsar of Russia, its King.

The change came after the speech of 1881 in which Solovyev pleaded for clemency for the murderers of Alexander II. 'Soon after that', in the words of his brief autobiography, he left all, 'and became absorbed in religious studies, pre-eminently the problem of the reunion of Churches and the reconciliation of Christianity and Judaism'.[29] 'The year 1881—the turning point in Solovyev's life', writes K. Mochulsky; with it, 'begins the period of struggle, propaganda, and preaching. Solovyev turns away from Slavophilism and even from Orthodoxy; for a time he becomes a passionate apologist of Catholicism. His former friends become his bitterest enemies. After the breach with Aksakov, he goes over into the camp of the positivist-Westerners, whose ideology is at bottom totally foreign to him . . . he lives in a complete spiritual solitude [isolation]. . .'[30]

Starting with an attack on neo-Slavophilism which grew more and more devastating as he developed his thesis, Solovyev subjected the Slavophile nationalism to a merciless criticism—not only their political and social nationalism, but also their religious and spiritual nationalism, the hierarchy, the people, the Russian Church itself, and finally Orthodoxy as such.

Slavophilism, he wrote, is not a Christian philosophy—

I do not doubt at all the sincere personal religiousness of this or that warrior of the 'Russian foundations'; only it is clear to me that in the system of the Slavophile ideas there is no legitimate place for religion *as such,* and if it got

---

[28]According to Solovyev's construction, the historical function of the Roman Church was to represent the Priesthood of Christianity, as contrasted with the function of Christ's Kingship which was represented in history by the Orthodox monarchies of Byzantium and the Slavs.

[29]Quoted by K. Mochulsky in *Vladimir Solovyev, His Life and Teaching;* p. 131.

[30]Ibid.

there, it was only through a misunderstanding, with someone else's passport, so to speak.[31]

It is but 'a zoological patriotism'. The messianic idea of the old Slavophiles became transformed into 'zoomorphic nationalism', and an idolatrous worship of the nation and everything in its past.

Only he who was born blind cannot see that the Russian society has been deluded all this time with a *harmful absurdity* and has forgotten its real duty. As I belong to those whom God has delivered from that delusion . . . I consider it my right and my obligation to say to the Russian society once more: repent now, afterwards it will be too late.
Your sin is one in two species.
[i.] You have abnegated the true Christianity, and instead of moderating and removing the old historical offences which separate mankind, you started weighing them with new burdens, multiplying them with new inventions. . .
[ii.] You have not done anything—not only for the spiritual education of the people in the Christian truth[s], but even for its physical nourishment, to secure for it its daily bread.[32]

The religious spirituality of old has degenerated into a mere 'confessional form', he wrote, the Russian people are spiritually 'sick', the religion of the Slavophiles themselves is not Orthodoxy but 'orthodoxing', 'the spiritual development of Russia has been arrested and deeply perverted. . .'[33]

The underlying cause of all these evils lay in the nationalist particularism of the Russian Church—which was, fundamentally and originally, the denominational and national particularism of Byzantine Orthodoxy. It was the Greek Church which had originally separated itself from the whole body of Christianity, and it is the Russian Church which separates itself from it now; according to Solovyev, not the Roman See, as all Easterners argue. And Solovyev charged that separatist attitude of the Eastern Church with the guilt of fratricide, of bringing death into the Body of Christ, the Universal Church, and of rendering the Christian religion, Antichrist's.[34]

In the article, 'St. Vladimir et l'Etat Chretien',[35] written on the occasion of the 900th anniversary of the Christianization of Russia, Solovyev asserted that the Russian Church in its separateness was no longer that Church against which the gates of hell shall not prevail, which was founded by Christ. The idea of the universal Church is expressed in Russia not by the official

---

[31]V. Solovyev, *Slavophilism and its Degeneration;* Works, V, p. 185. (1889).

[32]V. Solovyev, op. cit. p. 272 Paragraph arrangement somewhat modified for clarity.

[33]V. Solovyev, *Our Sin and Our Duty;* Works, V, p. 445. (1891).

[34]Ibid. p. 391.

[35]Published in *L'Univers;* No. 4, 11, 19, 1888.

Church but by the 12-15 million nonconformists, who consider it to be the church of the Antichrist.[36]

Repent! appeals Solovyev to the Slavophiles—and to the Russian Church—repent of that nationalist particularism, and return into the fold of the one true Church, the Catholic Church.

If he agreed with the Slavophiles that Russia had a unique mission in history, that mission, he maintained now, was not to recall the Latin Church from its errors to the fullness of the Christian truth and life preserved in the Orthodox fold, not to bring fresh streams of spiritual life and love to the spiritually exhausted Western humanity: it is the great act of repentance of the historic sin of the Greek Church.

'Solovyev becomes a convinced apologist of the idea of Pan-Catholicism, a fervent defender of the principles of singleness of ecclesiastical power, authority, and discipline'[37]—those of St. Peter, in the Roman Catholic Church.

K. Mochulsky does not believe that so complete a re-orientation of Solovyev's point of view could have been the result of a mere logical development of his ideas. He mentions the fact, related by Prince Eugene Trubetskoy, for example, that Solovyev had a 'prophetic' dream in which he saw a papal Nuncio blessing him to labour for the cause of the re-union of Christendom; the dream left a deep impression on the mystic mind of Solovyev, especially since it was actually fulfilled. Solovyev earnestly believed the dream was a mystical call to that great service. Mr Mochulsky also emphasizes the important emotional crisis in Solovyev's private life (in his love for Mrs Hitrovo) which took place at about the same time, 1883. It was then, too, that he fell very ill with typhoid fever, and came near dying. In the course of recuperation, Solovyev read sixteenth century polemics concerning the problems of the Uniat Church (in Polish), and Dante and Petrarch (in Italian). 'The study of Dante, especially his treatise "De Monarchia", helped Solovyev to come to the final formulation of his conception of the three-fold theocratic power: of the High Priest, the King, and the Prophet'.[38] Solovyev perceived for the first time 'the spiritual reality of the Church', says Mr Mochulsky, it was 'a new mystical experience', 'enormous in its significance' for the whole life of Solovyev, a 'sudden break-through, a transcensus'.[39]

Yet there is no doubt that that manifold crisis in Solovyev's life merely actuated and dramatized the formulation of a preceding development of his philosophical, theological, and historical ideas. With

[36]K. Mochulsky, op. cit. p. 182.

[37]Ibid. p. 140.

[38]K. Mochulsky, op. cit. p. 157.

[39]Ibid. p. 158.

his epistemological theory of integral knowledge, via the metaphysical conception of the universal unity as the synthesis-stage in the self-realization of the absolute—which is God—he came to regard history as the process of a gradual deification of mankind in the ever-growing realization of Christ's God-manhood on earth. This latter is effected—and this is the new perception, expanded into a vast vision of Theocracy—in the threefold manifestation of Divine power in the establishment of the Kingdom of God upon earth: the prophetic, the priestly, the monarchical, but *in and through the Church.*

St. Peter's successor is the High Priest in the nascent Theocracy; the Russian Tsar, its King. The King is to assist the Priest in the realization of the Divine rule on earth externally, in the secular domain. The mission of Russia is thus purely political, that of an Imperial magistrate. The Russian Church is to merge with the Catholic See, under Roman obedience, thus forming—at the long last—the One, truly universal Church.

Solovyev went to Europe several times to confer with the Uniats and later with the Jesuits; Archbishop Strossmeyer communicated his ideas to Cardinal Rampolla in Rome, to the papal Nuncio in Vienna, and to the Pope himself; in May, 1888, he had an audience with the Pope, at which he was to receive the papal benediction for his work towards the re-union of the two Churches.

In 1886 the Procurator of the Synod of the Russian Church (who represented the authority and power of the Imperial Government in the Church organization) forbade Solovyev any and all public activities as harmful to both the State and the Church of Russia. Several of his works had to be published abroad (*La Russie et l'Eglise Universelle, The History and Future of Theocracy,* the articles *St. Vladimir et l'Etat Chrétien; L'Idée Russe,* etc.). His former friends turned away from him. He had to go to his former ideological antagonists, the pro-Western positivists, to secure work for his livelihood by writing in their maga-zine, the *Messenger of Europe,* and then working for the Russian Encyclopaedia (1890-91).

All this time he continued his crusade for the realization of the Universal Theocracy, restricted as he was. When, under the stress of the general disapproval he went to a Russian monastery and thought very seriously of becoming a monk, he decided against the idea and in-clination only because the Orthodox monastic authorities would not permit him to continue his pro-Catholic propaganda. Perceiving, at length, that his ideas of Theocracy under the Bishop of Rome found no response amongst the leading cultural forces of Russia, he tried to ap-peal with his plans directly to the Tsar, but in vain. Then he even thought of organizing a revolution and earnestly tried to find 'a Bishop and a General' as its leaders, in order to set up his Theocracy by a coup of force.

Gradually, however, he came to realize the futility of all these efforts; not only his Orthodox friends and the Russians generally, but even his Catholic friends grew cold to him; 'my friends, the Jesuits, are strongly critical of my freethinking, dreamery, and mysticism', wrote he to the poet Fet (in 1899). His 'Free Theocracy' had no appeal—

The High Priest (Pope Leo XIII) declared it impossible of realization, the Tsar did not notice it, society scoffed at its prophet.[40]

Disillusioned, Solovyev was rapidly losing his hope of seeing Christ's kingship established among mankind.

It was then that he received the Holy Communion from Father Tolstoy.

Tired in spirit and body, he went on a long tour of Finland, Sweden, Scotland, and France, to rest from his arduous efforts; then he lived mostly in Finland, in the quiet of the country, on a lake shore, gradually returning to his old work in philosophy (*The Justification of the Good, Aesthetics*, and his translation of Plato, belong to this period). And in the quiet of that peaceful life, a new perception was formulated in his mind: the Kingdom of God is not to be had in the mundane realization for which he fought, it is a spiritual Kingdom, which will be fully effected only on the 'new earth' after this material world will have had its crucifixion, at the Second Advent. But before that—and the time is nigh at hand—comes Antichrist (the *Three Conversations* with the 'Narration About Antichrist', were written at this period). Only a few will remain faithful in those critical days: this simple scriptural fact made a deep impression on Solovyev, rendering Christianity much more a matter of private concern; and individual faith, of a much greater, more earnest, importance.

During the last two or three years of his life he was quieting down more and more; he visited old familiar places in the Russian countryside, returned to his old friendships, and was becoming reconciled with Russia, and the Russian Church. When he knew that the hour of death had come, he asked for a Russian priest, to receive the Orthodox ministration of the last rites. He died in full sacramental communion with the Russian Orthodox Church.

On his grave, next to an Orthodox ikon of the Resurrection with a Greek inscription, 'Christ has risen from the dead', was placed a Catholic ikon of the Blessed Virgin, with a Latin inscription: *In memoria aeterna erit iustus.*

---

[40]K. Mochulsky, op. cit. p. 192.

2. The background of Solovyev's ideas

A fuller understanding of Solovyev's problems and his solution of them requires at least a brief outline of the so-called Slavophile and the Pro-Western movements as the ideological background of his philosophy. For these movements and the controversy between them dominated Russian thought in the nineteenth century, especially during the third quarter of it.

They grew out of the upheaval of 1812. When, in the wake of Napoleon's retreat, the Russian armies had entered Paris, many young Russians of the educated class came into contact with the conditions, thought, and intellectual leaders of a France seething with the political, social and philosophic fermentation of that post-Revolution period. And when they returned to Russia, they brought back with them the great fervour of the conflicting aspirations not of France alone but of the whole West, then in the throes of the nativity of industrialism and its civilization.

It was, perhaps, the dual experience of that participation in the struggles and thought of Europe on the one hand, and on the other the great national triumph of Russia, 'holy Russia', Orthodox and Slavic Russia, which was exalted in the eyes of the world from its former position of a far-away, half-barbaric country to the illustrious position of the saviour of Europe, with the Russian, the Orthodox Russian Emperor presiding at the sessions of the Holy Alliance—it was, perhaps, that twofold experience which led to the two different reactions in Russian hearts and minds: one, a pro-Western trend of thought; the other, the politically and religiously nationalist current of Orthodoxy and Slavophilism.

German Idealism was at first the philosophic catalyst of both currents of thought. But while the Slavophiles continued their development under its influence, and especially that of Schelling, the 'Westerners' soon turned from idealism to the theories of socialism. Following the initial interest in utopian socialism, the greater part of the Westerners commenced working out the European socialist ideas into a new, distinctly Russian social philosophy in which the Western ideals were transcribed in terms of the predominantly agrarian pattern of economics and culture of Russia and integrated in the spirit of the Russian psychological collectivism (cultivated in the course of centuries by the spiritual tenor of Eastern Orthodox Christianity). A smaller group of sociological publicists, more radically pro-Western, embraced Marxism—and pursued it with an enthusiasm which grew into a dogmatic fanaticism. The apostles of the Russian agricultural socialism (the 'Populists') were largely agnostic; the disciples of Marxism were atheistic. The Slavophiles were nationalist Orthodox first and last.

Fundamentally, however, the Westerners' and Slavophile movements were reverberations of the same major forces which swayed the whole European development throughout the nineteenth century: the tendencies of liberation, with all their many shadings, in the political, economic, social, cultural, and religious spheres; and those of conservatism. Since Russia was now brought into the pattern of the interests of Europe, the interplay of forces and the events in Western countries inevitably evoked a reaction to them as well as an echo of the same tendencies, in the Byzantine-Varangian, Slavic-Mongolian complex of Russia's historical tradition. And the more so, the more she furthered the adoption of Western education, Western forms of Government, and industrialism.

Voltaire and Bentham on one side, Chateaubriand and de Maistre on the other, and the years 1830 and 1848, may be said to delineate the conflict—the ideals of republic, democracy, socialism, versus those of the aristocratic monarchy married to the Church, the 'Contrat Social' versus the theory of legitimacy:

These strangely contrasted appreciations may be taken as generally typical of the two schools of political thought which came into prominence at this period and were destined to play so conspicuous a part in the controversies of the nineteenth century. One aim was common to both, for alike they sought in a quaking world for some firm foothold of authority. The one found it in religion, and in the divine right of the established order; the other in inductive science, and the duty of men to build . . . a social order which should conduce to 'the greatest happiness of the greatest number'.[41]

With the revolutions of 1848—in France, Italy, Germany, Austria, Hungary—autocracy in Russia was enforced. The Russian Empire seemed to be the only 'bulwark against the revolution'. But the extraordinary influence exercised by Russia in European affairs terminated. A severe blow to the national self-respect, the defeat in war in spite of the heroic defence of Sevastopol brought to the forefront the polititcal social, and economic evils at home, especially those of serfdom: 'Reforms seemed inevitable'. A liberal Government was formed by Alexander II as soon as he ascended the throne to inaugurate broad internal reforms, which culminated in the emancipation of the serfs in 1861.

Solovyev was eight years of age then. The carrying out of the great reform occupied the following decade, and the social and ideological consequences of the emancipation, the economic and cultural readjustments it implied—echoed later on in the chopping down of the 'Cherry Orchard', Chekhov's parable for the passing away of the Russian landed gentry class and culture—took up the balance of the century. Solovyev died in 1900.

But—'The reform of 1861 was tragically inadequate.' Dissatisfaction

[41]W. Alison Phillips, 'The Congresses, 1815-22' in *The Cambridge Modern History*; X, p. 4.

spread among the peasants as well as among the intellectuals and leaders of public opinion. The Westerners, in succession—Hertsen, Bekunin, Chernishevsky, Dobrolubov, Pisarev, Lavrov, Mikhailovsky—at home or from exile, pressed for further, more democratic, even more socialistic measures. A whole series of movements appeared throughout the country such as 'The Will of the People', formed by the followers of Bakunin, or 'To the People!', which drew hundreds of university students and graduates into a crusade of preaching to the peasants the gospel of the Russian agrarian socialism; or the 'Land and Liberty', a secret, outright revolutionary, society. Then, amidst this rising ride of demands of all degrees of liberalism, sounded the unfortunate shot of Karakozov (1866)—the first attempt at the assassination of the Emperor-Liberator, whose name remains for ever paired with that of Abraham Lincoln.

Repressions followed. The revolutionary movement went under cover, inaugurating a new campaign of clandestine terrorism against the higher officials, and hunting the Emperor again.

Solovyev at this time was busy with his studies in philosophy. *The Crisis of Western Philosophy: Against Positivism*, published in 1874, was the first public statement of his reaction to the current issues in philosophy as well as in the political developments at home and abroad. *The Three Forces*, an address delivered in 1877, *The Philosophical Principles of Integral Knowledge*, published in the same year, and the *Lectures Concerning Godmanhood*, published in 1878, further developed his position in regard to the problems stirring both Russia and Europe: Russia, he believed in common with the Slavophiles, was to evolve a new solution for the political, social, and cultural order of society in a synthesis of the Occidental and Oriental anthropological patterns—and this synthesis was to be had in the Orthodox, Russian, or rather pan-Slavic, theocracy.

On March 1st, 1881, the Emperor signed a proclamation granting the country its first constitution, limited as it was; before it could be announced, however, a group of six terrorists murdered him with a bomb the explosion of which tore to bits the lower half of his body.

If in the seventies the country was widely in favour of progressive measures, after the assassination public opinion turned sharply against not only the revolutionaries but the whole liberalist movement.

It was at this time that Solovyev became preoccupied with religious and ecclesiastical problems exclusively. If his vision of the Orthodox, Easter-Christian theocracy, indicated in the *Lectures Concerning Godmanhood*, was his general answer to the Russian pro-Western sociologists, the *Three Discourses in Memory of Dostoyevsky* (1881-83), *The Spiritual Foundations of Life* (1882-84), *The History and the Future of Theocracy* (1886), and *La Russie et l'Eglise Universelle* (1889) represent a complete turning away from the sociological issues towards interests decidedly theological, spiritual, and ecclesiastical.

Nor was he alone in that change: even some of the Westerners showed a renewed interest in religion in the hushed atmosphere of the political reaction of the decade, perhaps not altogether without an influence of Solovyev. Thus P. L. Lavrov, himself a leading Westerner, scornfully remarked that 'With the beginning of the eighties, the manifestations of a revival of religious element [interest] in Russia occurred more frequently and assumed a more definite form. . . Everywhere there was a striking mixture, fantastic for the most part, of Orthodoxy with philosophical idealism, of populism with a clever mixture of [other] ideas, accessible only to a small minority. . . More painful than anything else was the fact that the growing youth, brought up in the epoch just preceding on the sober thought of Belinsky, Hertsen, Chernishevsky, and Dobrolubov, [now] learned to throng around the chairs of enthusiastic preachers who conceal the contradiction of science and religion; these [young people] have learned to look at the religious aspirations and the metaphysical positions of the teachers of this school, as natural and proper elements of human thought . . . (they have tired themselves out reading works which) with all the talent of their authors, formerly would not have been even published.'

The Slavophiles, on the other hand, always firmly maintained a definite religious approach in all their philosophical constructions. It has been customary to trace the Slavophile doctrine to German Idealism; but while there is no doubt that in its technically philosophical aspect Slavophilism was wholly based on Hegel and still more fully followed Schelling, it should not be forgotten that for the Slavophiles philosophy, especially metaphysics and epistemology, was subsidiary to their major theme of the Church and the State viewed in the light of the Christian conception of history. Henry Lanz emphasizes that religious and spiritual aspect of Slavophilism when he says: 'Hegel's influence was indeed very great in Russia, but to call such a complex spiritual phenomenon as Slavophilism a provincial branch of Hegel's philosophy, is quite absurd. The spiritual influences which tended to determine the philosophical aspect of Slavophilism seem to lie in the direction of the Orthodox theological tradition and by no means in that of German Idealism'. Likewise he finds that although Schelling's realism superseded the influence of Hegel, it was 'utterly incapable of attaining the ideal of true knowledge'—and *that*, the *spiritual*, super-rational and super-empirical, concept of knowledge, was one of the major weapons with which the Slavophiles fought all Western philosophy. 'Slavophilism', from Lanz's point of view, 'is not a [Russian] patriotic perversion of German Idealism, nor a reaction against modern rationalism. It is simply and solely a modern continuation of the religious tradition which dominated Russian life since the time of St.

Vladimir, which was temporarily driven under ground by the violent reforms of Peter the Great and his successors'.

For Slavophilism was essentially a doctrine of Russian Orthodox nationalism: the Orthodox teaching of Christianity taken in relation to society and in the perspective of history, and elaborated with the aid (and inclusion) of the philosophical trestles of the major concepts of German Idealism into a Christian philosophy of the State, society, and history—Christian, that is, again in the sense of the Eastern Orthodox meaning of that word.

Kireyevsky and Khomyakov were its two outstanding representatives. Like all Slavophiles, they were decidedly hostile to the West and opposed to anything Western in Russia. They criticized all departures from the Russian (pre-Petrine) traditions, all measures taken by the Government in the Europeanization of Russia. The Western nations presented to them a panorama of disunity and conflict which, they held, manifested their internal disintegration. The disintegration was not only political, social, and economic but also ideological and spiritual; the whole European civilization was deteriorating, according to the Slavophiles. This degeneration of Western humanity was wrought by the negative forces of materialism, individualism, and rationalism, they said—and of these, rationalism was the fundamental power of evil. Rationalism itself, finally, was rooted in the Latin, i.e. the *rationalistic*, conception of Christianity, they maintained. Not only Protestantism but even the subsequent anti-Christian philosophies, in their eyes, were but logical offsprings of the Roman rationalist theology.

Founded upon the ideals of Byzantine Christianity and the traditions of Russia as the Orthodox Empire, Slavophilism held the Church and the Tsar to be the two agents of God jointly effecting the care of divine Providence over Russia: the Church safeguarded the spiritual well-being of the Russian people, with the benevolent support of the (wholly Orthodox) Monarchy; and the Emperor looked after their secular welfare, with the fullest blessing of the (thoroughly monarchical and monarchist) Church. It was with this point of view that the Slavophiles greeted the Imperial Manifesto of 1856 in which, announcing the termination of the Crimean War, Alexander II proclaimed from the throne a broad programme of internal reforms, which led to the emancipation of the serfs.

With the help of Heavenly Providence, (rang the words of the Manifesto) which at all times showed Itself so beneficent toward Russia, may the internal order of its Commonwealth be improved and fortified.
May the Supreme Truth and Grace reign in the Courts of Justice, so that all may enjoy the fruits of their rightful labours, under the dome of laws equal to all and providing equal protection for everyone . . .

For the Slavophiles, these reforms were a free gift of God given by the hand of the Tsar, God's anointed one: not a concession wrested from autocracy by the pressure of restive masses, as it would have been in Europe and as the Russian Westerners would also have it in Russia. It really seemed to the Slavophiles as if Russia were starting on a new path, a path quite its own, unknown to other nations: in the general rejoicing of the country, they saw the Tsar, with the benediction of the exultant Church and the enthusiastic support of the elders of the land, launch forth wide changes designed to bestow upon the Russian people full measure of political, economic, social, and judicial benefits. And, overflowing the vast boundaries of Russia, this benevolence of the Heavens they saw reach out (by the arm of the Tsar) to the other Slavic peoples, liberating them from the Turkish yoke: and thus bringing into being the grand Pan-Slavic union of the Eastern Orthodox Church.

And more than that.

The Western civilization, in the understanding of the Slavophiles, was not only mechanistic in its industrialization of the externals of human life, but also increasingly atomistic in its social individualism and in the rationalism of its mentality: this atomistic individualization of all Western life and society, they prophesied, was irresistibly carrying the nations of Europe to an inevitable catastrophy—and it is the historical mission of the Orthodox Russians, they preached, to save their Western brethren from that impending doom by bringing to them the fullness of the Christian truth, life and love, held in the possession of the Orthodox Church and people. The celebrated address of Dostoyevsky at the unveiling of Pushkin's monument—after his return from the Siberian exile, Dostoyevsky was one of the most ardent Slavophiles—was a striking expression of that attitude, a fervent appeal, a call burning with outflowing Orthodox charity toward the 'perishing' West, to forsake its fratricidal particularism, to repent the pride of rationalism, to return to the Christian life of love: 'Repent, thou, proud man!' besought Dostoyevsky the Western intellectual; for the life and love of God is to be had only in Christ-like humility.

The patriarchal Russian culture, balmily ripening amidst the peaceful wheatfields which rolled endlessly eastward, secure under the wings of the Double Eagle—the Slavonic-Byzantine Church and Monarchy —the Slavophiles regarded as the only extant manifestation of a full social and political, as well as religious, realization of Christianity; the Russian people, as the only example of a truly-Christianized humanity: the 'God-bearing people', 'holy Russia', they called them. And that was so, they reiterated, because the Eastern Church alone preserved the full and true faith of the Fathers of the Church. It was there, in the basic divergence of the Catholic rationalist formalism (and materialism) from the true spirituality of the Patristic Church and teaching, that all the subsequent differences between the Roman-Gothic and Byzantine-Slavic developments had been rooted, the Slavophiles asserted. The East was now called upon to save the West because the Latin conception of the God-man-God relationship erred from the Greek conception of it, which was the original and the only correct one.

At this point the Slavophiles went beyond the Apostolic and Nicene Fathers, whom they studied diligently—beyond even the Oecumenical Councils, whose decrees the Orthodox Church maintained inviolate in opposition to all the later claims of the Papacy and innovations introduced by it—to the Hesychast mysticism and its doctrine of the 'Divine Light'.

Hesychasm, or the contemplative silence assumed under special vows in advanced ascetic monasticism, has been known as the apophatic Eastern mysticism dedicated to the attainment of a vision of the divine Light, that Light of divine Glory which the three chosen disciples of Christ beheld at His Transfiguration at Mt. Thabor.[42] Essentially, however, it was an inference from the early conception of God and man, found among the writers of the Neoplatonic School of Alexandria, in particular. God, according to the teaching going back to St. Gregory of Nissa and Dionysius the Areopagite, cannot be known by human reason, or expressed in any word or concept. He is Spirit, absolutely transcendant to all being and thought. His very name is ineffable. And man, a tiny microcosm reflecting and uniting in himself the whole created world, its master and the centre of the universe, was originally created not only 'in the image of God' but also 'after His likeness'; after the original sin, man remained a being formed in the image of God, but lost his Godlikeness. The ordering of one's life and thought after the ten commandments is the first and absolutely necessary step in the restoration of the lost Godlikeness; the purifying of one's heart from all inordinate affections—and *that* is the purpose of asceticism, not the Manichean slaying of the flesh as evil in itself—is the next step; and then comes the constant 'doing' of an inner prayer, in perpetual silence, as the means for the attainment of spiritual union with God, known in Western mysticism as the unitive prayer; and, finally, the vision, even the acquisition, of the divine Light. 'Not the soul alone or the body alone was named man, but one and the other together, created in the image of God'.[43] 'The intellectual and vocal nature of the angels possesses both the mind and the word which proceeds from it . . . (it) could be called a spirit . . . but that spirit is not creative of life'.[44] 'But the intellectual and vocal nature of the soul,

[42]Seminarium Kondakovianum, VIII, p. 100, footnote 2.

[43]St. Gregory Palama, (in Greek, Prosopopiie), in Mignelatrologia Graeca, (P.G.) 150, 1361 c.Quoted by Vissily Kuvoshein in Seminarium Kondakovianum, VIII, p. 104.

[44]Ibid, 150. *KEQ* P.G. 1145-D-1148B.

because it was created together with the earthen body, received from God the life-creating spirit as well; it alone, and in a measure greater than the angels, was created by God in His image'.[45] It is the *spiritual* nature of man which is developed through the inner, 'mental', prayer in silence; with his *spirit*, in prayer, man feeds on the spiritual grace of God, grows Godlike, and may be filled with the divine Light so that even his body may be permeated with It—and thus of a truth become a 'temple of the Holy Spirit', 'an habitation of God'.

Especially developed among the monks of Mt. Athos, the Hesychast practices of asceticism and this 'mental' or 'artful' (the Western translation of the Greek word for it is 'scientific') prayer, date from an early period of the Eastern Church. Besides Dionysius the Areopagite, Theodore the Studite and Maxim the Confessor were among the forerunners of the Hesychast mysticism; Simeon the New Theologian (949-1022) was the father of it. Its teachings were formulated some three hundred years later, by St. Gregory Palama (1296-1359). Opposed by Varlaam, a learned monk from Celabria, and many others, in the course of a complicated struggle of the Church and Court parties in Constantinople, the views of St. Gregory were fully adopted by the Council of 1351, and subsequently were made a part of the Orthodox dogma. The Council of 1368, confirming the teaching, canonized him.

The controversy at the Hesychast Councils—there were seven of them—centred on the nature of the divine Light of Mt. Thabor. Clearly a manifestation of the divine nature in Christ, was it of the same essence as God is in Himself, or was it different? St. Gregory believed, and the Council resolved, that the relationship of the Light to the essence of the Godhead was similar to that of the sun-rays to the sun[46] itself; that in this sense it was of a lower order of Divinity, as it were, as are also all the other manifestations of God (Palama called them 'energies'); but that, together with those other actuations of Divinity, the Light in question was of the same uncreated and eternal nature as God's essence.[47] But man as a created being, it was stated, can experience or know only these energies of God: never God Himself.

[45]Ibid.

[46]It may be of interest for Catholic readers to compare St. Gregory's use of that simile with its employment by St. Catherine of Sienna (1347-80) in her *Dialogue*.

[47]God's essence is 'higher' than His 'energies' in a manner in which the cause of something may be said to be higher than the effect. The name of God applies to His energies and essence alike. The distinction does not make Divinity complex, as some critics asserted. These were other major points of the teaching of St. Gregory Palama incorporated into the Orthodox dogma by the Council.

From Mount Athos, through the Balkan Slavs, these ideas reached the Russian Church-thought first in the fifteenth century, when they were taken by St. Nil Sorsky (1433-1508), the first Russian theologian of national magnitude, for the foundation of his works; and then again in the eighteenth century, when they were translated into Slavonic by the venerable monk Paisi Velichkovsky (1722-1794) in a collection of books under the general title of 'Dobrotolubie' (The Love of Goodness) which soon became a manual for the Russian convents and monasteries. Among these, the hermitages of Optina and Sarov were especially active in the dissemination of that teaching; the elders of Optina published Velichkovsky's translation of it. Attracted by the saintly fame of Seraphim of Sarov, Russia's greatest saint, and of the disciples of Paisi at Optina, thousands of people and many intellectuals of nineteenth century Russia made pilgrimages to these spiritual centres of Russian Orthodoxy; among them were virtually all the leaders of Slavophilism, as well as men like Gogol, Leo Tolstoy, etc. With his friend Dostoyevsky, Solovyev came there more than once.

Resurrected from oblivion in the eighteenth century, these ideas . . . streamed into Russian religious thought and found in Optina the base for themselves—and from there exerted their influence upon Slavophilism.[48]

The Hesychast teaching would seem to have been even more responsible for the religious nationalism of the Slavophiles than the historical differences between the Eastern and Western forms of Christianity, or the original points of controversy between the Church of Constantinople and that of Rome. For the Hesychast teaching asserted, directly as well as by implication, that the Eastern Church alone secured for its faithful the real, spiritual grace of God (the Western conception of grace came to be condemned by the Orthodox as too substantialistic, or even as materialistic). It was thus that the Orthodox people were regarded as the only ones who had the true means of human deification, in this 'true' grace, the actuation of the 'essence' of God. And were they not—for the Slavophiles—the true children of God, were they not fully leavened with the life and love of the Spirit of God? Does not the Russian brotherly charity, the Orthodox 'sobornost' of the Church and people, and the whole peaceful, integrated, Christian order of the Russian culture manifest that they 'dwell in love'? It is love which attests the life of grace, life in God. For 'God is love; and he that dwelleth in love dwelleth in God, and God in him'.[49]

[48]G. Florovsky, 'New Books About V. Solovyev,' in the *Bulletin of the Bibliographical Society of Odessa*, 1913.
It should be noted that Florovsky's estimate of that influence has been disputed by at least one contemporary Church authority.

[49]I John iv.16.

The love of God, and the love of neighbour—*not* atomistic in-dividualism and strife—are the earmarks of a Christian society, of Christian people. For '*this* commandment have we from Him, *That he who loveth God love his brother also*'.[50]

He that dwelleth in love, dwelleth in God: '*and God in him*'—of a truth the Russian people was a 'God-bearing' people, as the Slavo-philes saw it.

And they loved the meek, charitable, God-fearing Russian people; as a nurse solicitous over children, the Slavophiles cared for it—it was for the people's sake they wanted Monarchy in Russia, from the point of view of the peasants' needs they wished the Tsar to grant the re-forms. Their philosophy of the Church and the Crown was no eulogy of the monarchical Government; the latter had its own philosophers laureate, such as Katkov or Pobedonostsev. The Slavophiles were hostile to the bureaucracy, and were disliked, even persecuted by it. In their estimation the bureaucracy was a Westernist corruption of the old Russian order of things, one of the evils started by Peter the Great. The Orthodox Faith, the Tsar, and the people—in this trinity of the Slavo-philes' sociological creed, the people were the self-sufficient social value, with all the political organization to be ordered around it and for it, even the Tsar: for it was God's people, the 'God-bearing' people. The Tsar was to have a small council of the elders of the land for his counsel, but the administration of the country's government was to be almost entirely local self-government, the government 'of the land', according to the Slavophile system of Orthodox democracy, or 'popul-ism', as it was called.

Humble and meek was the Russian peasant, it was true; but that was only one more proof that he had regained man's Godlikeness—for so was Christ Himself. And indeed, had not the Hesychast—or the Alexandrian, originally—conception of God and man tended always to instill a very deep humility in man's estimation of himself? God, so transcendantly, so dreadfully great in His unutterable and incompre-hensible Majesty; and man, an infinitesimal microscopic creature of flesh and human weakness, not worthy, not capable of receiving more than crumbs of divine grace, an emanation of the infinitely distant, un-knowable essence of the thrice-holy God before whom Powers and Principalities of Heaven, and the four and twenty Elders fall down, prostrate, in awe and adoration. (No wonder the people, in their ap-proach to that ineffable God in prayer, humbly sought the intercessions of the many saints, thought of in the hierarchical order of the Byzantine imperial court.)

But if such was the anthropological echo of the Alexandrian Neo-platonic conception of Christianity in Russia, was not Solovyev's con-

---

[50]Ibid. verse 21. Italics are mine.

ception of the 'unconditionally One' also an outgrowth of that, fundamentally Platonic, approach to theology? Was it at Optina that he had overcome the Aristotelian metaphysics, while he sat with Dostoyevsky at the feet of a holy elder?

His ineffably transcendant conception of the absolute—of which the very being is but an attribute—developed in his analysis of the interrelationship of the three Persons in One God, is strangely akin in spirit to the Hesychast teaching of St. Gregory Palama, even though in construction it is quite Hegelian.

It was here, in connection with the mysteries of the inner nature of God, and the problems of relationship between His uncreated essence and the created world, including the finite creature of man, that the Slavophiles and Solovyev passed from the Patristic theology to the metaphysics of German Idealism—and found Schelling as incomplete as Fichte and Hegel. In treating of the metaphysics of Divinity and of the phenomenal world, or in their social philosophy, they perforce had to have recourse to Kant, Plotinus, and Plato, as well as to Spinoza and Aristotle; but only as auxiliary material—the Eastern Orthodox Russia remained, throughout, their theme.

Not only in terminology, but in all major conceptions, in the treatment of basic ontological, epistemological, and historical problems, Solovyev was a most forthright pupil of Hegel; yet he somehow transcended his master's dialectic and Protestant concept of the *Idée* as the ultimate being—transcended it, and filled it with the great riches of the Orthodox trinitarian God. And, sure to see some manifestation of the truth—*the* Truth, or Logos—in every doctrine, Solovyev attained an integration of philosophies and religion, of metaphysics, sociology, and theology, in a synthesis of God, man and the universe. That synthesis is expressed in the concept of the Godmanhood of Christ, who is the only link between the ineffable God and the phenomenal world of man—acting in man through the medium of the 'world-soul' or Sophia—and who is to receive unto Himself all redeemed humanity and the whole transfigured universe: the 'Son of Man' in whom 'dwelleth the fullness of God'.

3. The place of the idea of Godmanhood in the structure of Solovyev's philosophy

A sense of strange inadequacy of the labours of Western thought seemed to grow with Solovyev as he followed the course of its development in his studies. He devoted two of his major works, *The Crisis of Western Philosophy* and the *Criticism of Abstract Principles,* to technical analysis of the extant philosophical teachings. In them, he first presented a brief, brilliant summary of their fundamental propositions in

the form of two syllogisms—the historical sequence of rationalism and
empiricism—and then demonstrated that they really came to a negation
of what they had set out to do.

The quest for the understanding of what 'really is' through the study
of what it is we know, resulted in the discovery of the mere forms of
knowledge, he asserted:

Rationalism :

1. *Major* of Dogmatism (Descartes, Spinoza, Leibnitz, Wolff):
   True being is cognated through *a priori* cognition.
2. *Minor* of Kant: In the latter, however, are cognated only the
   forms of human thinking.
3. *Conclusio* of Hegel: *Ergo*, the forms of human thinking are the
   true being.

Empiricism :

1. *Major* of Bacon: True being is cognated in man's actual (sensory) experience.
2. *Minor* of Locke (and other empiricists): In experience, however, are cognated only the states of human consciousness.
3. *Conclusio* of Mill: *Ergo*, the states of human consciousness are
   the true being.

Both rationalism and empiricism thus came to the same point, says
Solovyev—'both equally deny the being of the known itself as well as
of the knower, transferring the whole truth into the *act of cognition*'.[51]
The exclusive rationalism and empiricism are, then, but two counter-
parts of one generic concept, formalism; and 'if there is neither the
subject nor the object of knowledge, there remains only the *form* of
cognition'.[52]

Having set out to determine the true nature of the world around us
as the content of knowledge, i.e. *what* man knows, Western thought
has thus come to two different, though complementary, answers as to
how man knows.

But it is imperative to determine the true nature of reality, the real
nature of being. It is imperative to know it not only for its own sake
but also—and more especially—because upon the nature of the real,
the ultimate being (and upon our correct understanding of it) depends
the nature of the ultimate *moral* principle:

. . . in order to do good in the right [true] way, it is necessary to know the
truth: in order *to do that which one ought to do, one must know what is.*[53]

And that—the ultimate principle of morals and ethics as the basic
criterion for the determination and establishment of the true, or really

[51]V. Solovyev, *The Crisis of Western Philosophy;* Works, I, p. 135.
[52]Ibid.
[53]V. Solovyev, *Criticism of Abstract Principles;* Works, II, p. 192.

good, order of society, and of humanity as a whole—was Solovyev's paramount concern.

If, then, the nature of the moral principle (and its effective power, says Solovyev) is based on the true nature of the ultimate being; in determining what the true nature of being is, philosophic inquiry must consider the problem of the criterion of truth; and that brings it to the problem of knowledge.

Ontology, as the ultimate basis of morals and therefore of social and political philosophy, itself depends upon epistemology: and now it appears that the Western development of the epistemological-ontological problem has brought results of an almost desperate futility —reality, the universe, the being as such, i.e. the content of knowledge, has dropped out entirely; only the forms (the mechanics, we would say to-day) of cognition remain.[54]

At the end of its development, abstract realism came to the conclusion that all is phenomenon, i.e. man's experience; and in a like manner, abstract rationalism concluded that all is concept, i.e. man's thought. Therefore, states Solovyev, 'for the true knowledge it is necessary to assume an unconditional being of the object [of knowledge]'—which is the 'truly extant', or the 'true being' (which is, of necessity, 'all-inclusive, the "all-one"')' —'and its actual relation to us, the cognating subject[s] [of knowledge].'[55] Furthermore: 'This principle [element] as the all-one, cannot be absolutely external to the subject of knowledge, it must have an inner relation to him, [for it is] by virtue of [this inner relation that] it [the being, the object of knowledge] is actually cognated; and by virtue of that same connection, the subject [of knowledge] can be also internally connected with all that exists [externally to him], as existing in the totality of being, and to really know ALL [the totality of being].'[56]

For, indeed,

When I say, 'I am', by this 'am' as distinct from 'I', I mean precisely all the actual and possible modes of my being, thoughts, sensations, volitions, etc. But logically I cannot affirm that these modes of being exist in themselves in the same sense in which I assert that I am; for they are in me only as predicates are in their subject, while I am in them as [in] my predicates; but I exist only independently of them, since they comprise but a certain part of my existence, never embracing it in its entirety. My thought is [exists] as *belonging* to me, but I am as *possessing* it. The word 'being' is thus used in two meanings, not

---

[54]Apart from the unsuccessful attempts of Hartman to synthesize the logical (Hegel) and the sensory (Mill) in the concept of the unconscious, and the even less successful efforts of Schopenhauer, the problem, according to Solovyev, remains (and, in fact, has not been perceived).

[55]Ibid. p. 288.

[56]Ibid. pp. 288, 289.

only different but contrasting as well. Therefore when it is said, 'this thought is' or 'this sensation is', it is only grammatically that thought and sensation can be admitted to be subjects with the predicate, extant; logically, however, since they are themselves predicates of him who thinks and senses, they cannot possibly be regarded as actual subjects—and therefore existence in no wise could be their predicate. So that such assertions [as] . . . 'thought is', 'sensation is', mean only 'someone thinks', 'someone senses'; or 'one who thinks, is', 'one who feels, is'; and finally, 'being is' means 'the extant one is'. A not fully clear realization of this truth, seemingly so simple, or the failure to apply it to the full extent, is precisely what has been the major sin of all abstract philosophy.

All its significant fallacies come from either conscious or unconscious hypostatization of the predicates; one of these philosophic currents (rationalism) takes the general, or logical, predicates, and the other (realism) confines itself to the specific, empirical ones. For the sake of avoiding these fallacies it is necessary to recognize first of all that the real [proper] subject of philosophy as true knowledge is extant in its predicates, but in no wise these predicates taken abstractly: only then will our cognition correspond to that which really is, and will not be an empty thinking void of content.

Thus . . . the real object of every knowledge is not this or that being or this or that predicate taken in themselves (for predicates cannot exist by themselves) but that to which this being belongs, what is expressed in this being, or that subject to which the given predicates are related. According to this, true knowledge in its universality, i.e., philosophy, has as its object not the being in general, but that to which being generally belongs, i.e. the unconditionally extant one, or the extant one as the ultimate beginning [source] of all being . . . It is the subject or the inner beginning.[57] of every being, and in this sense [it] is distinguished from every being; therefore if we supposed that it itself was being, we would have thereby asserted a certain super-being above all being, which is absurd. Thus, the beginning [principle] of all being cannot itself be regarded as being; but it cannot be designated as the non-being, for under non-being is understood the simple absence of being, or nought; whereas to the unconditionally extant one, on the contrary, *belongs* every being . . .[58]

Through an interesting development of the Hegelian idea (fundamentally, that of Aristotle) that the active manifestation of the absolute, i.e. of this ultimate subject of being requires an opposite of itself, its own antipode—'its other one'—Solovyev comes to defining it in relation to the phenomenal being. As the subject of being, the absolute is the I of 'I am', the Jah of Jahve; the being, or His 'am', is Spirit—God's substance, the *content* of the absolute: the predicate of Jah. In Himself, God is One; but any manifestation of Him would necessarily bring forth a pluralized antipode of Him as the Subject of being—a

[57]*Beginning* in the sense of the principle as well as of the starting point and source.

[58]Ibid. pp. 304, 305. It is the unconditional (*causa sui*) *subject* of all being, of being as such: being is merely its predicate.

multiplicity of particular 'beings', objects called forth from non-being into existence, as bits of nought *becoming* this or that phenomenon in response to His mere wish, intention to reveal His existence. Since there never was, is, or can be anything outside of Him—only nought is outside the absolute—the apparitions thus brought forth to phenomenal life perforce come within the scope of His existence (by *it* have they 'become'), and the absolutely One becomes the *All*-One, the living unity of all as well as the totality of the scope of His existence: the 'other one' of the One Subject of being is the phenomenal universe, the multiplicity of particular becomings. The inner force of cohesion of that living unity of all (as well as the 'breadth, and length, and depth, and height' of it) is Love, the inner essence of the creative, life-generating Spirit of God, i.e., of God Himself. And while His own being is this pure Spirit, the being of the phenomenal 'becomings' is material, i.e. the physical, chemical, biological (and even psychological) processes and structures: Hegel's 'petrified Intelligence', or rather a pattern(al)ized reflection of the creative Spirit of God in the non-being energized into appearances of being of diverse categories. The highest created pattern is that of man, in which are integrated all other created patterns and which is also an 'image' of the Creator—himself a *subject* endowed with a replica of the creative, intellectual, and spiritual powers of God, a microcosmic reflection of the macrocosmic Subject of all being.

If in the whole created universe the Creator manifests His being, in man He makes Himself known—and more than that: fully externalizes Himself in him. Man is the 'other one' of God. As the antipode of the 'absolutely extant One', he is the 'absolutely becoming one', 'at once nothing and God', matter—flesh and soul—in which grows a grain of the Spirit of God.

Jahve, who eternally is what He is, eternally *becomes* in man; and man eternally becomes God.

While this external manifestation of Himself has been a voluntary act on the part of God—something He could have, or could have not, done—in Solovyev's application of Hegelian dialectics to theology it appears to have been almost inevitable, once God, in all eternity, had expressed Himself within Himself, or 'for Himself'. And that had been an absolute inner logical compulsion with the Absolute: the same dialectic necessity had caused an eternal threefold relationship within itself.

'God is *the extant One*, i.e. He possesses being'.[59] But being in general, the abstract being, is a contradiction of terms; actual being implies 'not only a subject and an object, about which it is said that it *is*, but also a certain objective content, or essence, as the predicate'—'if

[59]Solovyev, *Lectures Concerning Godmanhood;* Works, III, p. 83.

grammatically the verb "to be" comprises merely the connection between the subject and the predicate, so logically also *being* may be
thought of only as *the relationship of the subject of being* [the extant one]
to its objective essence [substance] *or content*—the relationship in which
it posits, asserts, or expresses that its content, that its essence'.[60] A
being which would not in any *manner* posit, assert or express *any content,* could not be logically admitted to be any being at all (and 'herein
is the deeply-correct meaning of the famous paradox of Hegel, with
which he opens his *Logic,* namely, that being as such, i.e. the pure,
empty being, is identical with its opposite, i.e. is nought').[61]

But if the being of God is to be understood, thus, as having a certain
content; and if, on the other hand, there is not anything which could
be conceived as outside the absolute: it is obvious that the content of
the being of God is His own essence. 'God as the Subject of being is in
a certain relationship to His content or being'.[62] He is first seen 'as possessing this content in its immediate substantial oneness'; then 'as expressing or realizing His absolute content, contrasting it with Himself
or segregating it from Himself in the act of self-determination'; and,
finally, 'as retaining and asserting Himself in that His content, or as
realizing Himself in the activated, mediate, or differentiated unity with
this content or essence, i.e. with *all*—in other words, as finding Himself in "His other one", or eternally returning to Himself and in Himself abiding'.[63]

Furthermore, since 'in the absolute being there cannot be three suc-
cessive acts, one replacing another; and, on the other hand, three eternal
acts, by definition mutually exclusive, cannot be conceived as taking
place simultaneously in *one* subject . . . it is necessary to suppose
three eternal subjects (hypostases), of which *the second, immediately
generated by the first,* is the direct image of His hypostasis, expresses
the existential content of the first by His activity, serves as His *eternal
expression or the Word, and the third, proceeding from the first as already having His expression in the second, affirms Him as expressed or in
His expression'.[64]

Not only are the three Persons united in the oneness of the *substance*
of God, or His *being*—which is Spirit—which is the common, or rather
the one, substance of each of the three Persons: they are One also as
the Subject of being, as it may be seen from the illustration used by St.
Augustine in his *Confessions,* cited by Solovyev. In our human spirit

---

[60]Ibid. pp. 83, 84.

[61]Ibid. p. 84.

[62]Ibid. p. 85.

[63]Ibid. p. 90.

[64]Ibid. p. 94.

we distinguish its immediate being (*esse*), knowledge (*scire*) and will (*velle*); these three manifestations or actions of our spirit are identical not only in their content, inasmuch as the extant one knows and wills itself—their oneness goes much deeper: each one contains in itself the two others, and thus each contains in itself the whole fullness of the triune spirit. Indeed, I am, says Solovyev, but not just 'am'—I am as he who cognates and wills (*sum sciens et volens*), i.e. my being includes my knowledge and volition; when I know, I recognize my being and my will (*scio me esse et velle*), so that in my knowing is implied my being and my volition; and I myself necessarily as existing and mentally conscious (*volo me esse et scire*), the will embracing both being and thought. Solovyev might have drawn the simple inference a little further—as it is the same I in all cases of my experience, so it is also the same One God in His three Hypostases.

Besides the threefold general logical form of being-in-itself, being-for-itself, and being-by-itself, manifest in God as the ultimate First Principle or Self-extant Spirit, as the Word or the eternal expression of that eternal Subject of Being, and as the Spirit ratifying the Logos-expression of the eternal self-extant Spirit and, in returning unto the First Principle, completing the triune oneness of God, Solovyev distinguishes in the relationship of the three Persons of God the three modes of His existence as the will, representation, and sensation, to which correspond the 'three images of the essence' of God: Goodness, Truth, and Beauty. And these are united, or are One, in the underlying, all-pervading power of the Spirit of God, which is Love—in a sense, Goodness, Truth, and Beauty are but three 'different images' of Love.[65]

Love is the very innermost essence of the nature of God, the ultimate, last, secret of His own Being: the internal, Life-generating, magnetic power of Unity of the Spirit of God—conditioned, it would appear, by the metaphysical polarity inherent in His very oneness:

. . . in order to be what it is, it [the absolute] must be its own opposite, or the unity of itself with its antipode,

> *Denn Alles muss in Nichts zerfallen*
> *Wenn es in Sein beharren will.*

This supreme law of logic is but an abstract expression of the great physical and moral fact of love. Love is the self-negation of a being, the assertion by it of another being, and yet in that self-negation is effected its highest self-assertion. . . Thus, when we say that the absolute prime beginning, by its very definition is the unity of itself and of its self-negation, we repeat, only in a more abstract form, the word of the great apostle: God is love.

As the striving of the absolute for its opposite, that is, for being, love is the

[65]Ibid. p. 110.

beginning of plurality; for the absolute by itself, as supra-extant, is unconditionally one. . .[66]

Being is the relationship of the Subject of being to Its content; in
that primeval self-contained being of God in which, prior to all
eternity, the first stirring of His will had been the first manifestation of
His existence—as yet within Himself—He willed, desired, His content,
His own essence, as its Subject. The very link, association, between the
subject and the predicate of being is love, the exerted power of unity,
the extraverted force of magnetism, returned—with the inclusion of
its own essence, as its spoil—unto itself. And the essence—the subject's
content—is it not also that same unity or love?

The will of the good is love in its internal essence, or the primeval source of
love. The good is the unity of all or of everyone, i.e. love as *the desired*, as the
beloved one—consequently, here we have love in a special and paramount
sense as the idea of ideas: this is unity *substantial*. The truth is the same love,
i.e. the unity of all but as objectively represented [perceived]: this is unity
ideal. Finally, beauty is the same love (i.e. the unity of all) but as manifested
[as sensible]: this is the *real* unity. In other words, the good is unity in its
positive potentiality (and corresponding to this, the divine will may be
designated as the principle immediately-creative or *powerful*), the truth is
the same unity as necessity, and beauty—the same unity as the real . . . *the
absolute realizes the good through the truth, in beauty.*[67]

The three ideas or three common unities, being but three sides or aspects of
one and the same unity, form together in their mutual interpenetration a new
concrete unity, which represents the full realization of the divine content,
the wholeness [integrity] of the absolute essence, the realization of God as the
all-One, in whom 'dwelleth [all] the fullness of the Godhead bodily'.[68]

In this full determination the divine principle appears to us in Christianity.
Here, at last, we come upon the ground of the Christian revelation.[69]

In the historical development of religious consciousness, gradually attaining the fullness of truth, the pagan world which blossomed out in Hellenism
established divinity as primarily the *all*. Of the two necessary momenti of the
divine actuality: the personal or subjective and the ideal or objective—that
world perceived and expressed in a definite way only the second. Judasim,
on the contrary, comprising in this respect the direct opposite of Hellenism,
perceived and in a definite manner realized the first momentum, that of the
personal or subjective actuality: it cognated Divinity as the extant one or as
pure Ego.[70]

But religion which conceived divinity only as ideal cosmos or har-

[66]V. Solovyev, *Criticism of Abstract Principles;* Works, I, p. 310.

[67]V. Solovyev, *Lectures Concerning Godmanhood;* Works, III, pp. 110, 111.

[68]Colossians, ii.9.

[69]V. Solovyev, *Lectures Concerning Godmanhood;* Works, III, p. 111.

[70]Ibid. p. 74.

mony of all, was purely contemplative, without any positive pragmatic bearing upon the individual and social life of man; for Socrates and Plato, for Stoicism, as well as for Buddhism, 'the moral aim consisted of a simple hushing down of the human will'.[71] On the other hand it is true that divinity *is not only the one, but also the all, is not* only the individual but also the all-embracing being; not only the extant one, but also the substance'.[72]

God is all; i.e. all in the positive sense, *or the unity of all, comprises the proper content, object, or the objective substance of God. . .*[73]

So that in willing, desiring, loving His content, God, as the Subject of being, willed desired loved, *all.* But Solovyev is careful to guard this assertion from any confusion of it with pantheism, either naturalistic or idealistic the 'all' does not mean 'the particular conditional reality of the natural world':

all can be the object [matter, content] of the absolutely extant One only in its internal unity and integrity.[74]

The eternal God eternally realizes Himself, realizing His content i.e. realizing all. This 'all', in contradistinction with the extant God as the unconditionally One, is plurality as the content of the unconditionally One, as overcome by the One, as reduced to unity.[75]

The idea of unity is the central, cardinal conception of all Solovyev's philosophy, the cornerstone of all his ideological constructions, the fundamental criterion in his approach to any and all problems.

God is primevally One; in the pre-eternal unity of the Subject of being with His substance or content, that content—His being—potentially contained the plurality of all possible beings in their unity with Him, and therefore among themselves; His eternal existence eternally realizes that potential content and its unity in the created cosmos which He willed and posited forth as His 'other one'; the simple unity of the unconditionally One becomes the All-unity of God in His full self-realization. Everything else follows, in Solovyev's mind, from this fundamental truth about the ultimate nature of the ultimate being, the truth of unity as the ontological thesis willing, and working out, the theo-cosmic All-unity as its own predetermined synthesis (which is but the full and ratified expression of the Subject of being in Its own 'other one', Its own essence—the Word of God, Logos, actuated and in His fullness confirmed by the Spirit).

[71]Ibid. p. 73.
[72]Ibid.
[73]Ibid. p. 84.
[74]Ibid. p. 110.
[75]Ibid. p. 113.

The conception of All-unity, in Greek, *en ke pan,* is the central thread in the philosophy of Solovyev.[76]

All the universe is to be brought into unity with, and thus into, God. It is to become *His content,* therefore it *must* be brought into conformity with Him, with *His* nature, His internal organization, i.e. must be patterned after the manner of His intra-deital relationships. And man, especially shaped after the very image of God, most especially so.

But not all elements of the phenomenal world can be so brought into God, into conformity with His being—only that which constitutes unity in all things, the unifying factor in each item of creation. For there are also other factors in the world of nature, forces which work not towards the unity of all, but oppose it—the forces of self-assertion on the part of each individual created entity. They are the factors of evil.

Individualism is evil because its self-asserting will is directly contrary to the will of God, which is the will of the most fundamental good: that of the unity of all with Him who is the source of all good, the source of life, of existence itself. The divine will for unity is the life-generating Love of God; the individualist particularism not only monopolizes the portion of being it received from the absolute, but also wills—craves, covets, desires—that of the others, *for itself* i.e., not only deprives the others of its co-operation and the benefit they might receive from association with it, but tends to rob them of what they have in themselves as their little share from the source of all being and good. And even more—in that centripetal attitude of self-centred isolation, individualism, by the very logic of its particularism, works contrary to or *against* the will of God, disrupts the unifying forces of His Love, and introduces, instead, envy, hatred, and death: 'all creatures become subjected to the vanity and slavery of corruption', 'the world-organism is transformed into a mechanical conglomeration of atoms', 'the unity of the whole creation falls apart'.[77] Solovyev calls the egotist particular existence a 'heavy, torturous dream' of our reality.

The 'constant forms of natural phenomena, their harmonious relations and immutable laws, the whole ideal content of this world' appear to the mind as the 'clear reflection of eternal ideas',[78] as the norm, as the right order of things or 'that which ought to be'. But the self-assertion and egoism of particular existence common to all nature is definitely evil, something which 'ought not to be', the *ab*-normal.

Man is the connecting link of that polarity of the universal unity and

[76]William Henry Dunphy, *The Religious Philosophy of Vladimir Solovyev,* p. ii. (Private Edition, Distributed by the University of Chicago Libraries. 1939).

[77]Solovyev, *Lectures Concerning Godmanhood;* Works, III, p. 142.

[78]Ibid. p. 129.

the individualist particularism, between the divine and the natural worlds; he 'combines within himself all possible opposites, which are all reducible to one great polarity between the unconditioned and the contingent, between the absolute and eternal essence and the transitory phenomenon or appearance'.[79]

As a phenomenon, man presents 'in his physical aspect only a spatial group of elements, and in his psychological aspect—a temporal series of separate states'; neither the physical nor the psychological organism possesses any real unity, only a correlation of arbitrarily chosen divisions or units. If, however, as a phenomenon man is but 'a temporary, transitory fact' of empiricism, as the ideal essence 'he is necessarily eternal and all-embracing'. What is this ideal man? asks Solovyev. It is a being at once individual and universal, mankind in its ideal unity, he says; and gives this being the name of Sophia.

Just as the divine forces form one whole, absolutely universal and absolutely individual, organism of the living Logos; so all human elements form a like whole, an organism at once universal and individual—the necessary actualization and receptacle of the first one—the organism of the whole humanity as the eternal body of God and the eternal soul of the world. As this latter organism, i.e. Sophia, in its eternal being necessarily consists of a multiplicity of elements, of which she is the real unity, so each of those elements, as a necessary component part of the eternal godmanhood, must be recognized as *eternal* in the absolute or ideal order.[80]

It is this ideal essence in man, man as a part and a partaker of the ideal humanity, which is the *real* nature of man.

And in the light of this ideal meaning of man, 'in the ideal contemplation (as also in purely scientific knowledge) every individual separateness, every particularity of a real empirical phenomenon, is but "a fleeting dream", only an indifferent transitory chance, a mere sample of the general and the unitary; what counts here is not the real empirical existence of an object, but its ideal content, which is something perfect in itself and fully clear to the mind'.[81]

In the light of the ideal contemplation we do not feel and do not assert ourselves in our separateness: here the torturing flame of personal will is extinguished, and we recognize our essential oneness with all else. But such ideal state lasts in us only a moment; and except for these bright moments, in the whole remaining course of experience our ideal unity with all the 'other' [other than we] appears to us as a phantom, as immaterial; for our actual reality we take only our separate, particular *I*: we are secluded in ourselves, impenetrable for others, and therefore they are likewise impenetrable for us . . .

[79]Ibid. p. 121.

[80]Ibid. p. 127.

[81]Ibid. p. 130.

This same abnormal attitude toward all outside of us, this exclusive self-assertion or selfishness, all-powerful in practical life even though it is rejected in theory, this opposition of ourselves to all others and the practical denial of them—is precisely the root of evil in our nature: and as it is an attribute of everything living, for every living being in nature, every beast, every insect, and every stalk of grass, in its own existence separates itself from everything else and strives to be all for itself, absorbing or repulsing the 'other' (from whence comes the external, material existence) it follows that evil is a common attribute of all nature, being in one respect, i.e. in its ideal content or in its objective forms and laws merely *a reflection of the all-one idea*, in another respect, namely in its real, segregated, and severed existence, appears as something foreign and hostile to this idea, as something which ought not to be, or as evil. And it is evil in a twofold sense. For, if egotism, i.e. the striving to put one's own exclusive ego in the place of all, or to replace all with itself, is evil *par excellence* (the moral evil) then the fatal impossibility actually to realize that egotism, i.e. the impossibility of being everything, remaining in one's own exclusiveness—is the root of suffering, in regard to which all other sufferings are only particular instances of the general law. Indeed, the common basis of every suffering, moral as well as physical, is in the last analysis the result of subjection of a being to something external to it, some external fact which forcibly binds and oppresses it; but such external subjection obviously would be impossible if the given subject was in an internal and actual unity with all else, if it felt [found] itself in all: then there would not be anything ultimately foreign or external for it, nothing could forcibly limit or oppose it; sensing itself in concord with all the 'other', it would sense the action of all the 'other' upon itself as concordant with its own will, as agreeable to itself, and consequently would not experience any actual suffering . . . evil is the exerted condition of the will of an individual being asserting exclusively itself and negating all the 'other'; and suffering is the inevitable reaction of the 'other' to such will . . .[82]

Suffering is thus only 'the inevitable consequence of moral evil', and evil itself is but the negative attitude of individual beings towards each other: the 'actual existence of the natural world is abnormal, or such as it ought not to be, in so far as it opposes itself to the divine world (as the ultimate norm)'.

In itself, the divine beginning is the eternal all-One, abiding in absolute repose and immutability; but in relation to multiplicity of the finite being which left it, the divine beginning appears as the *active* force of unity—Logos *ad extra*. The multiple being in its discord rises against the divine unity, negates it; but Divinity, the principle of all-unity by its very nature, is merely aroused by the negative action of the disintegrated existence to positive reaction, to the manifestation of its unifying force, at first in the form of external law and then gradually realizing a new positive unification of these elements in the form of absolute organism or internal all-unity.[83]

[82]Ibid. pp. 130, 131.

[83]Ibid. p. 145.

But Logos by Himself cannot unify the discordant and rebellious phenomenal beings, according to Solovyev; 'because the divine beginning cannot immediately realize its idea in the disunited elements of the material being'[84]—the divine beginning of unity, of oneness, cannot act in the medium of disunity, of discord, he argues. But instead of resolving the conflict through the Crucifixion of Christ—in which these negative powers of the created existence had been once and for all conquered by the Word of God by absorbing in His *infinite*[85] suffering and bodily death the destructive power of the *Genus* of all negative forces—Solovyev makes recourse to the medium of Sophia as the 'world-soul', a concept not altogether unlike that of the different demiurges of Alexandrian gnosticism.

The Greek word for Wisdom, Sophia is scripturally but another name of the Word of God in His pre-eternal existence 'in the bosom of His Father', distinctly denoting the Word of God as being also the Spirit of God, the spirit of absolute holiness,[86] 'the Wisdom of God' in St. Paul's Epistle.[87] For Solovyev, it is on one hand the world-soul, the ideal humanity, the principle of unity in created nature; and on the other hand, 'Sophia is the body of God, the matter of Divinity,* permeated with the beginning of divine unity'.[88]

Christ is the most universal (and therefore the most individual) organism, the ultimate expression of God. And in every organism there are 'necessarily two unities on one hand, the unity of the acting principle which subordinates the plurality of the elements to itself as one; and on the other, that plurality as reduced to unity, as the determined [formed, expressed] image of that principle . . . or unity as the principle (in itself) and unity in phenomenon'.[89]

In the divine organism of Christ the active unifying principle, the principle expressing the unity of the ultimately-extant One, is obviously the Word or Logos.

The unity of the second kind, the resultant unity, in the Christian theosophy bears the name of Sophia. If in the absolute we distinguish, in general, the absolute as such, i.e. as the ultimately-extant One, from its content, essence, or idea, then the direct expression of the first we shall find in the Logos, and

[84]Ibid. p. 146.

[85]Because offered and accepted by in infinite love of God.

[86]Proverbs viii.22-30; The Wisdom of Solomon vii.22-7; Colossians i.17.

[87]I Corinthians i.24.

*'Such words as "body" and "matter" are employed here only in the most general sense, of course, as relative categories, without any association with them of those particular notions which may be applicable only to our material world but are perfectly unthinkable in relation to Divinity.'

[88]V. Solovyev, *Lectures Concerning Godmanhood;* Works, III, p. 115.

[89]Ibid. p. 114.

of the second—in Sophia, which is thus the idea expressed or realized. And, as the extant One is distinct from His idea and simultaneously One with it, so also Logos, being different from Sophia, is internally united with it. Sophia is God's body, the matter of Divinity,* permeated with the principle of divine unity. Christ, who accomplishes this unity in Himself, or is the bearer of it, as the integral divine organism—at once universal and individual—is both Logos and Sophia.[90]

If in the divine being—in Christ—the first or the forming unity is Divinity proper, God as the active force, or Logos; and if in this first unity we have, thus, Christ as the divine being: then the second, the produced unity, which was given the mystical name of Sophia, is the principle of humanity, the ideal or normal man. And in this second unity, Christ as a participant of the human principle, is a man, or, in the expression of the Holy Scripture, the second Adam.[91]

The unfolding or self-expression of Divinity requires the objective stratum in which It could express Itself, says Solovyev, true to the old Aristotelian notion that form, or the forming principle, has to have matter to which it would give form and upon which it could act.

Consequently, the eternal existence of God [taken here] as Logos or active God, obligates the assumption of the eternal existence of real elements which receive the divine action, i.e. obligates the assumption of the existence of a world subject to the divine action or *as giving in itself place* to the divine unity. But the world's own unity, i.e. the produced unity—which is the centre of the world and at the same time the circumference of Divinity—is humanity.[92]

Representing the realization of the divine principle, being its image and likeness, the proto-form humanity, or the soul of the world, is simultaneously all and one; it occupies the mediate [mediating] position between the multiplicity of living beings, which comprise the real content of its life, and the unconditional oneness of Divinity, which represents the ideal beginning and the norm of that life. As the living focus or the soul of all creatures and at the same time the real form of Divinity—the extant subject of created being and the extant object of divine action—participant of God's unity and at the same time embracing the whole multitude of living souls, the all-one humanity or the soul of the world, is a dual being: including in itself both the divine beginning and the created being, it is not defined exclusively by either one or the other; the divine beginning inherent in it frees it from created nature, and the latter makes it free in regard to Divinity . . . In so far as it receives unto itself the divine Logos and is determined by Him, the soul of the world is humanity—the divine humanity of Christ—Christ's body or Sophia. Assimilating the divine beginning, one in itself, and binding with that oneness the whole multiplicity of beings, the world-soul thereby gives the divine be-

*Solovyev's footnote appears on the preceding page.
[90]V. Solovyev, *Lectures Concerning Godmanhood;* Works, III, p. 115.
[91]Ibid. p. 121.
[92]Ibid. p. 122.

ginning full actual realization in all; through her mediation God is revealed as the living active force in all creation, or as the Holy Spirit. In other words: being determined or formed by the divine Logos, the world-soul makes it possible for the Holy Spirit to be actualized in all; for that which in the light of Logos unfolds in ideal images, by the Holy Spirit is brought into being in real action.[93]

Thus the incarnation of the divine idea in the world, which constitutes the goal of the whole world movement [development], is effected through the uniting of the divine beginning with the soul of the world; the first represents the active, determining, forming, or fertilizing element, and the world-soul appears as the passive force, which receives the ideal beginning and provides matter for the development of the received, the shell for its full self-revelation.[94]

This is Godmanhood.

The nativity of the Christ-child in Bethlehem, the first manifestation of the Incarnate Word, had been preceded by countless preparatory stages in the progressive subjugation of the 'chaos of disjunct elements' to the unifying power of the 'absolute idea', or Logos, acting through the nascent Sophia; and has *continued* after the Ascension of Christ, mainly (but not exclusively) through the Church He founded and empowered with the Spirit of God at the Pentecost for action, in the *continued* incarnation of the divine idea, 'or the deification (theosis) of all that exists by bringing it in'—as a subdued captive of the unifying power of the divine Love or Idea—'into the form of the absolute organism' of Logos-Sophia, or Christ, as the ever-widening manifestation of the Subject of being in its 'other one', i.e. in the phenomenal world of nature. For Sophia is not only the ideal humanity but also the 'world-soul', the unity of all created world.

After many stages of cosmological process, in which the divine principle 'uniting closer and closer with the world-soul, overcomes the chaotic matter more and more and finally brings it into the perfect form of the human organism', when nature has thus produced 'an external shell for the divine idea', a new process commenced—that of 'the internal all-unity, in the form of *consciousness* and free activity', in man:

'In man the world-soul for the first time unites with the divine Logos internally, in consciousness, as the pure form of all-unity. Only one out of the multitude of phenomenal beings in nature, man has in his consciousness the capacity of conceiving all, or the internal bond and meaning (logos) of all that exists; and thus appears, in idea, as the *all*, i.e. is, in this sense, the second all-unity, the image and the likeness of God.'[95] In man nature outgrows itself as it were, reaching out into the

[93]Ibid. pp. 140, 141.
[94]Ibid. p. 146.
[95]Ibid. pp. 149, 150.

eternal realm of the ideal; and man becomes the *mediator* between the natural world and Divinity. But,

Man not only possesses the same internal essence of life—the all-unity—which is possessed by God; he is also free, like God, to desire the possession of it, i.e. may of himself desire to be like God. Initially he has that essence from God . . . But, by virtue of being unlimited, he (or the world-soul in him) is not satisfied with that passive unity. He desires to possess the divine essence of himself, wants to take possession of it by himself to assimilate it. And in order to have it not only from God but also by himself, he asserts himself as separate from God, outside of God, falls off or secedes from God in his consciousness.[96]

and thus starts the long, painful, step by step return to God of the mind of man who had fallen into the abject enslavedness to the 'beggarly elements' of the phenomenal world of nature. Solovyev traces out a definite logical evolution in the development of religious thought, from the most primitive through Buddhism and the Graeco-Roman conceptions, to the Old Testament. But, he observes, throughout that whole period 'the wicked and suffering will' of man had remained at the basis of all human life: firmly rooted in its evil ways since the estrangement of man from God in his assertion of himself apart from God, that human will had been acted upon in those religious conceptions only *externally* by the divine beginning, through limitations or repression at first, and then through ideal enlightenment. Only since the incarnation of God in man has the divine beginning found its way into the human soul, has become a living personal force *within* man: and only then was he *regenerated*, born again spiritually, i.e. was again united with God in his will—now voluntarily, by a free choice.

The incarnation of the divine Logos in the person of Jesus Christ is the appearance of a new, spiritual man, the second Adam. As the first, the natural, Adam connotes not only a single person among other persons, but the all-one personality which includes the whole natural mankind; so also the second Adam is not only *that* individual being but at the same time the universal [being] which embraces the whole regenerate, spiritual humanity. In the sphere of the eternal divine existence, Christ is the eternal spiritual centre of the Catholic organism. But as this organism, or the Catholic humanity, falling into the stream of phenomena becomes subjected to the law of external existence and must through labour and suffering restore, in time, what it had abandoned in eternity, i.e. its internal unity with God and nature—so also Christ, as the active beginning of that unity, must come down for its restoration into the same stream of phenomena, must subject Himself to the same law of external existence, and from [being] the centre of eternity, become the centre of history, coming down at a definite moment—in the fullness of time. The evil spirit of discord and enmity, eternally powerless against God, at the beginning of times had overpowered man; in the middle of time it had

[96]Ibid. pp. 150, 151.

to be overcome by the Son of God and the Son of man, as the first-born of all creation, in order that at the conclusion of times it could be expelled from all creation—this is the basic meaning of the incarnation.[97]

With his vivid sense of the reality of evil, Solovyev regarded the cause of Christ not merely as a juridical satisfaction rendered to God the Father for the breach of His law by man—the theory of Anselm of Canterbury, so widely accepted in the West—but the real, dramatic and heroic struggle with evil, the victory over it, the liberation of humanity from its power and tyranny.

Man is a union of the divine beginning with his natural being, which implies, according to Solovyev, the third element—the human element properly so called—as the medium uniting the first two. This 'properly human element is reason (ratio), i.e. the ratio [inter-relationship] of the other two'[98] elements. Only in their perfect union in the (one) person of Christ could the 'natural' nature of man and his 'natural' will—which is *the* source of evil—be subjected to the divine nature and will of Christ, by the *voluntary* submission of the former to the latter; and only through Christ, in Christ, could humanity, subsequently, be brought into a similar reconciliation-sonship—with God: by a voluntary, may it be said again, acceptance and reception of Christ.

The original ('immediate') unity of the two beginnings, given in the first Adam and lost in the fall of man, could not be simply restored: it had to be *attained*, and attained only through a free and twofold heroic self-denial—that of God, temporarily laying aside His glory and infinite power in the assumption of human limitations, in the incarnation of God the Son; and that of man, abnegating his natural will in favour of the will of God the Father, in the twofold but indivisible person of Christ.

We have seen before how the interaction of the divine and the natural beginnings determined the whole life of the world and mankind, and [how] the whole course of this life consists of the gradual reapproachment and mutual interpenetration of these two beginnings . . . permeating each other deeper and deeper, until in Christ nature appears as the soul of man, ready for a complete self-denial and God [appears] as the spirit of love and mercy, communicating to that soul the fullness of the divine life: not repressing it by force, nor enlightening it with understanding, but quickening it in His loving kindness.[99]

The self limitation of Divinity in Christ liberates His humanity, permitting his natural will to abnegate itself voluntarily in favour of the divine beginning [in favour of the divine will] [regarded] not as external force (in that case the self-denial would not be voluntary) but [recognized] as [its] internal good,

[97]Ibid. p. 163.
[98]Ibid. p. 166.
[99]Ibid. p. 167.

and thereby to really acquire that good. Christ, as God, freely abnegates His divine glory, and thereby as man begets the possibility of *attaining* that divine glory.[100]

The attainment involves the overcoming of 'the temptations of evil', of which there are three categories, corresponding to the three elements comprising man: the material or natural; that of reason, or the human element properly so called; and the moral or spiritual (the divine) element. The three 'typical' temptations of Christ, as well as His suffering and death in the flesh, are important not so much in themselves, as because through His victory over them, Christ has attained the victory over them for all men. Ahungered, he rejected the temptation 'to make the material good the aim, and His divine power the means for attaining it'. 'If thou be the Son of God, command that these stones be made bread', said the tempter; not by bread alone, but 'by every word of God shall man live', answered Christ. Freed from subjection to the material instinct, He faced the temptation 'to make His divine power the means for the self-assertion [on the part] of His human personality, to succumb to the sin of the mind—[that of] pride'. In answering the devil, 'Thou shalt not tempt the Lord thy God', the Son of man received the power over the minds of all men who would be the children of God.

The enslavedness to the flesh and to the pride of reason have been removed: the human will finds itself on a high moral grade, realizes it is above all other creatures. In the name of this high moral status, man may desire authority over the world in order to lead the world to perfection: but the world lies in sin and will not voluntarily submit to moral superiority—it would seem necessary therefore to force it into submission, to exert His divine power, [even] as oppression, for the subjugation of the world. But the use of such oppression, i.e. of evil, for the attainment of a good would be [tantamount to] a recognition that the good in itself has no power, that evil is stronger—it would mean *falling down before* that *beginning of evil which dominates the world* . . . having overcome the temptation of the lust for power under the guise of purposing a good, the human will of Christ voluntarily submitted to the true good, and rejected any agreement with the evil reigning in the world.[101]

Having conquered the sin of the spirit, 'the Son of man received the supreme power in the realm of the spirit', and over the spirits of men; 'having rejected subjection to the mundane power for the sake of dominance over the earth, He gained the service of the powers of heaven: "and, behold, angels came and ministered unto Him". '

Thus Christ had brought His human will into agreement with the divine will, 'deifying His humanity after the inhumanization of His

[100]Ibid. pp. 168, 169.

[101]Ibid. p. 170.

Divinity'—the Russian use of the term inhumanization, in addition to that of incarnation, seems to have been very much more fruitful in maintaining the true perspective of the meaning of Christianity—but the cause of His incarnation was not fulfilled until it was consummated on the cross. Conquered by the inner self-denial of His human will, the evil beginning had to be despoiled of its power over the flesh, i.e. over created nature: 'this latter, purified by the death on the cross, lost its material "separatedness" and its weight, became a direct expression and instrument of the spirit of God, the true *spiritual body*. With such body Christ had risen and appeared to His Church'.[102]

This same task of attaining anew the due relationship between Divinity and nature, as the latter is represented in man, since the Resurrection of Christ has become the task of all humanity, and constitutes the meaning and purpose of history.

Hence follows the development of Solovyev's *practical* philosophy; all his subsequent writings and activities were given to the elaboration of the pragmatic consequences of this general epistemological-ontological-theological theme, and to working out the practical means for the realization of 'Godmanhood', i.e. the deification of all mankind.

But if he was quite certain in his vision of that general pattern of the universe and its meaning—the Subject of being manifesting Himself in His 'other one' (first, His own substance, then the created universe, then man) and reclaiming that 'other one' for Himself through gradual deification of it by Logos, concomitantly with the reduction of self-assertion of the created sessionist entities to compliance with the unifying power of God's love, which, however, was not *really* effective until the divine principle of unity *entered inside* the created nature in the person of God-man, and the evil of nature's selfedness was overcome by Him in the subjugation of the human will to that of God—Solovyev wavered in his attempts at charting the continuation of Christ's task very greatly.

Godmanhood, the universalization of Sophia as the task bequeathed to mankind by Logos on return to His Father in Heaven, was certain; but how was it to be realized in the given historical circumstances?

At first, when he was inspired primarily with the belief in the inner and voluntary acceptance of the principle of 'all-unity' by the soul of man as its freely preferred good, Solovyev enthusiastically believed, with the Slavophiles, that the Orthodox Church was the only one which had retained that true, inner, live, spiritual meaning of Christianity—the Roman Church appeared to him to be fundamentally false in its deadly formalism and external subjugation to the hierarchical and papal authority set forth in the stead of life in Christ's spirit and love. But then he came nearer to Catholicism, perceived truth in some

[102]Ibid. p. 171.

of its claims and assertions—while, conversely, the Orthodox zeal in guarding 'the fullness of truth' of the early Christian tradition in the seclusion of national and denominational aloofness, appeared to him as a very gross evil of exclusiveness, particularism, self-centredness, as the same individualist separationism which to him was the essence of all evil in the whole created nature.

Was not *unity* the good, the truth, and the beauty of God—were they not but three aspects of His love, *the* innermost nature of His very being, and the inner power of unity? Was not the attainment of 'all-unity' the purpose of all creation? *The purpose of history* is to achieve it among mankind, manifestly and chiefly in the Church: how may any part of the Church persist in self-assertion (Solovyev's earlier charge against Rome) or in maintaining aloofness (his subsequent accusation of the Orthodox Church)?

Since all humanity represents the same three basic elements as a single man, namely, his spirit, mind, and sensual soul; the temptation of evil is also three-fold for all mankind—but in a sequence different from [that experienced by] Christ. Mankind has already received the revelation of the divine truth in Christ, it already possesses this truth as actual *fact*—the first temptation therefore is to use this truth for wrongful purposes, yet in the name of this same truth, i.e. to do evil in the name of the good—the sin of the spirit. . .[103]

Christianity could be received either internally, through an inner or spiritual rebirth; or externally, as a mere recognition of the truths of redemption in Christ, and an outward compliance with the letter of the commandments.

The historical appearance of Christianity had divided mankind into two parts; the Christian Church, which possesses the divine truth and represents the will of God on earth—and the remaining outside world which does not know the true God, and 'lieth in sin'. And it may appear to the 'outward' Christians, those who believe in the truth of Christ but were not regenerated by it, that they should, nay, ought to, subjugate to Christ and His Church that outside and hostile world: and, as the world which lieth in sin will not voluntarily submit to the sons of God, that it should be subjugated *by force*. To this temptation of the ecclesiastical lust of power fell a part of the Church led by the Roman hierarchy, carrying with it the majority of Western mankind in the first great period of its historical life—in the middle ages.[104]

To assume that the truth of Christ, 'i.e. the truth of eternal love and unconditional lovingkindness', requires for its realization the means of force and deceit, is to profess that truth as impotent, to manifest the lack of faith in the good, in God.

And this unbelief, at first hidden in Catholicism as an imperceptible germ, later on was displayed openly. Thus in Jesuitism—the clearest and utmost

[103]Ibid. p. 173.
[104]Ibid. p. 174.

expression of the Roman-Catholic principle—the love of power became the direct moving force, not the Christian zeal: the peoples were being subjected not to Christ, but to the ecclesiastical authority . . . Here Christian faith becomes a chance form, and the essence and purpose is posited in the dominance of the hierarchy. . .[105]

The falsity of the Catholic path was early recognized in the West, and finally that realization found expression in Protestantism. Protestantism arises against the Catholic way of salvation as [against] a merely external fact, and requests personal religious relationship of man to God. . .[106]

Personal faith, however, lacks the necessary assurance of its correctness, of its verity; the Holy Scripture, accepted by Protestantism as the criterion, requires correct understanding; thus *personal reasoning* 'becomes the source of the religious truth', says Solovyev—'Protestantism naturally evolves into Rationalism'. The 'self-assurance and self-assertion of human reason' in pure Rationalism is the second temptation to which Western humanity had fallen—the pride of reason, the sin of the mind. Reason, furthermore, is a 'ratio' of the divine-being to the phenomenal becoming (and vice versa) in man, of the ontological truth in him to his sociological experience (and conversely, again); extolled as the source of truth in itself, this 'ratio' could but manifest the insolvency of the claim—and, since it was proclaimed *the* sociological arbiter (by the French Revolution) the inevitable result was the exaltation of the phenomenal, i.e. of the natural, elements in the lives of men. This exaltation of the material interests represented the temptation, the sin of the flesh (and this is the meaning of socialism). Thus the Western peoples had succumbed to the three temptations of Christ, which they encountered in the course of European history in the reverse order of succession.

The East had not succumbed to the three temptations of the evil beginning— it retained the truth of Christ; but, guarding it in the soul of its peoples, the Eastern Church has not realized it in external reality, has not given it actual expression, has not created any Christian culture, as the West has created the culture of the Antichrist.[107]

And the East could not have created the Christian culture, says Solovyev; for the Christian culture implies the establishment in all humanity and in all its actions of the same interrelationship of the three elements of man which was established in Christ, i.e. of the voluntary integration of the two lower elements (matter and reason) in the divine beginning in man; but 'in the Orthodox Church, an enormous majority of its members was captivated into obedience to the truth through immediate attraction', not through the conscious, mental realization of

[105]Ibid.

[106]Ibid. p. 175.

[107]Ibid. p. 178.

the Christian principles in the external actuality of cultural relations and institutions.

If the true society of Godmanhood, organized after the image and in the likeness of God-man Himself, ought to represent a free concord of the divine and human beginnings, then it is obviously determined by the co-operative force of the latter as well as by the active power of the former. It is required, consequently, that society would, first, preserve in all purity and power the divine beginning (Christ's truth) and, second, develop to the fullest extent the beginning of human initiative and activity.[108]

And this is precisely what has been accomplished in history by the Eastern and Western halves of humanity:

The East clave with the entire force of its spirit to the divine, and preserved it, developing in itself the conservative and ascetic attitude necessary for that; while the West spent all its energy for the development of the human beginning, which of necessity was to the detriment [of the preservation] of the divine truth, at first disfigured and then altogether rejected. Thus it is obvious that these two directions do not in the least exclude one another but [on the contrary] are perfectly necessary each for the other and for [the attainment of] the fullness of the stature of Christ in the whole mankind.[109]

Thus Solovyev had not only reconciled but integrated—for himself—his original problem of the polarity of the East and West, as well as his own religious aspirations and sociological interests, the Orthodox ideals of Slavophilism and the stark reality of the European industrial civilization, including even its rationalism and materialistic socialism; yes, even its individualism now seen as having had its part in the full development of the 'human beginning', necessary for the complete realization of Godmanhood in society.

As in the pre-Christian historical course, the base or matter was the human nature or element: the active or forming principle was the divine mind, the logos of God; and the result [was] (the nativity) [of] Godman, i.e. God who assumed human nature: so in the course of Christianity, the base or matter has been the divine nature or element (the Word which became flesh, and Christ's body, Sophia); the active or forming beginning is human reason; and the result is man-god, i.e. man who assumes Divinity. And, as man can assume Divinity only in his absolute totality, i.e. in the integrity with *all*: man-god is necessarily collective and universal, i.e. the all-humanity or the Universal Church.[110]

The Eastern Church had given the thesis, the Western civilization has evolved the antithesis: the synthesis requires the fertilization of the West with the true spirit of Christ, with the life and love of His Spirit, and the differentiation and development of the human elements

[108]Ibid. p. 179.
[109]Ibid.
[110]Ibid. p. 180.

in the society and culture of the East, still bound with the swaddling clothes of the thesis-stage. But how is their synthesis to be effected— how will the two be brought together?

Neither the civilization nor the Church of the West had any interest in the proffers of brotherly love which came in the nineteenth century from the Russian Pan-Slavist enthusiasts. Salvation may indeed be from the East, but . . . industrialism was not interested, and the Vatican had its doubts. As a matter of fact, the official Russian Orthodox Church was even more indifferent to any ideas of Church re-union.

Yet the realization of Godmanhood implied the universal development of man-godhood. 'Man can assume Divinity only in his absolute totality', Solovyev insisted, 'the man-god is necessarily collective and universal, i.e. [man-godhood is] the all-humanity or the Universal Church.'

Readings in Dante and in the old Uniat controversy, during the major crisis in his life (1882), gave Solovyev new ideas about the Church and the State. A new light shone in and about him—he found in his readings the solution for the seemingly irreconcilable conflict between Rome and Moscow. The realization of Godmanhood on earth is to be accomplished by the Church which is to bring all mankind into voluntary obedience to the divine beginning through the universal establishment of *Theocracy*. In this Theocracy, the ecclesiastical government is to be carried on by the Roman Church, for to it has been historically delegated the priestly[111] function in the realization of Godmanhood in this world: while the Orthodox Tsar is to effect the Kingship of the Son of God, the function represented historically by Byzantium, by the Slavic nations of the Balkans, and by Russia, as the Christian secular power collaborating with the Church in that establishment of the Kingdom of God on earth. The Orthodox Church is to acknowledge the Bishop of Rome as the High Priest of the whole of Christendom, accepting his jurisdictional authority in addition to the primacy of honour, which was granted him by the first Oecumenical Council; and Rome is to accept the retention of all Orthodox rites and traditions by the Eastern Church. This healing of the rift in the Body of Christ, caused by the schism of 1054, would bring about in the Church the revivification of the real Spirit of Christ, of the original spiritual fervour and true Christian love—and that would be certain to bring the Protestant groups into the fold of their Mother-Church of Apostolic succession. Thus reunited, the One, truly Universal Church could then earnestly go about its 'Father's business' of bringing the whole world into obedience to His Son.

---

[111]Solovyev, quite erroneously, regarded it as a prerogative of God the Father: the Church and the Scripture speak of Christ as the High Priest, *He* is 'the Priest forever after the order of Melchisidec'.

For the second great commandment, 'Love thy neighbour as thyself', extends beyond the individuals unto the nations, Solovyev asserted; for *one* Cup was given by the Lord of all to His apostles, and by them—from them, on—to all peoples.

Solovyev spent many years (1883-99) in arduous activities propagating his ideas of the Universal Theocracy before he conceded the futility of his efforts. Then he came to the problems of individual salvation; and it was in the working out of these problems (in the *Justification of the Good* and other works of that period) that he perceived at last the simple Scriptural truth that salvation will not be accepted by the whole world: that 'when the Son of man cometh', He will not be greeted by glad mankind, to the last man converted to His glorious truth—He will hardly find any faith upon earth . . . 'nation shall rise against nation, and kingdom against kingdom: and there shall be famines, and pestilences, and earthquakes', 'many false prophets shall rise, and shall deceive many. And because iniquity shall abound, the love of many shall wax cold'.[112] Solovyev understood that the Transfiguration of Christ was not a symbol for the world—that, rather, Golgotha was the forecast for the Church; that the earth and all mankind had to go through their crucifixion before the phenomenal universe could become fully deified Sophia: even Christ's *most holy* Body had to undergo the death of the cross. Hence Solovyev's *Narration About Antichrist* in the *Three Conversations;* hence a renewed emphasis on individual salvation: and hence the reconciliation with his Russian friends, and with the Russian Church, so aloof from the problems or politics of the world. Only a minority, even among Christians, will be found faithful when the Son of man cometh for Judgment—and that is near, Solovyev believed, 'even at the door'.

*   *   *   *

Few men encompassed the range of human problems as fully as Solovyev; and fewer yet attempted an integration of that vast domain of existence and thought, from the primitive notions of nature worship through all the complexities of the metaphysics of Idealism.

Permeated with the consciousness of the universal presence of the truth, Solovyev sought and found it everywhere: he saw it in the most diversified prismatic angles, in every, or more exactly, above every human teaching. It is not surprising [therefore] that in his conception of the universe became integrated the most diverse trends of religious and philosophic thought.[113]

Solovyev had an almost organic quest for, love of, belief in, the inherent unity of all being and thought. It was a deep conviction of his whole person that all things in the life of men and the universe have

[112]St. Matthew, xxiv. 7-12.

[113]Prince Eugene Trubetskoy, *The World-View of V. S. Solovyev;* I, p. 35.

come from God—who is the very oneness of unity—and will freely re-unite with Him, and in Him, after they will have come to know themselves and will have fully revealed themselves in their independence of Him. Because then they will also come to know *Him*, and perceive Him to be so great a good—the good itself and the source of all that is good, true, or beautiful—that they will freely choose Him and the return to Him, will choose their re-union with Him as *their own* greatest particular good: whether they be saints, heathens, molecules, or political nations.

The whole creation had room in Solovyev's heart, was genuinely, organically, dear to him. Not only did he throw himself into that one-man crusade for bringing together the Orthodox and the Catholics; he defended the Protestants as certainly a part of the one Church of Christ, however much they may have deprived themselves of the fullness of grace and truth because of their separation from the main body of the historic Church; and he prayed fervently all his life for the Jews, that they too would come into the fold of Christ's sheep, according to the word of St. Paul that in the latter days they will be released from their 'unbelief', i.e. their inability to perceive the Messiah in Jesus. Solovyev regarded all men, of whatever faith or station in life, as in some way, in some measure, carrying out God's will and purpose. He awaited the redemption of all the creatures of this world, groaning 'until now' because of man's sin,[114] which Solovyev felt as his personal guilt before them. Is not the whole of nature also a part of Sophia, in the large sense of the term?

This concept of Sophia is perhaps the most changeable in the whole construction of Solovyev's philosophy. It takes on different connotations in different contexts, although its basic meaning remains the same—that of the passive medium through which alone Logos can reduce humanity to divine obedience and deify it, and through it, in it, all created nature. In the pre-creation plan, Sophia appears to Solovyev as the divine substance or matter—a perfectly spiritual one, to be sure—the 'Wisdom of God', the *ideal* essence, *with* which or out of which God created[115] the universe *by* His Word, Logos. In Christ, it is the human part of His two-fold nature; but human, again, in the ideal sense, i.e. in the sense of the idea of humanity, or humanity as it was planned in the mind of God, and as it will be after its redemption and resurrection. In created mankind, Sophia is the collective soul of humanity, and in this sense 'the soul of the world'. As the medium through and *in* which Logos assumed humanity, as that ideal humanity

[114]Repentance, in the true Christian sense, ought to be not only individual but also collective, by each nation as a whole, according to Solovyev.

[115]This conception of Wisdom was refuted as un-Christian as far back as the second century, by Tertullian.

which enshrined Him, Sophia is likened to and linked with the Holy Virgin, Mother of Christ, in a mistaken interpretation of the scriptural passage, 'Wisdom hath builded her house, she hath hewn out her seven pillars'.[116] Yet there is no complete identification of Sophia with the Virgin Mary: Solovyev made much of a Russian ikon (known as the ikon of Sophia) which portrays the Blessed Virgin by the side of another woman's figure, that of Sophia.[117] The passivity of her auxiliary function (as the co-operative stratum necessary for the action of Logos in humanity) suggests the notion of the feminine character of Sophia; and, of course, the linquistic use of the feminine gender in regard to the term has had undoubted influence on the formation of the concept. It was 'the eternal feminine' for him; and also the Church, the Bride of Christ. At the same time Sophia is also 'the idea', an abstract beginning.

Perhaps the most complete single formulation of the term will be found in the following passage:

The central and perfect personal manifestation of Sophia is Jesus Christ; her feminine complement is the most Holy Virgin, and her universal propagation is the Church. In her feminine personality she is called Mary, in her masculine personality—Jesus; while by her proper name of Sapientia or Sophia is denoted her whole and universal manifestation in the perfect Church of the future—the Bride of the Word of God.

Treated by most of the mystics, this subject has found a renewed interest in certain contemporary Orthodox writers, such as N. Berdyaev and S. Bulgakov—no doubt, under the influence of Vladimir Solovyev. It will not be amiss to mention that two of the Russian Orthodox Synods, one of the Russian Church abroad and the other inside Russia, officially condemned the teachings of Sophia as heretical. According to St. Paul, it was noted above,[118] Wisdom is simply and definitely another name of the Second Person of the Holy Trinity, the Word of God.

Students of religion will find Solovyev's schematic synthesis of the development of religious thought in history[119] one of the most illuminating works on the subject. Students of philosophy will not fail to appreciate his keen critical analysis of the Western schools (in *The Crisis of Western Philosophy, Criticism of Abstract Principles*, and

[116]Proverbs, ix. 1.

[117]With John the Baptist on the other side of Sophia, Christ is shown behind her, having His arms stretched upward, toward the book of the four Gospels, which signifies Him as the Word of God.

[118]See p. 51, above.

[119]The third, fourth, and fifth lectures. (See also *The Mythological Process in Ancient Paganism, Judaism and the Christian Problem*, and other essays and articles on the subject of religion in 'Collected Works'.)

separate articles) as well as his positive constructions (in *The Philosophical Foundations of Integral Knowledge, The Justification of the Good*). The *Narration Concerning Antichrist* affords a striking reading of contemporary interest generally.

The most noteworthy, however, the most technically important contribution to philosophy, will be found in Solovyev's concept of the absolute as the *Subject* of being. Since it was developed in another work, the *Criticism of Abstract Principles*, it could have been but touched upon on these pages, which are concerned with his treatise on Godmanhood. Yet without question it was the fundamental grasp of that crucial problem of ontology and epistemology which made possible the entire run of subsequent integration in Solovyev's work, an inspired perception which gave the impetus to the whole unifying momentum of all his philosophy. In his brilliant analysis of rationalism and empiricism, he revealed that the confusion of the logical and grammatical concepts in the formation of the different ideas of the absolute has been the source of major philosophical errors: boldly dissecting the predicate from the subject, he asserted that being is a mere predicate, an attribute of the absolute, and that the absolute itself is the '*Subject* of being', indefinitely beyond the 'being' as such, completely ineffable in the Kantian as well as in the mystical sense. The conceptions of the Idea, of Substance, of Spirit, are merely hypostatizations of the predicates of the subject of being. 'The absolute, which is not subject to any definition (for the general conception of it is only for us), defines itself, manifesting itself as the unconditionally extant one through the positing forth of its antipode'[120]—first, within itself, realizing itself as the triune God, and then in the universe and mankind He has created: it is the Jah of Jahve, the absolute Subject— 'I am that I am'—of whom Hegel's *Idée* is the Word, Logos, expressing the being of God the Father, and whose *being*, or Spinoza's substance, is Spirit, the Holy Spirit of God, 'the Lord and Giver of Life'. In His being—which is His 'other one', His antipode—God possesses all, and is in all; in Himself, He is totally unknowable, incomprehensible: the absolute 'cannot reveal itself as it is in itself, as an external object' (external to the human mind). Only in

Divesting ourselves of all definite forms of being, of all sensations and thoughts, we can find the unconditionally extant as such in the depth of our spirit, i.e. find it not as manifest in being, but as freed, absolved of all being.[121]

The very word Absolute, says Solovyev, signifies just these two meanings—first, that it is freed, absolved of all, and then as including all, 'the completed', 'fulfilled', 'whole'—i.e. the absolute as the subject of

---

[120]V. Solovyev, *Criticism of Abstract Principles; Works*, II, p. 311

[121]Ibid. p. 307.

being, and then also as the 'being' which is Its opposite, Its substance, which the Subject of being posits forth and which gives being to all that exists and includes all particular being:

The second pole is substance, or 'prima materia' of the absolute, while the first pole is the absolute as such; it is not any new substance, different from the absolute, but is [the absolute] itself which has asserted itself as such through the assertion of its opposite.[122]

Logos, the Word of God, is the expression ('word') and at the same time the *ratio* (the Greek 'logos' = the Latin 'ratio'), the relationship between the Subject of being and His being: the *unity* between the two —the very unity of the absolute within itself—and hence the principle and the power of unity as such, and in all being.

Since all being, issuing forth from God, is organized by the Word; and He, the Word, is the unity, the inner order of God in Himself: is it much wonder that in describing His unifying ordering of phenomenal creation—and of mankind in the historically nascent Godmanhood as the fullest manifestation of Himself in that creation—Solovyev found unity and order, meaning and purpose in the vast panorama of the cosmic and historic unfoldment of the revelation of the Word, the expressed image of His Father?

'By Him' are all things;
That in the dispensation of *the fullness of times he might gather together in one all things in Christ,* both which are in heaven, and which are on earth; even in him.[123]
And in the meantime,
To justify the Faith of the fathers, to elevate it to the highest level of rational consciousness, and to show how this ancient Faith, freed from the chains of inner seclusiveness and national self-love, coincides with the eternal and immutable truth.[124]

to integrate the philosophical verity of the mind with the religious truth of the faith—this was, in Solovyev's own words, the aim of his life.

That integration was not complete until he had fully perceived the truth of Christ Crucified. His Christianity was still the pantheistic Christianity of the natural world, 'of the world' and *for* the world, when he sought to bring all mankind under the sceptre of Christ the King: only after his acquaintance with Western Christianity did he come to realize that Christ's sceptre has won—and can be won—only by the agony and the death of the Cross; and that this applies to the world as well.

[122]Ibid. p. 311.

[123]Ephesians, i.10. Italics are mine.

[124]V. Solovyev.

LECTURE ONE

I AM going to discuss the truths of positive religion—subjects which are far away from contemporary consciousness, foreign to the interests of contemporary civilization. The interests of contemporary civilization, however, were not here yesterday and will not be present tomorrow. Is it not permissible to prefer matters which are equally important at all times?

I will not dispute those who at the present time maintain a negative attitude toward the religious principle. I shall not argue with the contemporary opponents of religion—because they are right. I say that those who at the present time refuse religion are right, because religion appears in reality not what it ought to be.

Religion, speaking generally and abstractly, is the connection of man and the world with the unconditional beginning, which is the focus of all that exists. It is evident that if we admit the reality of this unconditional beginning, it must define all the interests and the whole content of human life; consciousness must depend upon it; and to it must be related all that is essential in what man does, learns, and creates. If we admit the existence of such an unconditional centre, then all points on the circle of life must be linked to that centre with equal radii. It is only then that unity, wholeness, and accord appear in the life and consciousness of man. It is only then that all his deeds and sufferings in life, great or small, are transmuted into intelligent, inwardly necessary *events* from a state of aimless and senseless *phenomena*. It is quite certain that such all-embracing, central importance must belong to the religious principle, once it is admitted at all; and it is equally indubitable that in reality, for the contemporary civilized humanity, even for that part of it which recognizes the religious principle, religion does not possess this all-embracing and central importance. Instead of being all in all, it hides in a very small and remote corner of our inner world, and appears as one of a multitude of the different interests which divide our attention.

Contemporary religion represents a very pitiful thing: properly speaking, religion as the dominating principle, as the centre of spiritual attraction, does not exist today; instead, there is the so-called religiosity as a personal mood, a personal taste: some people have this taste, others do not, just as some people like music and others do not.

In the absence of the unconditional centring [of all interests in religion] we have as many relative, temporary centres of life and consciousness as we have different requirements and interests, tastes and inclinations, opinions and points of view.

It would be superfluous to dwell upon the mental and moral discord and the lack of principle, at present prevalent in the realm of society as well as in the minds and hearts of the individuals, for that fact is too well known to anyone at all introspective or observant.

That lack of principle, that discord, is an undoubted and obvious fact; but it is also an undoubted and obvious fact that humanity is not content with that, that it is at least seeking some uniting and integrating principle. We see, in fact, that contemporary Western civilization, having repudiated the religious principle as something that in its given form proved to be subjective and impotent, even that civilization is trying to find certain binding principles for the [human] life and consciousness outside of the religious sphere, is endeavouring to substitute something for the gods which it has cast away. Although according to the prevalent conviction all the ends and beginnings of human existence are reduced to the present reality, to the given natural existence, and our life is locked 'in a narrow ring of sublunal impressions'; yet even in that narrow ring contemporary civilization is labouring to find a unifying and organizing principle for mankind.

All modern civilization is characterized by this striving to organize humanity outside of the unconditional religious sphere, to establish itself and make itself comfortable in the realm of the temporal, finite interests.

Most logically, with the greatest consciousness and fullness, that trend is manifested in two contemporary constructions: one of these—*socialism*—can be referred pre-eminently to practical interests of social life; while the other—*positivism*—has to do with the theoretical realm of scientific *knowledge*.

Neither socialism nor positivism stands in any direct relation to religion, either negatively or positively: they would simply occupy the empty space that religion has left in the life and knowledge of modern civilized humanity. It is from that point of view that they should be evaluated.

I am not going to refute socialism. It is usually refuted by those who fear its truth. But we stand upon principles for which socialism holds no menace. Thus, we can talk freely about the *truth of socialism*.

First of all, we can say that it is justified historically, as a necessary consequence, as the final word of the Western historical development which preceded it.

The French Revolution, with which the essential character of Western philosophy became well defined as extra-religious philosophy, as an attempt to build an edifice of universal culture, to organize mankind upon purely secular, external principles—the French Revolution, I say, proclaimed as a basis of social order the rights of *man* instead of the former divine right [established as such a basis formerly]. The *rights* of man can be reduced to two main rights, those of *liberty* and *equality*, which are to be reconciled in brotherhood.[1] The great Revolution proclaimed freedom, equality, and brotherhood. It proclaimed them, but did not realize them: the three words remained empty words. Socialism is an attempt to realize these three principles actually. The Revolution established civil liberty. But with the existing social inequality, the emancipation from one dominating class is a subjugation to another. The power of monarchy and feudal lords was merely replaced with the power of capital and of the bourgeoisie. Freedom alone does not give anything to the popular majority if there is no equality. The Revolution proclaimed the latter also. But in our world based on struggle, on unlimited competition of the individual, *equality of rights* means nothing without the *equality of powers*. The principle of equality, of equal rights, proved to be real only for those who at the given historical moment possessed power.

Historically, however, [state] power changes hands, and the bourgeoisie, as the property-owning class, took advantage of the principle of equality for its own benefit, because at the given historical moment it had the power. In a like manner, the 'have-not' class, the proletariat, naturally strives to take advantage of the same principle of equality for its own benefit as soon as the power will pass into its hands.

Social order must rest upon some positive basis. That basis either has the unconditional, supernatural and superhuman, character, or it belongs to the conditional sphere of the given human nature; the social order rests either upon the *will of God* or upon the *people's will*; the will of men. One cannot argue against this dilemma by stating that social order can be defined as the state-power of the government, for this state power itself, as government, also rests upon something: either upon the will of God or upon the popular will.

The first member of the dilemma was rejected by Western civilization; the French Revolution, having broken with traditional principles, resolutely established the democratic principle according to which social order rests upon the will of the people. The popular will, from this point of view, is nothing more than the will of the aggregate of the persons comprising the nation. Indeed, the great Revolution started with the proclamation that man, as such, has unconditional rights by virtue of his human dignity; and that, since the same general human dignity, which forms the source of all rights, belongs by nature to all persons, all persons necessarily have equal rights. Each of those individuals by himself as the legislative power and, as a result, the legislative power belongs to the majority of the people.

[1]If the supreme value of man as such, his status of being a law unto himself, is recognized, then the acknowledgment of his *freedom* follows naturally: for nothing can have power over him who is himself the source of all power; and, as the status of man belongs to all people, [their] equality follows from the same [premise].

If the will of the popular majority represents the basis, and the sole basis, of all the rights and of every law; if the will of popular majority naturally has as its object the welfare of that majority; then that welfare becomes the supreme right and law. If one class, if a minority of the people enjoys in reality a larger material welfare than the majority, then from this point of view it is a wrong and an untruth.

Such is the present situation. The Revolution which in principle asserted *democracy*, produced in fact only a plutocracy. The people is self-governed only *de jure*, while *de facto* the surpeme power belongs to its negligible fraction—to the wealthy bourgeoisie, the capitalists. As plutocracy by its very nature is generally accessible to everyone, it really represents the kingdom of free competition or rivalry. This freedom and the equality of rights, however, appear to the majority only as an abstract possibility. The existence of hereditary property and its concentration in a few hands, make of the bourgeoisie a separate, privileged class; while the immense majority of the working people, deprived of any property, with all their abstract freedom and equality of rights become in reality an enslaved class of proletarians, for whom equality is but the equality of pauperism, and freedom is very often but the freedom to die of hunger. The presence of a constant proletariat, however, which is a characteristic feature of contemporary Western civilization, in this civilization [more than in any other] is deprived of any justification. For if the old order rested upon the well known absolute principles, then the contemporary plutocracy can refer in its favour only to the force of fact, to historical conditions. Those conditions change, however: ancient slavery also was based upon historical conditions, but that did not prevent it from disappearing. And if we were to speak about justice, would it not be just that wealth should belong to him who produces it, that is to say, to the worker? Naturally, capital, that is to say, the result of [certain] previous labour, is as necessary for the production of wealth as the present labour; but at no time has anyone been able to prove the necessity of their exclusive partition, that is to say, that some persons must be *only* capitalists while others must be *only* workers.

Thus, the striving of socialism toward the equalization of material welfare, its effort to transfer that material welfare from the hands of the minority into the hands of the majority of the people, is absolutely natural and lawful from the point of view of those principles which were proclaimed by the French Revolution and were laid down as the basis of all contemporary civilization.

Socialism appears as a force historically justified, and one to which undoubtedly belongs the immediate future in the West. It does not, however, wish to be only an historical force, to have only a conditional justification; it wishes to be the supreme moral power, it pretends to actualize the unconditional truth in the realm of social relations. Here, however, socialism unavoidably, fatally, falls into a contradiction with itself, and its inconsistency becomes evident. It wishes to manifest the truth in society; in what does the [social] truth consist? Once more, in the equalization of the material welfare. One of two alternatives must be true: either the material welfare in itself is not the aim of socialism, and only the justice of its distribution is its aim; or the material welfare is an end in itself—then, since the striving toward the material welfare is but a natural fact of human nature, the affirmation of that aim as a principle can have no moral value. Socialism proclaimed, as soon as it appeared, the re-establishment of the rights of matter; matter does have its rights, and the striving for the realization of those rights is a very natural one; but it is only one of the natural demands of man, and certainly not the very best one—the unconditional truth certainly does not lie in it. To proclaim the re-establishment of the rights of matter as a moral principle is equivalent to proclaiming the re-establishment of the rights of egoism (in a socio-religious sect in America, the founder of the group actually did substitute for the ten commandments of Moses his own twelve, the first of which stated: 'Love thyself'—a requirement quite lawful, but in most cases superfluous).

Justice, in the moral sense, is a certain voluntary limitation of one's claims in favour of the rights of others; justice thus appears as a certain sacrifice, self-denial; and the more there is of this self-sacrifice, of self-denial, the better it is in the moral sense. Therefore, from the moral viewpoint it is impossible to attach any moral value to the demand on the part of the working class for an even distribution of the material welfare; for justice here—if there is any justice here—becomes coincident for that class with its own advantages; their demand, consequently, is seeking their own good, and therefore cannot have moral value.

Sometimes socialism manifests a pretention of realizing the Christian morals. In this connection someone made the well-known jest that there is but one slight difference between Christianity and socialism, which is that Christianity urges one to give away what is one's own, while socialism urges one to take what belongs to others.

Even if we admit that the demand for economic equality on the part of the non-possessing class is only the demand for getting its own, that which justly belongs to it, even then that demand cannot have any moral value in the positive sense; for to take one's own is only a *right*, and in no way a merit. In its demands, even if they be admitted to be just, the working class rests evidently upon the legal, not upon the moral point of view.

But if socialism cannot have any moral significance as the self-seeking aim of the non-possessing class, it is not thereby precluded from manifesting the moral character as a demand for social truth, irrespective of who presents that demand. Indeed, socialism is right in rebelling against the existing social untruth. But where is the root of

71

that untruth? Evidently in the fact that the social order rests upon the egoism of individuals, whence come their competition, their struggle, enmity, and all social evils.

But if the root of social untruth consists of egoism, then social truth must be based upon the opposite [of egoism], that is to say, upon the principle of self-denial or love [for others].

In order to realize that truth, every single member of society must set a limit to his exclusive self-assertion, must adopt the point of view of self-denial, must renounce his exclusive will, must sacrifice it. But in whose favour? For whom, from the moral standpoint, ought one to sacrifice one's will? Is it in favour of other particular persons, each of whom rests upon egoism, upon self-assertion? Is it to be in favour of all of them together?

It is impossible to sacrifice one's own will, one's own self-assertion, in favour of all men; for all, as an aggregate of separate persons, do not represent and cannot constitute the true aim of human activity; for totality is not a datum of experience, it is only a specific group of persons which is concrete. Self-sacrifice [in favour of particular persons] would be also unjust, because it would be unfair, while denying one's own egoism, to confirm it in others, to support someone else's egoism.

Thus, the realization of the truth or of the moral principle is possible only in relation to that which by its very nature is truth. The moral limit of egoism of a given person is not the egoism of others, not their self-asserting will, but only that which in itself cannot be exclusive and egoistic, that which in itself, by its nature, is truth. Only when all personally realize the truth and are participants of the unconditional moral principle, only then can the will of all be the moral law for me. Consequently, love and self-sacrifice in their relation to men are possible only when they manifest the unconditional principle which stands above men, the principle in relation to which all equally represent an untruth, and all equally must recant that untruth.

Otherwise, if such an unconditional principle is not acknowledged, if all other men appear only as conditional beings, representing a certain natural force, then subjection to them will result only in oppression on their part. Every power that does not represent the unconditional principle of the truth is oppression, and subjection to such a power can be only a forced one. The *free* subjection of each to all, then, is evidently possible only when all are themselves subjected to the unconditional moral principle, in relation to which they are *equal* among themselves, as all finite quantities are equal in respect to infinity.

At the same time it is quite unimportant who advances the claim to exercise that power, whether it be a single person, or the majority of the people, or even the majority of mankind; because quantity in itself does not, obviously, give any moral right, and the mass as the mass does not represent any inner pre-eminence. (If one was to speak about convenience, then undoubtedly the despotism of a single person is much more convenient than the despotism of the mass).

By nature men are not equal among themselves, because they do not possess equal powers; and as a result of the inequality of their powers, they necessarily find themselves in a state of forced subjection one to another; consequently, by nature they are not free either; finally, by nature men are strange and inimical towards each other—natural humanity by no means represents a brotherhood. If, thus, the realization of the truth is impossible on the ground of the given natural conditions, in the kingdom of nature, then it is possible only in the Kingdom of grace, that is to say, on the basis of the moral principle, as the unconditional or divine.

Thus, by its demand for the social truth, and by the impossibility of its realization on the finite natural bases, socialism logically leads to the recognition of the necessity of the unconditional principle in life, i.e., to the acknowledgment of religion.

Positivism leads to the same conclusion in the realm of knowledge. The so-called enlightenment of the eighteenth century proclaimed against traditional theology the rights of the human reason. Reason, however, is only a means, an instrument, or a medium of knowledge, but not its content. Reason gives the ideal *form*, while the content of reason or of rational knowledge is *reality;* and, as the supernatural, metaphysical reality is rejected by the rationalist enlightenment, there remains only the conditional reality of the given natural phenomena. Truth [verity] is the given fact, that which occurs or happens. Such is the general principle of positivism. One cannot fail to see in it a lawful desire to *realize* the truth, to actualize it in the far limits of reality, to demonstrate it as a visible, palpable fact; just as in socialism one cannot deny the presence of a lawful effort to realize the moral principle, to carry it out to the extreme limits of life, into the sphere of the material economic relations. In order that the [moral] truth could be manifested by man in a lower sphere of life, it must previously exist by itself, independently of man; in the same manner, before the truth [as verity] may become a fact for man, it must have its own reality. Indeed, as each separate given will does not represent by itself any good or any truth, but becomes righteous solely through the normal relationship or consent with the general will—general not in the sense of mechanistic union of the wills of many or of all, but in the sense of the will which is by its nature universal, that is to say, the will of Him Who is all, the will of God—in the same way, a separately taken fact, an individual phenomenon, obviously does not represent the truth by itself, in its detachment, but is acknowledged as true only in a normal relation, in a logical connection or accord with the whole or with the reality of the whole; and that, again not in a mechanistic sense, not in the sense of the totality of all phenomena or facts. For, in the first place, such a

73

totality cannot exist in our knowledge, because the number of facts and phenomena is inexhaustible and, consequently, cannot represent any definite sum; and secondly, even if such a totality existed, it would not have represented the truth by itself, because if each separate fact is not the truth, then obviously, the summing together of all such separate facts which are not the truth, will not obtain the truth (as a multitude of zeros will not produce a unit, and a multitude of rascals will not produce a single righteous man). Consequently, the reality of the whole, the universal, or the entire reality is the reality of *Him Who is all*—the reality of God. But that unconditional reality is accessible, as such, only to an immediate perception, in an internal revelation; that is to say, it represents the object of *religious* knowledge.

Thus, both socialism and positivism lead, when their principles are logically developed, to a demand for the religious principles in life and in knowledge.

Religion is the reunion of man and the world with the unconditional and integral principle. That principle, as integral and all-embracing, excludes nothing, and therefore the true union with it, the true religion cannot exclude, or suppress, or forcibly subject to itself any element whatever, any living force either in man or in his universe.

The re-union, or religion, consists in the bringing of all natural forces of human life, all particular principles and forces of humanity, into correct relation with the unconditional central principle, and through it, as well as in it, into correct, harmonious relationship among themselves.

As the unconditional principle, by its nature, cannot admit (any) exclusiveness or coercion, that union of particular aspects of life and individual forces with the integral principle, as well as among themselves, must be unconditionally free: at the same time, all these principles and forces, each inside of its own limits, the limits of its own function or its own idea, have equal rights for existence and development. As, however, they are all united into a single, common, unconditional whole, to which they are related as different but equally indispensable elements they mutually represent a complete solidarity or *brotherhood*.

Thus, from this point of view, the religious principle appears to be the only actual realization of liberty, equality, and fraternity.

I said that according to the meaning of the religious idea, the reunion of separate beings and particular principles and forces with the unconditional beginning must be free; this means that those separate beings and those particular principles must of themselves or by their own will come to a re-union and unconditional accord, must themselves deny their own exclusiveness, their own self-assertion or egoism.

The way toward salvation, toward the realization of true equality, true freedom and brotherhood, is that of self-denial. For self-denial, however, a previous self-assertion is necessary: in order to deny one's own exclusive will, it is necessary first to have it; in order that the particular principles and forces might freely reunite with the unconditional beginning, they must have first separated from it; they must *stand on their own*, must strive toward exclusive dominion and unconditional significance; for it is only actual experience, a tasted contradiction, the experienced fundamental insolvency of that self-assertion, that can lead toward a voluntary self-denial, as well as toward a conscious and free demand for a union with the unconditional beginning.

Hence can be seen the great meaning of the negative [or] the Western development, the great purpose of Western civilization. It represents the complete and logical falling away of the human, natural forces from the divine beginning, their exclusive self-assertion, the striving to found the edifice of universal culture upon themselves. Through the insolvency and fated failure of that trend comes forth self-denial, and self-denial leads towards the free reunion with the divine beginning.

A fundamental change, a great crisis in the consciousness of the Western part of humanity has already begun. A clear expression of it is manifest in the development and the success of pessimistic ideas according to which the existing reality is evil, deceit, and suffering; while the source of that reality and, consequently, of that evil, deceit, and suffering lies in the self-asserting will, in the will to live—which means that salvation is in the negation of that will, in self-negation.

This pessimistic point of view, which turns toward self-negation, has been manifested so far only in theory, in a philosophic system; but one can foresee with certainty that soon—namely, when the social revolution in the West will be victorious and, after it will have won its victory, will see its own insolvency, the impossibility of establishing a harmonious and correct social order, of realizing the truth upon the foundations of a conditional transient existence—when the Western part of humanity will be convinced by facts, by historical reality, that the self-assertion of the will, no matter how it may manifest itself, is the source of evil and suffering: then pessimism, the turn toward self-denial, will pass from theory into life, and Western humanity will be ready to accept the religious principle, the positive revelation of true religion.

According to the law of the division of historical functions, however, one and the same cultural type, one and the same nation cannot realize two universal ideas, perform two historical acts; and if Western civilization had as its task, as its world function, the embodiment of the negative transition from the religious past to the religious future, then the task of laying the foundation for that religious future is reserved for another historical force.

LECTURE TWO

I HAVE said that the purpose of the Western development, of the Western extra-religious civilization, was to serve humanity as a necessary transition from its religious past to its religious future.

We can obtain some idea of the general character of this future if we consider the sins of the religious past, the essence of its chief untruth, which necessitated its negation as well as a negative transition toward other forms.

The religious past about which I now speak is represented by Roman Catholicism. Although the insolvency of this form [of religion] by now has been understood, yet until a change from it to a new and better form, a still more positive and all-embracing one, will have taken place, until then Catholicism will retain both its conditional power and its conditional right. Until the positive creative principles of the future will become realized in the life and consciousness of civilized humanity, until then the positive past will continue to weigh over [dominate] the negative present. It can be nullified, and will be effectively and finally nullified only by a principle which will give more than it [the positive principle of the past] has given, but not by any feeble empty negation. That is why Catholicism still stands and carries on a stubborn struggle against the intellectual and social progress—the progress that will gain a fate-like unconquerable power over the old principle, but only at the time when it will reach positive deductions, when it will establish such foundations upon which it will be possible to build a new world, not only *freer*, but also *richer in its spiritual forces*.

Who would venture to say that modern Europe is richer in spiritual forces than, for instance, the Catholic and knightly Europe of the Middle Ages?

There is going on at present among our Western neighbours the so-called cultural struggle against Catholicism; in that struggle it is impossible for any impartial man to take a stand on either side. If the defenders of culture justly reproach Catholicism for having employed force against the enemies of Christianity, as if following the example of its patron, St. Peter, who drew his sword in the garden of Gethsemane in order to defend Christ; if they justly reproach Catholicism for its striving to create external, earthly forms and formulas for matters spiritual and divine, as if following the same Apostle in his wish to build material tabernacles for Christ, Moses, and Elias on Mount Thabor at the time of the Transfiguration: then the defenders of Catholicism can justly reproach contemporary culture in that, having denied Christianity and the religious principles in favour of a desire for material welfare and wealth, it [the contemporary civilization] followed the worse example of another apostle, one who betrayed Christ for thirty pieces of silver.

For reasons easily understood, it is seldom that we find an impartial attitude towards Catholicism, not only on the part of the Protestant and rationalistic point of view, but also on the part of one positively religious and ecclesiastical. Justly reproaching Catholicism for its inclination to 'lay upon the truth of God the rotted weight of earthly armour', people do not want to see it in that same truth of God even though it has been clothed in an unbecoming garment. As a result of the historical conditions, Catholicism at all times has shown itself the arch-enemy of our [Russian] people and of our [Orthodox] Church; but it is precisely on this account that we ought to be just towards it.

The following lines of the poet are quite applicable to the Roman Church:

> Heaven she did not forget;
> But she has also learned all that pertains to
> the earth—
> And the earth's dust got laid upon her.

Ordinarily we mistake this earthly dust for the very essence, for the idea of Catholicism, whereas, as a matter of fact, the general idea of Catholicism is first of all the truth that all secular powers and principles, all the powers of society and of the individual man must be subjected to the religious principle; that the Kingdom of God, represented on earth by the spiritual society—the Church—must possess [dominate] the kingdom of this world.

If Christ said: 'My kingdom is not of this world', it was precisely because it is not of this world, is higher than this world, and the world is to be subjected to Him; for it was also Christ who said: 'I have overcome the world'.

Since, however, even after that victory the duality of that which is God's and of that which is Cæsar's still remained, because the secular society did not merge with the spiritual, the Church did not assimilate the State: the problem about the correct relationship—such as it ought to be—between the two authorities, remained an open question. From the religious point of view only one general answer is possible to that question: if the Church is really the Kingdom of God on earth, then all the other forces and authorities must be subjected to it, must be its instruments. If the Church represents the unconditional divine beginning, then all the rest must be conditional, dependent, subservient to it. Obviously there cannot be two independent, two supreme principles in human life—one cannot serve two masters. There is talk of a strict division or demarkation of the ecclesiastical and civil spheres. The problem, however, is precisely in that—can the civil sphere, can the matters of the world be absolutely independent, have such unconditional independence as ought to belong to the divine affairs? Can the external civil interests of man be severed from his inner spiritual interests without destroying the vitality of both? Is not such a separation of the internal and the external principles that which has been called 'death and decay'? If the temporal life of man serves only as a means and transition towards the eternal life, then all the interests and acts of this life must be also only means and instruments for the eternal spiritual interests and matters, must in one way or another be conditioned by the eternal life and the Kingdom of God; and once the state and society have acknowledged themselves to be Christian, such a point of view must be obligatory for them.

The kingdom of the world must be subjected to the Kingdom of God, the worldly forces of society and man must be subjected to the spiritual force: but what manner of subjection is meant by that, and *how*, by what means and methods is it to be realized?

It is obvious that the character and the means of that subjection must correspond to the unconditional divine beginning in the name of which the subjection is required. If, moreover, God is acknowledged in Christianity to be love, reason, and free spirit, then, thereby, all oppression and slavery, every blind and dark influence, are excluded: the subjection of the principles of the world to the divine beginning must be voluntary and can be attained [only] through the internal power of the subjugating beginning.

'In my father's house are many mansions', said Christ.

Everything finds its place in the Kingdom of God, everything can be bound by an inner harmonious connection, nothing has to be suppressed or destroyed. The spiritual society—the Church—should subject worldly society to itself by raising it up to itself, by spiritualizing it, by making the worldly element its instrument and means, its body; then the external unity would appear by itself, as a natural result. In Catholicism, however, the external unity appears not as the result but as the foundation, and at the same time as the aim. For [the attainment of] an external unity as a [deliberate] aim, however, there is but one means—an external force; and Catholicism adopts it and [thereby] places itself in the ranks of the other external, i.e. the worldly, forces. But asserting itself as a worldly external force, Catholicism thereby obviously justifies also the self-assertion of those other external forces which it strives to subject to itself, and thus itself renders that subjection impossible.

As the higher principle, the principle of the general, Catholicism demands subjection to itself on the part of the particular and individual, the subjection of the human personality. By becoming an external power, however, it ceases to be the higher principle and loses its *right* of dominion over the human personality (which does possess internal power); while its factual domination appears only as coercion and suppression, provoking a necessary and just protest on the part of the personality—in which lies the essential meaning and justification of Protestantism.

Beginning with Protestantism, Western civilization represents a gradual emancipation of the human personality, of the human *ego*, from that historical bond, founded on tradition, which united but at the same time enslaved men during the period of the Middle Ages. The great meaning of the historical process which began with the Reformation consists in the fact that it has segregated the human personality and left it to itself in order that it might consciously and freely turn to the divine beginning, enter with it into a perfectly free and deliberate union.

Such a union would be impossible if the divine beginning were purely external to man, if it were not rooted in the human personality itself; in that case man could find himself in regard to the divine beginning only in a forced, fated subjection. The free internal union between the unconditional divine beginning and the human personality is possible only because the latter itself has an unconditional value. The human personality can unite with the divine beginning freely, from within itself, only because it is itself in a certain sense divine, or, more exactly, participant of Divinity.

The human personality—not, however, human personality in general, not the abstract idea of it, but [taken to mean] a real living person, an individual man—has unconditional, divine value. In this affirmation Christianity agrees with contemporary mundane civilization.

In what does this unconditionality, this divinity of the human personality consist?

Unconditionality, like other similar concepts (such as infinity, the absolute) has two meanings, negative and positive.

The negative unconditionality, which undoubtedly belongs to human personality, consists in the ability to transcend every limited content in the capacity not to be limited by it, not to be satisfied with it but to request something greater: in the capacity 'To seek beatitudes, for which there is no name or measure', in the words of a poet.

Not satisfied with any finite conditional content, man does, indeed, declare himself to be free from any internal limitation, declaring [thus] his negative unconditionality, which constitutes the surety of an infinite development. The dissatisfaction with any finite content, with any partial limited actuality is itself a request for full reality, full content. In the *possession* of the whole reality, however, of the fullness of life, lies the *positive* unconditionality. Without it, or at least without the possibility of it, the negative unconditionality has no significance, or, rather, means only an internal insoluble contradiction. The human consciousness of today finds itself in just such a contradiction.

Western civilization has liberated human consciousness from all external limitations, acknowledged the negative unconditionality of the human personality, proclaimed the unconditional rights of man. At the same time, however, having rejected every principle unconditional in the positive sense, that is to say, in reality, and by its very nature possessed of the entire plenitude of being; having circumscribed the life and consciousness of man with a circle of the conditional and transitory: this civilization has asserted [thereby] the striving and the impossibility of its satisfaction.

Contemporary man is aware that he is internally free, deems himself to be higher than any external principle independent of him, asserts himself as the centre of everything; but with all that, appears in reality to be only one infinitely small and disappearing [transitory] dot upon the circumference of the world.

Contemporary consciousness acknowledges that the human personality has divine rights, but does not give to it either the divine powers or the divine content; for contemporary man admits—in life as well as in knowledge—only a limited conditional reality, the reality of particular facts and phenomena—and from this point of view is himself but one of those particular facts.

Thus, on the one hand, man is a being with unconditional significance, with unconditional rights and demands; and [on the other hand] the same man is but a limited and transitory phenomenon, a fact among the multitude of other facts, on all sides limited by them and dependent upon them—and this is true not only [of] the individual man, but [of] the whole humanity. From the atheistic point of view it is not only the individual man who appears and disappears, like all other facts and phenomena of nature; according to that point of view the whole of humanity, having appeared on this globe as a result of natural conditions, may, as a result of a change in the same natural conditions, disappear without a trace from this globe, or perish together with it. Man is everything for himself, and yet his very existence appears to be conditional and constantly problematical [precarious]. If this contradiction were purely theoretical, if it pertained to some abstract problem and object, then it would not be so fatal and tragic, then it could be disregarded, and man could flee from it into experience, into [its] live interests. When, however, the contradiction lies in the very centre of human consciousness, when it concerns the very human *ego* and spreads over all his vital forces, then there is no way of fleeing from it, no escape from it. We have to adopt, one of the two parts of the [following] dilemma: either man really has that unconditional value, those unconditional rights which he, in his inner subjective consciousness allows himself to have—in such case he must have also the possibility of [means, innate endowments, for] realizing that value, those rights; or else man is only a fact, only a conditional and limited phenomenon that is present today but tomorrow may not exist, and in some few score years *certainly* will cease to exist;

in that case let him be only a fact. A fact in itself is neither true nor false, neither good nor evil—it is merely natural, merely necessary; [and if he is only a fact] then let man cease striving for the truth and the good, since there are merely conditional concepts, essentially but empty words. If man is only a fact, if he is inevitably limited by the mechanism of the external reality, then let him seek not anything greater than that natural reality, then let him 'eat, drink, and be merry'; and if he is not gay, then he can, perhaps, terminate that his factual existence with just as factual an end.

Man, however, does not wish to be a mere fact, to be only a phenomenon; and this unwillingness is already a hint that actually he is not a mere fact, that he is not a phenomenon only, but something greater. For what is the meaning of a fact which refuses to be [but] a fact? or of a phenomenon which does not wish to be [only] a phenomenon?

This does not, of course, prove anything beside the fact that, in accepting the first part of the dilemma, by resolutely and logically taking the side of the mechanistic point of view, we do not escape the contradiction but only make it sharper.

[Then], however, a question presents itself: what is the basis of this mechanistic point of view according to which man is but one of nature's phenomena, an insignificant wheel inside of the world mechanism?

In order to accept such a view—which delivers a mortal blow to all essential strivings of man and makes life impossible for anyone who would assume such a point of view fully and logically—in order to accept it, one must, obviously, have very firm reasons. If that point of view contradicts the human will and feelings, then it must be unconditionally necessary, at least for the intellect, [i.e.] it must possess an unconditional theoretical truth. And, in fact, it [the mechanistic point of view] does make that claim But the claim to absolute verity on the part of the view which recognizes only the relative and the negative, seems strange. It represents another contradiction. However, let us admit even that; let us admit that the mechanistic point of view *may* be unconditionally true; what is the reason which would compel us to recognize it to be really such? As Leibnitz has already noted a long time ago, every doctrine is true in what it asserts, and is false in, or because of, that which it denies or excludes. Thus, in regard to the mechanistic view, or materialism, (I am using here both terms without distinction, for I have in mind only that sense [of each] of them in which they coincide) we must acknowledge that its general fundamental assertions are perfectly true. They may be reduced to the following: first, *all that exists, consists of force and matter;* and, second, *all that occurs, occurs of necessity, or according to immutable laws.*

In their generality these propositions do not exclude anything and can be acknowledged even from the spiritual point of view. In fact, everything consists of matter and force, but these are very general conceptions. We speak of physical forces, we speak of spiritual forces. Forces of either kind can be real. In agreeing with materialism further, that forces cannot exist by themselves, but necessarily belong to certain real units or atoms, which represent the subjects of these forces, we can understand with Democritus the subject of these forces—the human soul—also to be such a real unit, a special atom or monad of a higher order which possesses, as all atoms do, eternity [eternal being].

If the general proposition stated above does not provide any grounds for denying the independence of spiritual forces, which are as real as physical forces; and if, in fact, the more philosophical, more logical minds among the representatives of the mechanistic point of view do not deny the reality and independence of spiritual forces (the reduction of spiritual forces to the physical ones, the assertion that the soul, or thought, is an emanation of the brain just as bile is the secretion of the liver, is true only of the poorer representatives, of the mechanistic world-view, of poor scientists and poor philosophers); if, I say, from this general point of view, there is no basis for denying the existence and independence of spiritual forces known to us, then there is not any more ground to deny from this point of view, the existence and the full reality of the infinite multitude of other forces, unknown to us, *occult* for us in our present state.

In the same way, agreeing that all that occurs, occurs of necessity, we must distinguish various kinds of necessity. It is of necessity that a stone, when let down, falls to the ground; a ball striking another ball, of necessity sets it into motion; it is of necessity also that the sun by its rays generates life in the plant: the process is determined, but the means of that determining action are different. A certain mental picture in the mind of the animal calls forth this or that movement; a sublime idea, once it has found its way into man's soul, stimulates him to noble exploits; there is [an element of necessity] in all these instances, but necessity of different kinds.

The idea of necessity [taken] in a broad sense—and there is no reason for understanding it in a narrow way—the idea of necessity does not by any means exclude freedom. Freedom is but one of the species of necessity. When freedom is contrasted with necessity, this contrast usually signifies the contrast between the *internal* and the *external* necessity.

For instance, it is necessary for God to love all and to manifest the eternal idea of the good in [all] creation; God cannot nourish enmity, in God there can be no hatred: love, reason, freedom, are necessary with God. We must say, [in other words] that for God *freedom is necessary*—which indicates that freedom cannot be a concept logically, unconditionally excluding the concept of necessity.

Everything occurs according to immutable laws; but in the different spheres of being, obviously, must obtain diverse laws (or to be more exact, different applications of one and the same law): and out of this diversity naturally follows the difference of the interrelations among particular laws, so that the laws of a lower order can appear to be subject [subordinate] to the laws of a higher order; as when we admit specific differences between universal forces, we have the right to admit also the difference in their relations, to admit the existence of the higher and more mighty forces capable of subjecting to themselves other forces.

Thus the fundamental propositions of materialism, which are undoubtedly true, by their generality and indefiniteness do not exclude anything and leave all problems open. Materialism appears to be a definite point of view only in its negative, exclusive aspect, in the assertion that there are no other forces except the physical [ones], that there is no other matter except that with which experimental physics and chemistry have to deal—that there are no other laws in nature except the mechanical laws which regulate the movement (and, possibly, also the laws, just as mechanistic, of the association of ideas within human consciousness). If we encounter in experience something which does not appear to have the mechanical character (for instance, life, creation), then it is only an illusion [materialism maintains]; *essentially* all is a mechanism and everything *must be* reduced to mechanical relations. On what grounds are this negation and this demand based? Certainly not on science, for science, studying the phenomena given in experience and the mechanism of their external relationships, does not set before itself ultimate problems which concern the essence of things. Undoubtedly, all that exists must have a mechanistic aspect, which is subject to exact science; but, obviously, it would be a very gross and arbitrary assumption to acknowledge the reality [only] of this one aspect. If exact science stops where mechanism ends, does it mean that the end of exact science is also the end of everything, or at least of all knowledge? Obviously this is the sort of a logical jump that is possible only in a mind completely possessed by a preconceived idea. Science deals with matters and forces, but what matter and force really are, that question is not any of its concern; and if a scientist should have from a metaphysician that matter is in reality but sense perception, and that force is really the will, then he, as a scientist, cannot say anything either for or against such an assertion. If, however, the negative principle of materialism is not—and it is certain that it is not—the result of exact science (which, in general, is not concerned with the universal and ultimate principles) then it is only a philosophical proposition. But in the realm of philosophical perception (as is well known to anyone who is but slightly familiar with this domain) not only is there no ground for denying the existence of the spiritual forces as independent of the physical forces, but there are solid philosophical grounds for the assertion that the physical forces themselves can be reduced to the spiritual. It would be inappropriate to try to prove that proposition here, but it is obvious that in philosophy whole doctrines—one can even say, the greater number of philosophical doctrines—accept the reducibility of the physical forces to the spiritual ones; so that materialism, at best, is only one of the philosophical opinions.

But if materialism as a theory is only one of the philosophical opinions, and, consequently, the acknowledgment of the unconditional correctness of that opinion is but an arbitrary belief—in what, then, does the indubitable practical strength of materialism consist? If that force has no positive basis, then it must have a negative one: it is based on the impotence of the principle opposite [to it], the spiritual principle, as the strength of any falsehood consists of the impotence of the [corresponding] truth, and the strength of an evil in the impotence of the [corresponding] good. The impotence of a truth lies, of course, not in truth itself, but within us, in our inconsistency: by not carrying out a truth to the end, we limit it—and any limitation of the truth provides an expanse for falsehood.

As truth cannot contradict itself, complete consistence [in carrying out the truth of any local pattern] will inevitably bring it to victory; just as the same consistence is fatal to falsehood, which maintains itself only by an internal contradiction [within a pattern].

The beginning of verity [in the subject under discussion] is the conviction that the human personality is not only negatively unconditional (which is a fact)—that is to say, that it does not wish and cannot be satisfied with any conditional, limited content—but that human personality is able to reach the positive unconditionality as well; that is to say, that it [the human personality] is able to possess the whole content, the fullness of being is not a mere fantasy, a subjective phantom, but a real, pregnant with forces, actuality. Thus one's faith in oneself, faith in human personality, is at the same time faith in God; for Divinity belongs to man as well as to God—with this one difference, that God possesses it in eternal reality, whereas man can only attain to it, to him it is granted; and that in the given state [of man], for him it is only a possibility, only an aspiration.

The human ego is unconditional in potentiality and infinitesimal in reality. This contradiction constitutes evil and suffering, in it lies the captivity, the inner slavery of man. Emancipation from this slavery may be had only in the attainment of that unconditional content, of that fullness of being which is asserted by the infinite striving of the human ego. '[Ye shall] know the truth, and the truth shall make you free'.

Before man can reach this unconditional content in life, he must reach it in his consciousness; before he can *know* it as a reality lying *outside of himself*, he must become *aware* of it as an idea *in himself*. A positive conviction [of the truth] of an idea is a conviction [of the certainty] of its [possible] realization; for an unrealizable idea is a phantom and deceit; and if it is madness not to believe in God, then it is still a greater madness to believe in Him only in part.

The old traditional form of religion has issued forth from the faith in God, but it has failed to carry out this faith to the end. The modern extra-religious civilization proceeds from the faith in man, but it, too, remains inconsistent—does not carry its faith to its [logical] end. But when both of these faiths, the faith in God and the faith in man are carried out consistently and realized in full, they meet in the unique, complete, and integral truth of Godmanhood.

Every reference to the unconditional character of human life, and to human personality as the bearer of the unconditional content—every such allusion generally meets with arguments of the most elementary nature, which can be refuted with considerations just as simple and elementary.

It is argued: What sort of unconditional content can there be in life, when it is a necessary natural process, conditioned on all sides, materially dependent, completely relative?

Undoubtedly life is a natural, materially-conditioned process, subject to the laws of physical necessity. But what is to be inferred from this fact?

When a man speaks, his speech is a mechanical process which is conditioned by the bodily structure of the organs of speech, which by their movement cause certain vibrations of the air, and the vibrating movement of the air produces in the listener—through the medium of other mechanical processes in his organs of hearing—the sensation of sound; but does this mean that human speech is only a mechanical process, that it has no special content absolutely independent of, in it- self having nothing in common with, the mechanical process of speaking? Not only is this content independent of the mechanical process, but this process, on the contrary, depends upon the content, is determined by it; for when I speak, the movement of my organs of speech are directed in one way or in another, according to sounds I have to use in order to express that definite idea, that content. In the same way, when we see actors on the stage, there is no doubt that their acting is a mechanical, materially conditioned process—all their gestures and mimicry are nothing other than physical movements [namely] certain contractions of the muscles, and all their words are sound vibrations resulting from the mechanical movement of the organs of speech— yet all that does not prevent the drama staged by them from being more than a mechanical process, does not prevent it from having its inner content, quite apart from the mechanical conditions of the movements which are made by the actors for the external expression of this content and which, on the contrary, are themselves determined by this content. And if it is self-evident that without the mechanism of the nerves and the muscles in charge of the movements, as well as without the use of the speech apparatus, the actors would be unable to present the drama materially—it is also equally evident that all these material organs, which are able to produce all sorts of movements, by themselves would be unable to produce any play at all if the poetical content of the drama and the intention to present it on the stage had not already been given independently of them.

Here, however, I hear the usual declaration of materialism that not only our words and bodily movements, but also all our thoughts—and, consequently, those thoughts which represent the drama [also]—are but mechanical processes, that is to say, movements within the brain. That is a very simple view indeed! Is it not, however, too simple? Leaving aside the fact that here the truth of the materialistic principle is presupposed in advance—a principle which is at least but a debatable opinion, so that to refer to it, as to a basis, is a logical error called petitio principii—leaving aside that fact, and even adapting the general materialistic point of view (that is to say, admitting that thought cannot exist without the brain), it is easy to see that the observation just made results only in a restatement of the problem, but in no way provides its solution in the materialistic sense.

Indeed, if in our words and gestures we must distinguish their *content*, that is to say, that which they express, from their *mechanism*, i.e., the means of that expression; then the same distinction appears necessary in regard to our thoughts, in regard to which the vibrating particles of the brain represent the same mechanism as the voice organs are for our speech (which is but a thought transferred from the apparatus of the brain to that of the voice).

Thus, admitting the necessary material connection between the thought and the brain, admitting that the movements of brain-particles are the material cause, (causa materialis) of the thought, we do not remove in any way the obvious *formal* difference, or even the incommensurability, between the external mechanism of the movements of brain-particles and the proper *content* of thought, which is expressed by that mechanism. Let us take a simple example. Let us suppose that at the present moment you are thinking about the Cathedral of St. Sophia in Constantinople. The picture of that temple appears in your mind, and even if this mental picture is conditioned by some movements of the brain-particles, yet in the mental image itself these movements are not present—only the imaged figure of the temple of St. Sophia is present in it, and nothing more. Hence it is clear that the material dependence of that representation upon some unknown movements in the brain in no way has anything to do with the formal contents of that representation; because the image of the temple of St. Sophia and the movements of the brain-particles are objects absolutely different, incommensurate one with another. If, for instance, at the time when you had the said representation, an outside observer could possibly see all that was going on in your brain (in the way that is pictured in the fairy tale of Bulwer's, *A Strange Story*), what would he see? He would see the structure of the brain, the vibration of the tiniest brain-particles; he would see, perhaps, phenomena of light proceeding from neural electricity ('the red and blue flame', as it was said in that story)—but all that would not at all resemble the mental picture which you had at the moment, and you may be quite ignorant of the brain movements and the electrical currents, while the outside observer sees only them; whence it follows directly that there can be no formal identity between the one and the other.

It is neither possible nor necessary to analyse here the problem of the relation of the thought to the brain, a problem the solution of which depends mainly upon the solution of the general problem as to the essence of matter; I had in mind only to explain by an example the obvious truth that the mechanism of any process whatever, and the ideal (ideological, to be more precise) content that is realized in it—in whatever relationship, in whatever material connection—represent, in any case, something [two categories] formally different and mutually incommensurate, in consequence of which any direct inference from the properties of one to the properties of the other (as, for example, the inference from the contingency of the mechanical process to the contingency of its own content) appears logically impossible.

To return to our subject: as soon as we admit that the life of the world and of humanity is not an accident without any meaning or purpose (and there is neither any theoretical ground for acknowledging it as such, nor any moral possibility of doing so) but represents a definite and integrated process, we are forced at once to give recognition to the content realized by that process—to which all material conditions of the process, all its mechanism, would refer as means to an end, as methods of expression to that which is expressed. As in our former example—that of the physical and spiritual natures in the actors—[in which we saw that] all their capacities and forces, as well as the movements derived from these forces and capacities, have significance only as methods of external expression of that poetical content which is given in the performed drama; so also the whole mechanical aspect of the life of the universe, the whole combination of the natural forces and movements can have significance only as the material and an instrument for the external realization of the universal content, which in itself is independent of *all* those material conditions, which is, thus, *unconditional*. Such content is generally called the *idea*.

Yes, the life of man and of the world is a natural process; yes, this life is a change of phenomena, a play of natural forces; but this play presupposes the players and that which is being played—i.e., [it] presupposes unconditional personality, and unconditional content or the idea of life.

It would be childish to pose the question, and argue, which is more necessary for the actual, complete life: the idea or the material conditions of its realization. Obviously, both are equally necessary, as in arithmetics both the multiplicand and the multiplier are necessary to obtain the product, both seven and five to get thirty-five.

It must be noted that the content or the idea is distinguished not only from the external but also from the internal nature; not only the external physical forces must serve as means, instrument, or a material condition for the realization of a certain content, but the spiritual forces also: the will, the intellect, and the senses have significance solely as means for the realization of a definite content, but by themselves do not constitute this content.

Indeed, it is obvious that—once these forces, the will, the intellect, and the senses, are given—it is obvious that there must be a definite *object* of desire, perception, and feeling: it is obvious that man cannot wish only for the sake of wishing, think for the sake of thinking (i.e. to think pure thought), or feel for the sake of feeling. As the mechanical process of physical movements is only a material ground for the ideal content, so likewise the mechanical process of spiritual phenomena, connected among themselves according to the psychological laws which are as general and as necessary as the physical laws, can have significance only as means of expression or realization of a definite content.

Man has to wish *something*, think *something* or about something, feel *something;* and this something, which constitutes the determining beginning, aim, and object of his spiritual forces and his spiritual life, is precisely what is sought, what arouses his interest, what furnished meaning. Because of his capacity for conscious deliberation, for reflection, man submits to judgment and appraisal all the factual data of his inner and exterior life; he cannot limit himself with wishing only because he would wish something, with thinking because he happens to be thinking, or with feeling because he is in the mood for feeling—he demands that the object of his will would have its own dignity in order that it may be desired by him or, to use school language, in order that it would be *objectively-desirable,* that it would be an *objective good;* in the same way he demands that the object and the content of his thought be *objectively true,* and the object of his feeling be *objectively-beautiful,* i.e., [true and beautiful] not for him only but for everyone unconditionally.

It is true that every man has his own small specific part in life; but that does not at all imply that he can content himself only with a conditional, relative content of life. In the performance of a drama every actor has his own specific rôle, but would he be able to play it well if he did not know the whole content of the drama? And as one expects from an actor not only that he *act,* but that he act *well,* so man and humanity are, likewise, not only to *live,* but to live *well,* It is said: What is the need of an objective definition of the will, i.e., of the definition of its unconditional object? It is sufficient that the will be good.

What, however, does define the good quality of the will if not its correspondence with that which is acknowledged to be objectively-desirable or is recognized as the good in itself? (It is clear to anyone that a good will aimed towards false goals can produce only evil. The inquisitors of the Middle Ages had the good will to defend the Kingdom of God on earth, but since they had bad conceptions of that Kingdom of God, of its objective essence or idea, they could bring only evil to mankind).

The same should be said about the object of knowledge and about the object of feeling; the more so as these objects are closely, inseparably interconnected or, rather, are different aspects of the same thing.

The simple, clear to all (one might say, trivial), distinction of the true from the false, of the beautiful from the ugly by itself presupposes the acknowledgment of the objective and unconditional principle in those spheres of spiritual life. Indeed, in this distinction man affirms that there is something *normal* in moral activity as well as in knowledge, in feeling, and in artistic creation that is born of feeling; and that this something *ought* to be because it is in itself good, true, and beautiful; in other words, that it is the unconditional goodness, truth, and beauty.

Thus the unconditional principle is required by the intellectual, normal, and aesthetic interest of man. These three interests in their unity comprise the religious interest; for as the will, reason, and feeling are forces of a single spirit, so the objects corresponding to them are but different aspects (ideas) of the single unconditional beginning which in its reality is the special object of religion.

It is quite evident that the reality of the unconditional beginning, as existing in itself, independently of us—the reality of God (as, in general, the independent reality of any other being, except ourselves) cannot be deduced from pure reason, cannot be proved by logic alone. The necessity of an unconditional principle for the higher interests of man—its necessity for the will and the moral activity, for reason and true knowledge, for feeling and creation—this necessity merely renders the actual existence of the divine beginning *probable,* in the highest degree; the complete and unconditional *certainty* of its existence can be given only by faith. And this refers, as it was previously noted, to the existence of any object at all, and of the whole external world in general. For, since we can know anything about the world only through our sensations, through what we experience, so that the whole content of our experience and [that] of our knowledge are our own states of consciousness and nothing more—therefore every affirmation of the external being corresponding to these states represents, from the logical viewpoint, only a more or less probable conclusion; and if we are, nevertheless, definitely and directly convinced of the existence of external beings (other men, beasts, and so forth), this conviction has no logical character (for it cannot be proved logically): it

is, consequently, nothing other than *faith*. Although the law of causality leads us to acknowledge external existence as the cause of our
sensations and ideas, yet since that same law of causality is but a form
of our own reason, the application of this law to external reality as the
cause of our sensations and ideas, yet since that same law of causality
is but a form of our own reason, the application of this law to external
reality can have only a conditional meaning,[1] and, consequently, cannot
give the unconditional, firm conviction of the existence of an external
reality: all proofs of that existence, reduced to the law of causality,
appear thus to be only considerations of probability, not evidences of
certainty—only faith remains to be such an evidence.

That anything exists outside of ourselves and independently of ourselves—that we cannot *know*, because all that we know (actually),
that is to say, all that we experience, exists within us, not outside of us
(as our sensations and our thoughts); and what is not within us, but
is in its own self, is *thereby* beyond the limits of our experience and,
consequently, outside of our actual knowledge; it can be asserted, thus,
only by an act of the spirit which can reach beyond the boundaries of
this reality of ours—and it is this act of the spirit that is called faith. We
know that two plus two equals four, that fire burns; these are facts of
our consciousness; but the existence of anything beyond the limits of
our consciousness (for example, the existence of a 'substantial' fire,
that is to say, of an entity or entities which produce on us the effect of
fire) obviously cannot be given in that consciousness, cannot be the
fact of it or its state (that would be a direct contradiction), and, consequently, can be asserted only by faith, which is 'evidence of things
not seen'.

But if the *existence* of external reality is supported by faith, then the
content of that reality (its essence, *essentia*) is given by experience: that
reality *is*, we believe; but *what* it is, we experience and know. Had we
not believed in the existence of external reality, then all that we experience and know would have had only a subjective value, would
have represented only the data of our inner physical life. Had we not
believed in the independent existence of the sun, then all the experi-
ential material contained in the conception of the sun (namely, the
sensation of light and heat, the picture of the solar disc, the periodical
solar phenomena, and so forth) would have been for us [only] states
of our own subjective consciousness, physically conditioned—a
continuous and correct hallucination, a part of an uninterrupted dream.
All that we know from experience about the sun, as experienced by ourselves, would give warrant only to our own reality, but in no way to
the reality of the sun. But once we believe in the latter, once we are con-

[1] That is to say, *if* our intellect has an objective power, *if* there must exist
objective knowledge and science, *then*, etc., etc.

vinced of the objective existence of the sun, then all the experimental facts about the sun appear as the action of that objective being upon us, and thus receive an objective reality. It is true, we have the same experimental facts about the external world whether we believe in its reality or not; but in the latter case the data would have no objective value: as the same banknotes may represent either so much paper or actual wealth depending on whether they have credit [back of them] or not.

The data of experience, along with the faith in the existence of external objects corresponding to them, appear as evidence of the actually extant, and as such form the basis of objective knowledge. For the fullness of that knowledge it is necessary that these separate evidences concerning that which exists were connected among themselves, that experience be *organized* into an integrated system; and that is attained by rational thought which gives form to empirical material.

All that has been said in regard to the external world is fully applicable ([and] on the same grounds) to the divine beginning as well. Its existence also can be affirmed only by an act of faith. Although the best minds of humanity were engaged in finding the so-called proofs of God's being, so far they were not successful; for all the proofs, based necessarily upon certain assumptions, have a hypothetical character and, consequently, cannot give unconditional certainty. As the existence of the outside world, so also the existence of the divine beginning for reason is only a probability or a contingent truth; unconditionally it can be asserted only by faith. But the *content* of the divine beginning, as well as the content of external nature, is given by experience. That God is, we believe; but *what* He is, we experience and cognate. Certainly, the facts of inner religious experience without the faith in the reality of their object are only fantasy and hallucination, but the facts of outside experience are similarly fantasies and hallucinations if we do not believe in the proper reality of their objects. In both cases experience gives only the psychic facts, facts of consciousness; the objective meaning of these facts is determined by the creative act of faith, With this faith, the inner data of religious experience are cognated as the actions upon us of the divine beginning, as its *revelation* in us, while it itself appears, thus, as the actual object of our consciousness.

But the data of religious experience, even with the faith in their objective value, appear by themselves only as partial information concerning the divine matters, not as complete knowledge about them. Such knowledge is attained by the *organization* of religious experience into an integrated, logically connected system. Thus, besides religious faith and religious experience, we must also have religious thought, the result of which is the philosophy of religion.

It is often said: Why philosophize about the divine matters; is it not enough to believe in them and feel them? Certainly, it is enough . . . in the absence of intellectual interest on the part of him who believes and feels. It is equivalent to saying: Is it not enough to believe that the sun exists, and to delight in its light and warmth? Why should we have any physical and astronomical theories about the sun and the solar system? They are not, of course, necessary for those who have no scientific interest. But on what grounds should the limitations of some people be made a law for all? If man has faith in the divine matters, and if at the same time he has the capacity as well as the need for thinking, then of necessity he must think about the object of his faith; and it is certainly desirable that he think about such matters correctly and systematically—that is to say, that his thinking be a philosophy of religion. More than that; since it is only a philosophy of religion, as a connected system and a complete synthesis of religious truths, which can give us an adequate knowledge about the divine beginning, as the unconditional or all-embracing—for without such a synthesis separate religious data are but disjunct parts of an unknown whole—then philosophy of religion is equally necessary for all thinking men, both those who believe and those who do not; for if the first ought to know what they believe, the second should certainly know what they deny (not to speak of the fact that in many instances the denial itself depends upon ignorance, and that those who believe 'not according to knowledge', who wish to turn the religious truth into a matter of blind faith and vague feeling, act obviously only in favour of the denial). The combination of religious experience and religious thought constitutes the content of religious consciousness. On the objective side, this content is *revelation* of the divine beginning as the actual object of religious consciousness. Since the human spirit in general, and consequently, the religious consciousness also, is not anything final, completed, but something that arises and occurs (develops), something that is in the state of process, the revelation of the divine beginning in that consciousness is necessarily gradual. As the external nature is only gradually revealed to the mind of man and humanity, in consequence of which we must speak of the development of experimentation and natural sciences; so the divine beginning also is revealed to human consciousness gradually, and we must speak of the development of religious experience and religious thought.

Since the divine beginning is the actual object of religious consciousness, i.e., one which acts upon that consciousness and which reveals in it its content, religious development is a positive and objective process, an actual interaction between God and man—a divine-human process.

It is clear that, as a result of the objective and positive character of religious development, not a single stage of it, not a single momentum of the religious process can in itself be false or erroneous. A 'false religion' is a *contradictio in adjecto.* The religious process cannot consist of a substitution of pure truth for pure falsehood, for in that case the former would appear suddenly and wholly without any transition, without progress—and then a question would arise: Why did this sudden appearance of truth take place at the given moment, and not at some other instant? And if it be retorted, Truth could appear only after the exhaustion of falsehood, then it would mean that the realization of falsehood is *necessary* for the realization of truth; that is to say, that falsehood *had to be;* but in that case it would not be falsehood, for we understand by the term falsehood (as well as by the terms evil and ugliness) precisely that which *ought not to be.*

The difference in the stages of religious revelation does not at all imply untruths in the lower stages. The reality of the physical sun reveals itself in different measures to the blind, to one who does see, to one who is armed with a telescope, and finally, to the learned astronomer who possesses all the scientific means and aptitudes. Does it follow therefore, that the sensations of the warmth of the sun, which represent the whole experience of the blind man about the sun, are less real and true than the experience of the man who can see, or the knowledge of the astronomer? But if the blind man would insist that his is the only true experience, and that the experience of the one who can see and the knowledge of the astronomer are false, then it would be only in that statement that falsehood and error would appear, not in the experience to which the statement refers. In the same way, in the development of religion falsehood and error obtain not in the content of any one stage of that development, but in the exclusive affirmation of one of them and in the negation of all others, for the sake and in the name of that one stage. In other words, falsehood and error appear in the impotent efforts to retard or to stop the religious process.

Furthermore, like the fact that the blind man's experience of the sun (the sensation of warmth) is not destroyed by the experience of one who can see, but on the contrary, is preserved in it, enters into it, and at the same time is enriched with a new experience (the sensation of light), which appears thus as *a part* of a more complete experience, whereas, before (for the blind man) this was *the whole* experience—so also in religious development, in their positive content the lower stages are not abolished by the higher, but only lose their significance of the whole, becoming a part of a more complete revelation.

It is evident from what has been said that the highest grade of religious development, the highest form of the divine revelation must, in the first place, command the fullest freedom from any exclusiveness and one-sidedness, must represent the greatest generality; and, secondly must have the largest wealth of positive content, must represent the greatest fullness and *integrity* (concreteness). Both of these conditions are united in the idea of the *positive universality,* which is directly opposite to the negative, formally logical universality, which consists in the absence of all definite properties, of all peculiarities.

Religion has to be universal and one. But for the realization of that it is not sufficient, as many think, to *take away* from the extant religions all their distinguishing, particular features, to deprive each of them of its positive individuality, and to reduce all religion to that simple and indifferent datum which is to be found equally in all actual and possible religions, such as, for example, the acknowledgement of God as the unconditional beginning of all that exists, without any further determination of Him. Such a generalization and unification of religions, such a reduction of all religions to one common denominator, obviously possesses, in the result, a minimum of religious content. In that case, why not go a step further and reduce religion to the ultimate minimum, i.e. to zero? And, in fact, this abstract religion reached by the way of logical negation—whether we call it the rational, natural religion, pure Deism, or something else—always does serve for consistent minds as a mere transition to complete atheism; only superficial minds, the weak and insincere characters hold to it [to the abstract religion]. If anyone replied in answer to the question, What is the sun? that the sun is an external object, and with that statement would wish to limit all our knowledge about the sun, who would regard such a man seriously? But then why seriously consider those who want to limit our knowledge about the divine beginning with similarly general and empty concepts, as for example, the supreme being, the infinite reason, the first cause, and so on. Undoubtedly all these general definitions are correct, but one cannot really base religion upon such a foundation, any more than one can base astronomy on a similarly true proposition, that the sun is an external object.

It is obvious that from the religious point of view, the aim is not the *minimum* but the *maximum* of positive content—the religious form is the higher, the richer it is, the more alive and concrete it is. The perfect religion is not that which is equally contained in all (the indifferent foundation of religion), but that which *contains all of them in itself* and possesses all (the complete religious synthesis). The perfect religion [by logical necessity] must be free from all limitation and exclusiveness, yet not because it is deprived of every positive peculiarity and individuality—such a negative freedom is the freedom of emptiness, the freedom of the beggar—but because it contains in its bosom all peculiarities and, consequently, is not attached to any one of them exclusively, possesses all of them, and, consequently, is free from them all. To the true conception of religion are equally repugnant the dark fanaticism which holds on to a single partial revelation, a single positive form, and denies all others; and the abstract rationalism which resolves the whole essence of religion into the fog of indefinite concepts and merges all religious forms into one empty, impotent, and colourless generality. The religious truth, coming from one root, has developed among mankind into many and varied branches. To cut down all these branches, to leave a naked, dry, and fruitless trunk which can be easily sacrificed to complete atheism—that is the goal of the rationalistic purification of religion. The positive religious synthesis, on the other hand, the true philosophy of religion, must embrace the whole content of religious development without excluding a single positive element, and to seek the unity of religion in [their] fullness, not in indifference.

Taking up the logical developments of the religious truth in its idea (idea-l) content (not touching, at the moment, upon the actual means of its revelation, for this would require different psychological and epistemological analyses, which would be out of place here), we shall follow the order in which the religious truth has been historically developed in mankind; for the historical and the logical order, in their content, that is to say, in their internal connection (and this is the one that we have in mind) evidently coincide (if it be acknowledged that history is a development, and not nonsense).

Originally we have three basic elements: these are, first, *nature,* that is to say, the given, present reality, the material life and consciousness; second *the divine beginning,* as the sought aim and content, which is gradually revealing itself; and, third, *human personality,* as the subject of life and consciousness, as that which passes from the given to the sought and, by adopting [assimilating] the divine beginning, reunites with it nature also, transforming the latter from the accidental into that which ought to be.

The very idea of revelation (and the religious development, as something objective, is necessarily a revelation) assumes that the unfolding divine being was originally hidden, that is to say, was not given as such; but even then it must have existed for men, for otherwise its subsequent revelation would have been quite unintelligible: consequently, it existed and acted, but not in its own definiteness, not in itself, but in its antipode [in its 'other' manifestation, in that which is *not* it], that is to say, in [the created] nature; which is possible and natural in so far as the divine beginning, as the unconditional and therefore the all-embracing, embraces nature also (but is not embraced by it, since the larger covers the smaller, and not vice versa). This first stage of religious development, in which the divine beginning is hidden behind the world of natural phenomena and the direct object of religious consciousness consists only of subservient beings and forces, which act directly in nature and most directly determine the material life and fate of man—this first main stage is represented by polytheism in the broad sense of that word, that is to say, by all that mythological or the so-called *nature-religions.* I call this stage the *natural* or *immediate revelation.* In the next stage of religious development the divine beginning is revealed in its distinction from, and contrast with, nature, as its negation, or the nought, (the absence) of natural being, the negative freedom from it. I call this stage, which is marked essentially with the pessimistic and ascetic character, the *negative revelation;* its purest type is represented by Buddhism. Finally, in the third stage the divine beginning is gradually revealed in its own content, in that which it *is* in itself and for itself (whereas previously it was revealed only in what it is not, that is to say, in its antipode, or in the simple negation of that antipode, [and] consequently still in relation to it, but not as [it is in] itself); this third stage, which I call generally the *positive revelation,* itself represents several clearly discernable phases which are subject to a separate analysis. Now let us return to the first, the natural religion.

Since the divine beginning is known here *only* in the creatures and forces of the natural world, nature itself, as such, receives a divine significance, is considered to be something unconditionally self-existant. This represents the general meaning of the naturalistic consciousness; here also man is not content with the present reality, here also he seeks for another unconditional, but seeks for it and thinks that he can find it in the same sphere of the natural material existence—and therefore falls under the dominion of the forces and principles which act in nature, falls into slavery to the 'beggarly elements' of the world of nature. But since human personality distinguishes itself from nature, places the latter before itself as an object, and therefore comes to be not only a natural being but also something different and greater than nature, the dominion of natural elements over human personality cannot be unconditional—for that power is given to them by human personality itself: nature dominates over us in an external manner only because and only inasmuch as we submit to it internally; and we submit to it internally, we give it the power over ourselves only because we think it to possess that unconditional content which could give fullness of our life and consciousness, could answer our infinite striving. As soon as we, i.e., a separate man as well as the whole of humanity, are convinced by experience that nature, as the external mechanism and the material of life, is by itself void of content and, consequently, is unable to fulfil our demand, nature necessarily loses its power over us, ceases to be divine [for us]; we become inwardly liberated from it, and the full inner emancipation is necessarily followed by external deliverance also.

The inner emancipation from nature in the self-consciousness of pure personality was first clearly expressed in the Indian philosophy. There is, for example in the Sankhya-Karika, a work ascribed to the seer Kapila, the founder of the philosophical school of Sankhya and, in all probability, the nearest predecessor of Buddhism.

The true and perfect knowledge through which one reaches emancipation from all evil consists in the resolute and complete differentiation of the material principles of the natural world from the sensing and comprehending element, that is to say, from the ego.

The spirit (purusha) is the observer, the witness, the guest—it is lone and suffering.

Nature (prakriti) is a means for the spirit—it prepares the spirit for deliverance.

The union of spirit with Nature is similar to the union of the lame with the blind. Blind, but rich with its acting forces, Nature carries upon its shoulders the inactive but seeing (conscious) spirit. Through this all creation is effected. The spirit experiences the sufferings of life and death until it finally renounces its union with Nature.

In the same way as a dancing maiden, having shown herself to a gathered crowd of spectators, finishes her dance and departs; so creative Nature steps aside after it has shown itself to the spirit in all its brilliancy. The dancing maiden goes away because she has been seen, and the spectators leave because they have satisfied their sight: in the same manner breaks up the union of spirit with Nature through full knowledge. I saw her, have seen more than enough of her, says the spirit. I was seen, says Nature—and they turn away from each other, and there is no more reason for their union, or for the creation resulting from that union.[2]

Nature by itself is but a series of indifferent processes—a quiet and indifferent existence; but when it is endowed with the unconditional, divine value, when it is held to contain [in itself] the aim of life and the content of human personality, then nature necessarily receives a negative significance for man, appears as *evil* and *suffering*.

Indeed, the life of nature is all based on struggle, on the exclusive self-assertion of every being, on the inner and outer negation by the latter of all other [beings]. The law of nature is the struggle for existence, and the more highly and perfectly a being is organized, the greater development that law perceives in its application, the more complicated and the deeper is the evil. In man it reaches its fullness. Although, as the poet says,

> Es wächst hienieden Brot genung
> Für alle Menschenkinder
> Auch Myrten und Rosen Schönheit und Lust,
> Und Zuckererbsen nicht minder,

but even if it were so in reality, ([which it is not,] the above is but a *pium desiderium*), the struggle for existence has a deeper sense and is of a wider volume that a mere struggle for bread, for myrtles and roses. Heine forgot about the struggle for laurels and the still more frightful fight for power and authority. He who impartially observed human nature will not doubt that if all men were well fed and their lower passions satisfied, [nevertheless,] remaining on natural grounds, on

[2]See the translation of Sankhya-Karika, attached to the well known book of Colbroog on Indian philosophy in the French translation by Potie.

the ground of natural egoism, they would surely destroy each other in competition for mental and moral supremacy.

Further, nature by itself, as a combination of natural processes only, is a constant movement, a constant transition from one form to another, a constant attainment. But if there is nothing else outside of nature, independent of it, then that movement is a movement without aim, a transition without end—an attainment by which nothing is attained.

The processes and states of natural being can appear to the imagination as aims only until they are realized. The realization of a natural tendency or instinct, which consists of such a natural process, appears as the necessary content, as something satisfying and fulfilling [only] until the time when that realization has been accomplished, until the natural good has been reached. The attainment of it demonstrates however, that in reality it is not what it appears to be—that the imagination posited, gave definite forms and definite content, established as an object and purpose, that which in reality is but an indifferent process, void of content, that which itself needs a content and a purpose. Thus the natural life, when it is set up as the aim, proves to be not only evil, but also a deceit, an illusion: the whole content which man in his striving ties up with certain objects and phenomena, all that content, all the images and colours belong to him alone, to his imagination. It is not man who receives from nature something that he does not have, which could satisfy and fulfil his existence—on the contrary, he himself adds to nature all that she does not possess, that which he draws out of himself. Divested of that rich garment, which was given her by the will and imagination of man, nature appears only as a blind, external, alien force, a force of evil and deceit.

The subjection to this external and blind force is the fundamental source of suffering for man; but the realization that nature is evil, deceit, and suffering, is at the same time the realization of his personal superiority, of the superiority of human personality over nature.

If I acknowledge nature to be evil, it is only because within myself there is a force of the good, in relation to which nature appears as evil. If I recognize that nature is a deceit and phantom, it is only because I can find in myself a force of the truth, in comparison with which nature is deceit. And, finally, [if] nature causes suffering—not this or that partial, accidental suffering, but the general burden of natural existence, [as it were]—[it is] only because there is [in us] a striving and capacity for the beatitude and for the fullness of being which nature cannot give.

If, thus, human personality is something greater than nature, and nature's power over it depends on the personality itself; i.e. [if it is] man's own will, when turned towards nature, [that] ties man with the latter and leads towards evil, deceit, and suffering: then the emancipation or redemption from the power and domination of nature is in the emancipation from one's own natural will—in the renunciation of it.

The human will in all its acts is a striving for natural existence, the assertion of oneself as a natural being—and the abnegation of that will is the abnegation of natural existence. But since nature in the beginning is given as his *all*, since outside of it nothing exists for man in the given state of his consciousness: the abnegation of natural existence is the abnegation of any existence. The striving for liberation from nature is [thus] a striving for self-annihilation; if nature is all, then that which is not nature—is nought.

Of course, the recognition of nature as evil, deceit, and suffering; itself takes away from nature the value of the unconditional principle, but since outside of it [of nature] there is no other content for the consciousness of the natural man, then the unconditional principle, which is not nature, can receive only a negative definition: it appears as the absence of all being, as nothing, as *nirvana*.

Nirvana is the central idea of Buddhism. If in natural religion the unconditional beginning is merged with nature, with something that it is not, in Buddhism that beginning is opposed to nature [as principle]. But as the positive starting point [for Buddhism] is nature again, this unconditional beginning, which is opposed to it [as principle], can be defined only in a negative way, [i.e.] can be defined by what it is not. The sacred books of the Buddhists are all permeated with the theoretical and practical negation of life as well as of all that exists, for only in that negation is the divine beginning known to the Buddhist.

This (that is to say, all that exists in nature) is transient, it is beggarly, it is empty, it is void of substance.

All that is complex disappears (but all that exists is complex).

Contemplation does not affirm any state (that is to say, is unable to stop at anything, is unable to retain anything).

Nowhere, however, is the principle of Buddhism expressed with such sharpness and consistency as in the following paragraph of the Pradjna-Paramite, a book that is a part of the Abidarm, i.e., the metaphysical portion of the sacred writings of Buddhism:

The master is covered only then with the great armour, when such an idea presents itself to his mind: I must lead towards the perfect Nirvana an infinite multitude of beings—I must lead them; and yet neither they who must be led, nor I myself, who must lead, exist. They do not really exist, because non-existence is the proper character of all that is recognized as extant. It is as if a clever magician would evoke the appearance at the crossing of four large roads of an enormous crowd of phantom men who would fight one another, and then would all disappear; while, as a matter of fact, neither those who appeared, nor the killers, nor the slain, nor those who disappeared were there; likewise the Buddhas lead towards the perfect Nirvana an infinite multitude of beings, whereas, as a matter of fact, there are no leaders, nor the men who are led. If the disciple of wisdom, having pondered this truth, will not be disturbed and will not fear, and will nevertheless lead beings towards the full Nirvana, then it must be acknowledged that he is covered with the great armour.[3]

It is noteworthy that, as the religious attitude towards nature (the subjection to it of the life and consciousness of man, and its deification) finally led to a religious negation of nature and of all being, [i.e.] to a religious nihilism; so also the philosophical deification of nature in contemporary consciousness, the philosophical naturalism, has led towards the philosophical negation of all being, towards the philosophical nihilism, which, as is well known, has been developed in our days in the systems of Schopenhauer and Hartman.

It can be seen even from these facts that this nihilism, in its religious as well as in its philosophical form, is not anything accidental, is not a product of temporary historical conditions; that it has deeper significance for human consciousness and, indeed, this negative world view is a logically necessary step in the development of religious consciousness.

If man begins by confusing the unconditional beginning with the baggarly, powerless elements of the world (and as a finite natural being he has to begin with such a confusion); then, in order that he would realize and understand that unconditional beginning in its own reality, it is necessary that he should first separate it from, and oppose it to, those feeble and beggarly elements of the world: in order to understand what the unconditional beginning is, one must first reject with his will and thought that which it is not. This unconditional rejection of all finite, limited attributes is already a negative definition of the unconditional beginning itself; for the consciousness which does not as yet possess that beginning itself, such a negative definition is necessarily the first step towards the positive knowledge of it. For the contemporary consciousness, which has transferred the centre of gravity from the unconditional beginning to conditional nature, it is necessary to go through a complete and resolute rejection of that nature in order to be able, once more, to realize the supernatural, unconditional reality.

Ancient as well as modern Buddhism can be termed a negative religion, and this negative religion must necessarily precede the positive one as an unavoidable stage [of transition towards it], in the same way as in the ancient times those who wanted to be initiated had to go through the small mysteries before they could reach the great ones.

If the divine beginning is to be 'all' for us, then all that is not it [not the divine beginning] must be acknowledged by us as nothing. But if, as Christ said, we lose our soul in order to receive it back again— then we lose the world also in order that we may receive it back again;

---

[3]See: Eugene Burnouf, *Introduction dans l'histoire du Bouddhisme indien.*

because, as we shall see, if the natural world, regarded outside of the divine beginning, in severance from it, in itself, is evil, deceit, and suffering: then in the positive relation to that unconditional beginning, or viewed *from within* that beginning, the natural world becomes a necessary tool or material for the complete actualization, for the final realization of the divine beginning itself.

LECTURE FOUR

T HE negative religion—the universally-historical expression of which is represented by Buddhism—understands the unconditional beginning as nothing. It is indeed *nothing*, for it is not *something*, it is not any definite, limited being, or a creature among other creatures—for it is above any definition, because it is *free from all*. The freedom from all being (the positive nothingness), however, is not the deprivation [loss] of all being (the negative nothingness). The actual, positive freedom of an entity presupposes its dominion, a positive force or power, over that from which the entity is free. Thus, for instance, one cannot say about a child that he is free from passions or that he is above passions—he simply does not have them (and in this respect he is below them); only he can be considered to be free from passions who has them but holds them in his control, who dominates, but is not dominated by, them.

Thus the divine beginning, free from all being, from everything, is at the same time and thereby the positive force and power of all being, possesses all, all is its own content; and in that sense *the divine beginning itself is 'all'*. This is indicated in that the most general and necessary name which we have to give to the divine beginning—the name of *the absolute;* for the word *absolutum* means, first, *that which is absolved*, i.e., [divested] of all particular definitions; and, second, that which is *fulfilled*, accomplished, completed i.e. that which possesses all and contains all in itself. At the same time it is evident that both of these meanings are closely interconnected, so that only in possessing all can one abnegate all.

What is, then, that *all* which forms the positive content of the divine beginning? It cannot be merely the aggregate of natural phenomena, for each of the phenomena, and consequently all of them together, represent only a constant transition, a process, which bears only an appearance of being but [is] not the true, essential, and abiding being. If, thus, our natural universe, because of its purely relative character, cannot be the true content of the divine beginning; then that content, that is to say, *the positive all* (the all-integrity or the fullness of being) can be found solely in the supernatural domain which, in contradistinction with the world of material phenomena, is determined as the realm of ideal essences, as the kingdom of ideas.

The ideal cosmos forms the basic content—and the fundamental truth—of the Greek philosophy in its central system, the system of Platonism. In order to comprehend the truth of this system, we must review (although with the greatest haste) the whole mental path which separates it from the contemporary scientific world-view. Although it seems that between them lies an impassible abyss, yet, as I shall try to prove presently, an uninterrupted thread of logical thought must lead every consistent mind from the sensual experience of phenomena to the contemplative belief in ideas.

First of all, I must once again return to certain elemental truths. We are given natural phenomena, which form what we call the external, material world. That world, as such (that is to say, as external and material) is indubitably only an illusion and not a reality. Let us take some material object, this table, for instance. Of what is this object, really, composed? We have, first, a definite spacial image, a figure or a form, then a certain density or hardness; all of these represent but our own sensations. The colour of that table is only our sensation of sight, i.e., a certain change in our sensation of sight; the figure of the table being formed by a combination of our visual muscular sensations; finally, its firmness, or its corporateness, is the sensation of our sense of touch. We see, we touch that object—yet all that [what we experience] is only our own sensations, only our own states, which take place within ourselves. If we did not possess these external definite senses, then this material object, this table, could not exist for us such as it is, for all its fundamental properties depend directly upon our senses. In fact, it is quite evident that if the sense of sight did not exist, then there would be no colour, for colour is only a sensation of sight; if there was no sense of touch, if there were no creatures that are able to experience touch sensations, then there would not be that which we call hardness, for the phenomenon of hardness is but a sensation of touch. Thus this external object, this table, in such a form as it actually presents itself, that is to say, as a tangible, material object—is not a self-subsistent reality, independent of us and of our senses, but is only a combination of our sensual states, of our sensations.

It is generally thought that if all creatures capable of sensations disappeared from the world, the world would remain as it is together with all the variety of its forms, with all its colours and sounds. It is, however, an obvious error; for what is sound without hearing? or light and colour without sight?

Taking the point of view of the [now] dominant philosophies [based on] natural science, we must admit that if there were no creatures endowed with senses, the world would have changed its character radically. In fact, from this point of view, sound, for instance, all by itself, that is to say independently of the sense of hearing and of the organs of hearing—is only an undulating vibration of the air, but evidently the vibration of the air by itself is not what we call sound; in order that this vibration of the air might become a sound, an ear is necessary upon which that vibration might act and stimulate certain reactions in the nervous apparatus of hearing, appearing in the being to whom that apparatus belongs as the sensation of sound.

In the same manner, for the scientific point of view, light is but a vibratory movement of the waves of ether. The movement of the ether-waves by itself, however, is not what we call light; it [the movement] is but a mechanical movement and nothing more. In order to become light and colour it is necessary that it should act upon the organ of sight and, producing in it corresponding changes, in some way stimulate in the creature [endowed with sensorium] these sensations which are, properly, what we call light.

If I became blind, light would not, of course, cease to exist— but only because there would [still] be other creatures capable of seeing, having light sensations. If, however, there were no seeing creatures, then, obviously, there would be no light *as light*: there would be only the mechanical movements of ether, corresponding to light.

Thus the world we know in every case is only phenomena in us and for us, our representation [perception]; and if we place it wholly outside of ourselves, as something unconditionally self-determined and independent of ourselves, then it is [only because we misapprehend] a natural illusion.

The world is [human] representation. Since, however, this representation is not arbitrary, because we cannot at will create or destroy material objects—because the material universe with all its phenomena is, so to speak, imposed upon us; and although its sensible qualities are defined by our senses, and in this regard depend upon us, yet its very reality, its existence, does not depend upon us, but is given to us; therefore, although in its sensory forms the world is our representation, it must, nevertheless, have a certain cause or essence independent of us.

If what we see is only our representation, it does not follow that this representation did not have causes independent of us, which we do not see. The involuntary character of this representation makes the admission of these causes necessary. Thus, at the base of dependent phenomena is assumed an independent essence or an essential cause which gives us a certain relative reality. As, however, the relative reality of these objects and phenomena, which are multiple and multiform, presupposes the interrelation and interaction of many causes, therefore that essence, which generates them must also constitute a certain plurality, for otherwise it could not contain sufficient basis or cause of the given phenomena.

Therefore the general foundation [of the phenomenal world] appears necessarily as the aggregate of a great many elementary substances or causes of an eternal and immutable nature, which constitute the ultimate bases of all reality, out of which are composed all objects, all phenomena, all real being, and into which this real being can be decomposed. These elements, being eternal and immutable, cannot themselves be decomposed or divided. It is these fundamental substances which we call atoms, that is to say, the indivisible.

Thus, in reality, independently exist only the indivisible elementary essences which, through different combinations and multiform interactions, comprise what we call the real world. This real world is actually real only in its elemental foundations or causes—in the atoms—but in its concrete aspect it is only a phenomenon, only a representation that is conditioned by multiform interactions, only an appearance.

But what are we to think about these fundamental essences, about the atoms themselves? Vulgar materialism understands by atoms some infinitely small particles of matter; but that is obviously a gross error. Under the term matter we understand something that extends in space, something hard and solid, that is to say, impermeable—in a word, something corporal; but, as we have seen, all bodily matter is reduced to our sensations and is only our representation. Extension is the combination of visual and muscular sensations, hardness is a sensation of touch; consequently, matter, as something extended and hard, impervious, is only a representation; and therefore atoms, as elementary essences, as the foundations of [external] reality i.e., as that which is not representation, cannot possibly be particles of matter. When I touch any material object, then its hardness and impermeability are merely my sensations and a combination of these sensations which form [my representation of] a whole object, [i.e., are] only my sense-perception, are within me.

But the cause which produces this [sense-perception] in me, i.e., that because of which I get the sensation of impermeability—that which I encounter—evidently is not in me, is independent of me, is a self-extant cause of my sensations.

In the sensation of impermeability I encounter a certain resistance, which is what produces the sensation; consequently, I must suppose a certain *opposing force,* and it is only to that force that the reality independent of myself belongs. Consequently the atoms, as the fundamental or ultimate elements of this reality, are nothing other than elementary forces.

Thus, the atoms are acting or active forces, and all that exists is the result of their interaction.

This interaction, however, not only presupposes the faculty of acting, but also the faculty of receiving the actions of others. Each force acts upon another and at the same time experiences the action of this other or of these other [forces]. In order to act outside of itself upon others, the force must have a centrifugal or extravertive *striving.* In order to receive the action of another force, the given force must give it room, so to speak, must attract that force, or present it before itself. Thus every fundamental force is necessarily expressed in *striving and in representation.*

In striving it receives actuality for the others, or acts upon the others; while in representation, other [forces] have actuality for it, it is acted upon by the others.

Thus, the foundations of reality are forces—the striving [extraverted, active] forces, and those receiving [action, i.e., acted upon], or the representing ones.

By experiencing the action of another force upon itself, by giving it place, the first force is limited by the other one, is distinguished from it and at the same time turns, so to speak, unto itself, burrows into its own reality, becomes defined [within itself and therefore] for itself. Thus, for example, when we touch or strike a material object, we first sense this object, this 'other one', this external force; it becomes real for us; but in this sensation of ours we also become aware of our own selves, because it is *our* sensation; by this sensation, we witness, as it were our own reality, as [the reality] of those who feel; we come to be something [objective] for ourselves. Thus, we have forces which, first, act outside of themselves [and thus beget external] reality for others; and, second, those which receive the action of that [which in relation to them is their] 'other one', for which that 'other one' possesses [external] reality, or is represented by them; and, finally, [forces] which [themselves] beget reality for themselves—that [reflection of forces upon themselves, or their awareness of themselves] which we call consciousness in the broad meaning of that word. Such forces are more than forces—they are *beings.*

Thus we must assume that atoms, that is to say, the fundamental elements of every reality [besides being mechanical forces] are elementary living beings; or what, since the time of Leibnitz, has received the name of monads.

Thus the content of *all* consists of living and acting beings, eternal and abiding, which by their interaction form all reality, all that exists.

The interaction of the basic beings or monads presupposes a qualitative distinction among them; if the action of one monad upon another is defined by its striving towards that other one, and of that striving properly speaking consists, then the basis [origin] of that striving will be found in the fact that other basic beings, other monads, represent something qualitatively different from the first one, something that would give to the first being a new content which it itself does not possess, which would complete its being; for otherwise, if these two fundamental beings were fully identical, if the second [monad] was exactly alike with the first one, then there would not be any sufficient ground, any reason, for the first [monad] to strive towards the second one. (In order to elucidate this problem one can point to the law of polarity, which obtains in the physical world: only the opposite or diversely named poles attract each other, because they complete one another, are mutually necessary.)

The interaction of basic beings requires that each one of them have its own specific quality which makes it different from all others, because of which it becomes the object of the striving and action of all the others, and it itself is able, in turn, to act upon the others in a certain manner.

The beings not merely act upon each other, but act in a certain specific way, and in no other.

If all the external qualitative differences known to us belong to the realm of phenomena, if they are conditional, unstable and transitory, then the qualitative differences among the fundamental beings, which are eternal and immutable, must also be eternal and immutable, that is to say, unconditional.

This unconditional quality of a fundamental being, which allows it to be the content of all the others, and in consequence of which all the others can be the content of it—this unconditional quality which determines all the acts of a being as well as all its [receptory] reactions (because the being not only acts according to what it is, but also receives the actions of the others according to what it is [itself])—this unconditional quality, I say, represents the being's proper inner, immutable character which makes it what it is, or constitutes its *idea*.

Thus the fundamental beings, which comprise the content of the unconditional beginning, in the first place, are not only indivisible units or atoms; secondly, they are not only living, acting forces, or monads: they are, [in addition] beings defined by the unconditional quality of being, or ideas.

In order that *all* could be the content of the unconditional beginning, it is necessary that this all should itself represent a definite content i.e., it is necessary that every unit which composes this whole, that each member of that whole, be something specific, that it could not be replaced or confused with something else; it is necessary that it be an eternal, abiding idea.

The doctrine of ideas, as of the eternal and immutable essences which lie at the basis of all the transitory existences and phenomena, and constitute the real content of the unconditional beginning, or the eternal, immutable *all*—that doctrine, first developed, as is known, by the Greek philosophy in the person of Plato, constituted in the revelation of the divine beginning the next step after Buddhism. Buddhism says: 'The given universe, the natural being, all that exists, is not the true being, is a phantom; if so, if what is, is not the truth then the truth must be that which is not, or nothing.' Platonic idealism states the opposite: 'If that which, for us, exists immediately, [namely,] the natural being or the world of phenomena, is not the truth, is not the really-extant'—and at this point Platonism agrees with Buddhism—'then this being this reality can be acknowledged as untrue only because there is another reality, which does possess character and truth and essentiality.' The given reality is untrue or not genuine only in relation to another, the true and genuine, reality; or, in other words, the natural reality has its truth, its real essence in another reality, and this 'other' reality is the idea; and at the same time, since the true, genuine reality cannot be poorer, cannot include in itself less than the phantom reality contains, then we must necessarily assume that to everything that is found in the latter (i.e., in the visible or phantom reality), corresponds something in the true and genuine reality—in other words, [we must assume] that every being of this natural world has its own idea or its true and genuine essence. Thus this true reality, this genuine essence is defined not simply as an idea, but as the ideal *all* or as the world of ideas, the kingdom of ideas.

A clear understanding of what the idea is may be gained in a reference to the inner character of human personality.

Every human personality is first of all a natural phenomenon, subjected to external conditions and determined by them in its acts and perceptions. In so far as the manifestations of this personality are determined by the outside conditions, in so far as they are subjected to the laws of external or mechanical causality, in that measure the properties of the acts or manifestations of this personality—properties which form what is called the empirical character of this personality—are but natural conditional properties.

Together with this, however, every human personality has in itself something absolutely unique which defies all external determination, which does not fit any formula, and yet imposes a certain individual stamp upon all the acts and perceptions of this personality. This peculiarity is not only something undefinable, but also something unchanging: it is completely independent of the external direction of the will and action of this person; it remains unchanging under all circumstances and in all the conditions in which this personality may be placed. Under all these circumstances and conditions the personality will manifest that indefinable and elusive peculiarity, that its individual character, will put its imprint upon every one of its actions and perceptions.

Thus the internal individual character of the personality appears to be something unconditional, and it is that [unconditional element] what comprises its own essence, the particular personal content or the specific personal idea of the given being, the idea by which is determined the essential value of the being in everything, the part which it plays and for ever will play in the universal drama.

The qualitative distinctions of the fundamental beings are necessarily expressed in the diversity of their relations: if all the fundamental beings were unconditionally identical, then they would be related one to the other in unconditionally similar ways; but if they are not identical, if every one among them represents its own specific character or idea, every one of them must be related to all others in its own particular manner, must occupy in *all* [in the pattern of totality] its own definite place: and it is that relation of each being to *all* that constitutes its *objective* idea—which represents the full manifestation or realization of its inner peculiarity, or its *subjective* idea.

But how, in general, is the relation between fundamental beings possible when they are qualitatively different and separate? Obviously, it is possible only when they come together or are equated in something that is common to them, although they differ from each other immediately; and in case of the *essential* relation between ideas, it is necessary that that common [element] itself should be essential, i.e., that it be a specific idea or a fundamental being. Thus the essential relation between ideas is similar to the formally-logical relation among different concepts—here, as well as there, we have a relation of a greater or lesser commonness and breadth. If the ideas of several beings relate to the idea of a single being as the concepts denoting species are related to genus-concept, then this latter being covers all those others, contains them in itself: different among themselves, they are equal in relation to it [to the genus-being] and it appears, as their common centre, equally fulfilling them with its [own] idea. Thus appears [comes into being] the complex organism of beings; several such organisms find the centre in another being with a still more general or broad idea and then become parts or organs of a new organism of a higher order, which responds to, or covers with itself, all the lower organisms related to it. Thus, gradually ascending, we reach the widest and most general idea which must internally cover with itself all the others. This is the idea of the unconditional goodness, or more exactly, the idea of the unconditional grace [benevolence], or Love. In reality, every idea is a good —[good] for the bearer of it—his good and his love. Every being is what it loves. If, however, every specific idea is a certain specific good and specific love, then the general universal, or absolute idea is the unconditional good and the unconditional love, i.e., such love which equally contains in itself all [i.e., the ideas of all entities], which corresponds to all. The unconditional love is precisely that ideal whole, that universal integrity, which comprises the proper content of the divine beginning. For the plenitude of ideas may not be conceived as their mechanical aggregate, but is [instead] their inner unity, which is love.

LECTURE FIVE

T H E doctrine of ideas, when it is correctly developed, indicates for us the objective essence of the divine beginning, or what constitutes the proper metaphysical realm of its being, which is independent of the natural world of phenomena, although connected with it. We have learned what is to be thought of those fundamental bases and ultimate elements of all existence, which on the one hand, are related to the visible world of phenomena as its substantial principles or generating causes, and on the other hand form the proper content or the inner fullness of the divine beginning. In order to reach it[this understanding] we have gone through three mental stages, and the answer we have got represents, in school language, three momenti: (1) In order to be the *bases of reality,* the essences in question must be indivisible units not subject to differentiation, [or] ultimate centres of being—the atoms.[1] (2) In order *to produce actual* multiformity of being these central units must act and receive action, i.e., must be in a state of interaction among themselves; and, consequently, they must be acting or living forces—the monads. (3) Finally, in order to constitute the essential whole, or to be the content of the unconditional beginning, these individual forces must themselves comprise a certain content, i.e. be definite ideas.

Different metaphysical systems dwelt primarily upon one of these three momenti, losing sight of the other two; although logically they do not exclude one another but, on the contrary, require one another, so that the full truth of the answer to the fundamental metaphysical question is found in the synthesis of these three concepts, the atom, the living force (the monad), and the idea—in the synthesis which can be expressed by the simple word of general use, a *being.*

Indeed, the concept of a being internally unites in itself these three concepts. For a being, in order to be a being, must, first, form a separate unit, a specific centre of being; because otherwise it would not be an independent being but would be merely an attribute of another being. In the second place, a being must possess an active force, must be capable of action and change; for a dead or inert mass is not a being. And, finally, a being must have a qualitatively definite content, or ex-

[1]Here we have in mind, so far, only their relations among themselves and that outside phenomenal existence in regard to which they are bases and centres. In relation to the absolute being, they cannot have the significance of unconditionally real centres: in relation to it they appear to be permeable, inasmuch as they themselves are rooted in it. Therefore, in speaking of the indivisible units or atoms, we are using only a relative definition.

press a certain idea; for otherwise it would not be an actual, i.e. this specific being, and not some other one. In other words, a being, as such, is necessarily at one and the same time an atom, a living force (a monad), and an idea.

It is necessary to acknowledge the *plurality* of these basic beings, and to think of the unconditional *all* as their aggregate; for action is impossible without such plurality—because every action is a relation of one being to another—and consequently, *actuality as a system of actions, and reality as their result,* are impossible. And if in such a case the world becomes a pure phantom, the being of God is also deprived thereby of its necessary condition: for God, deprived of an object of action, Himself loses all actuality, becomes a pure possibility or a pure nothing. If, however a denial of the plurality of being leads at once to the denial of both God and the world, the opposite admission, [the postulation] of unconditional plurality, i.e., of many unconditionally self-extant beings, leads exactly to the same result. Indeed, as unconditionally independent, i.e., as possessing everything of themselves, these beings would be deprived of every necessary internal connection among themselves, would have no basis for any interaction; and, consequently, all actuality and reality, which proceeds from such interaction, would be impossible. On the other hand, with the full self-subsistence of many beings, they would be also independent of the single unconditional principle, would be perfectly foreign to it; it would not have in them [any portion of] its own inner content, and would itself remain a dead unity, an indifferent, empty existence; limited from outside by independent beings, it could not be unconditional or absolute—more than that: having the whole totality of being *outside of itself,* it would itself be reduced, thereby, to pure nought.

If, thus, the admission of unconditional singleness as well as of unconditional plurality of beings lead to negative results, and renders any intelligent view of the universe impossible; then the truth lies, obviously, in the unification of the two, or in the admission of a *relative* oneness and a *relative* plurality. To assert the impossibility of such a unification is an evident *petitio principii:* it is indeed impossible, if we acknowledge in advance the opposite terms to be *true in their exclusiveness,* i.e., [true] separately one from the other. If it be asserted that the one can exist as such only by itself, excluding all plurality: then, of course, there is no transition from that one to plurality at all. In the same way, if it be asserted that absolute plurality is by itself without any internal oneness, then it is evident that there is no transition from such plurality to the one. But the acceptance of exclusive oneness or of exclusive plurality as the starting point is, precisely, that arbitrary thought which cannot be justified by reason; the very impossibility of . reaching any satisfactory result, if that point of view be taken as the premise, indicates its insolvency. Contrariwise: since logically we can start only with the unconditional, and the unconditional, by the very conception of it, cannot be anything exclusive, i.e. limited, and therefore cannot be *only* single or only *plural;* we must straightly acknowledge, therefore, in agreement with logic as well as with the external and internal experience, that there is not and cannot be either pure oneness or pure plurality; that all that is, is necessarily both one and many. From this point of view, the many (beings) do not have existence in their separateness or in unconditional particularization, but each of them can exist in itself and for itself only in so far as it is at the same time in a state of interaction and interpenetration with the others, as inseparable elements of a single whole; for the particular quality or character of each being in its objectivity consists precisely in the definite relation of that being to the whole, and, consequently, in its definite interaction with *all.* But this, obviously, is possible only in case those beings have among themselves an essential commonness; i.e., if they are rooted in a single general substance, which forms the *essential medium* of their interaction, embracing all of them in itself but not contained [entirely, exclusively] in any one of them separately.

Thus, the plurality of beings is not the plurality of unconditionally-separate units, but is merely the plurality of the elements of a single system, conditioned by the essential unity of their common beginning (as the life of natural organisms known to us is also conditioned by the unity of the organic soul, by which they are determined). Such an organic character of the basic beings depends, on the other hand, on the fact that those beings are ideas. Indeed, if the basic beings were only real units or only acting forces and, consequently, were related one to another purely externally, if each existed only in itself and outside of others—in such case, their unity also would be only external, mechanical, and then the very possibility of such a unity, the possibility of any kind of interaction, would be questionable. Since, however, as we had to admit already, the fundamental beings are not only units possessing force, or units of forces, but are also definite ideas; and, consequently, their connection consists not only of their external action on each other as real forces, but is first of all determined by their ideal content which gives to each one a specific importance and a necessary place in the whole: it follows directly that there is an internal connection among all beings, by virtue of which their system appears as the *organism of ideas.*

As it was already noted in the last lecture, the general character of the ideal cosmos represents a certain correspondence with the interrelation of our intellectual conceptions—namely, the fact that particular beings or ideas are embraced by others, the more general ones, as the concepts of species are embraced by the concept of [their] genus.

On the other hand, however, there is a fundamental difference and even a contrast between the interrelationship in the domain of concepts and that of the ideas of beings. As it is known from formal logic, the volume [quantitative extent] of a concept is in inverse relation to the [qualitative] content; i.e., the broader any concept is, the larger is its scope, i.e., the larger the number of other particular concepts which come under it—the fewer are its symbols, the poorer is its [qualitative] content, the more general, more indefinite, it is. (Thus, for example, 'man' as a general concept embracing all human beings, and consequently of a scope broader than for instance, the concept of a 'monk', is much poorer than the latter in [its qualitative] content: for in the concept of 'man' *in general,* are included only such characteristics as are common to all men without exception, while in the idea of a 'monk' we can find, in addition, many other characteristics which constitute the specific character of monastic vocation; so that this latter concept, narrower than the concept of 'man', is at the same time richer by its inner content, i.e., richer in positive characteristics).

Such relation, obviously, depends upon the [manner of] origin of the general rational concepts. Because they result from a purely negative abstraction, they can have no independence, no content of their own, but are only the general framework for that concrete data from which they are abstracted. And abstraction consists in the removal or negation of those specific characteristics which define the particular concepts, entering the scope of the general concept. (Thus, in the example given above, the abstract concept of 'man' is formed by the removal or the negation of all those particular distinguishing characteristics which could be found in the concepts of the different sorts of men.)

With *ideas,* as positive determinants of particular beings, it is quite the reverse: *the relation of the volume* [scope] *to the content is necessarily direct;* that is to say, the broader the scope of the idea, the richer it is in content. If a general generic concept, as a simple abstraction, as a passive consequence of rational activity, can be defined by its constituent concepts only negatively, by the exclusion of their positive characteristics from its content-to-be; then the idea, as an independent essence, must, on the contrary, find itself in a state of active interrelation with those particular ideas which are covered by it, which comprise its volume; i.e., it must be defined by them positively. Indeed, since general idea is something in itself, or expresses an independent being; therefore, standing in certain relation to other particular ideas or beings, receiving their action and also reacting upon them in accordance with its own character, it (obviously) actualizes, thereby, upon them that its own character, develops its own content on different sides and in different directions, realizes itself in different relations; and, consequently, the larger the number of particular ideas with which it is in a direct relation, or the greater number of ideas in its volume—the greater the diversity and definiteness with which it realizes itself, the fuller, the richer is its own content. Thus, because of the positive character which necessarily belongs to the interaction of ideal beings, the particular ideas which comprise the volume of a general idea, comprise also its content; or, to be more precise, the content of this broader idea is directly and positively determined, in its realization or objectivity, by those narrower ideas which enter into its scope—and, consequently, the broader the scope [of the idea of a being], the richer its content.

Therefore, the well known dictum of Spinoza, '*omnis determinatio est negatio*'[2] (every definition is a negation), in no wise may be applied to an actual being, which possesses a positive content or idea; for in that case the determination, i.e., the action of others upon this being, encounters in it [in this being] a certain positive force of its own, which is called forth by this action to manifest or to actualize its content. As a living force, a being cannot react only passively to the action of others: it acts upon them itself; and, in being fulfilled with them, it fulfils them. Consequently, the determination of others is for it [for the being in question] at the same time its [own] self-determination; the result depends equally on itself and on the external forces acting upon it; and the whole relation has a positive character. Thus, for example, every human person, having his own character and representing a certain specific idea, by entering into interaction with others, in being determined by others and determining them himself, discloses thereby his own character and realizes his own idea, without which his character and idea would be [remain] a pure possibility: they become an actuality of the person and in that [actuality] the person is necessarily also determined by the others. Consequently, in this case the determination is not a negation, but a realization; it would be a negation only in case the person had no characteristics, represented no specific particularity, [i.e.] if he the person were an empty space; but that, obviously, is an impossibility.

From all that has been said it is clear that by [the term] ideas we mean perfectly definite, special forms of metaphysical beings, which belongs to them [to the metaphysical beings] as such, and in no way are the result of our own abstracting reasoning. According to this view, ideas possess an objective existence in relation to our cognition and at the same time a subjective being in themselves; i.e., they themselves are subjects, or more correctly, they have their own special subjects. Ideas are equally independent of both the rationalist abstractions and the sensual reality. Indeed, if material reality, perceived by our external senses, represents by itself only conditional and transitory phenomena,

---

[2]I take this aphorism in its general meaning, of course, for the elucidation of my thought, not analysing that particular meaning which it may have in Spinoza's system itself.

but not the self-existant beings of foundations of being; then these latter, although connected in a certain way with that external reality, must, nevertheless, formally differ from it, must have their own being independent of it; and, consequently, for the cognition of them as actual we need a special mode of mental activity, which we shall call by the term already known in philosophy, that of mental contemplation or intuition (*intellektuelle Anschauung, Intuition*), and which comprises the primeval form of the true knowledge, clearly distinguished from sense-perception and experience, as well as from the rational or abstract thinking. This latter, it has been shown, cannot have any positive content of its own: an abstract concept, by its very definition, cannot go beyond that from which it was abstracted, it cannot itself transform accidental and particular facts into necessary and universal truths or ideas. Nevertheless, abstract reasoning undoubtedly has a special, although a negative and mediatory, significance as a transition or demarcation between the sense-perception of phenomena and the mental contemplation of ideas. Indeed, every general abstract concept contains the negation of all phenomena which enter into its scope in their particular, immediate peculiarity, and at the same time, and thereby, their affirmation in some new unity and in a new content which the abstract conception, by virtue of its purely negative origin, does not give but only indicates. Every general concept is thus a negation of a particular phenomenon, and an indication of a universal idea. Thus, in the former example, the general concept of 'man' not only includes a negation of the particular peculiarities of this or that man considered separately, but also affirms a certain new, higher unity, which embraces all men, but is at the same time different from them all, and, consequently, must possess its own special objectivity, which makes it to be their generic objective norm (we directly point to such a norm when we say: 'be a man', or 'act in conformity with human dignity', and so forth). But this objective norm, this content of the higher unity which embraces all human actuality—and yet is free from it—we shall, obviously, never reach by way of an abstraction in which that new unity comes only as an empty place left after the negation of that which is not. Hence it is clear that abstract thought is a transitory state of mind [appearing] when it [the mind] is strong enough to liberate itself from the exclusive domination of sense-perception and to adopt a negative attitude towards it, but is not as yet capable of grasping the idea in the entirety of its actual objective being, to unite with it internally and essentially; [when the mind] can only touch upon its surface (to use a metaphor), [or] glide over its external forms. The fruit of such an attitude is not a living image or likeness of an extant idea but only its shadow, which outlines its external boundaries and configurations without, however, the plenitude of forms, forces, and colours. Thus abstract thought, deprived of its own content, must either serve as *an abbreviation* [summation] *of sense perception* or as an *anticipation of mental contemplation,* in so far as the general concepts forming it can be affirmed either as schemes of phenomena or as *shadows of ideas.*[3]

As far as the latter are concerned, even if the necessity for the acknowledgment of them was not based on clear logical foundations, we would still have to acknowledge them on factual grounds, which give them the authenticity of the universal human experience: the reality of ideas and of mental contemplation is indubitably proved by the fact of *artistic creation.* Indeed, those images that are embodied by the artist in his works are neither a simple reproduction of observed phenomena in their particular and accidental reality, nor a general concept abstracted from that reality. Both, observation and abstraction, or generalization, are necessary for the working out of artistic ideas, but not for their creation—otherwise every observing and thoughtful man, every scientist and thinker could be a true artist, which is not the case. Anyone at all familiar with the process of artistic creation is well aware [of the fact] that artistic ideas and images are not complex products of observation and reflection, but appear to mental vision at once, in their inner wholeness (the artist *sees* them, as Goethe and Hoffman directly testified about themselves), and the subsequent artistic work means merely their development and embodiment in material details. Everyone knows that abstract intellectualism, *as well as servile imitation of external reality, are equally deficiencies in artistic creation;* everyone knows that the truly artistic image or type requires an inner unity of a perfect individuality with a complete generality or universality; and it is this unity which comprises the essential or the proper definition of an idea mentally contemplated, in contradistinction with the abstract concept which possesses only universality, [on one hand,] and [on the other] with the particular phenomenon which possesses only individuality. If, thus, neither a particular phenomenon, which is perceived through external experience, nor the general conception, which is developed by intellectual reflection, can be the object of artistic crea-

---

[3]It is upon the confusion of ideas with concepts that the well known scholastic controversy between the nominalists and the realists was based. Both sides were really right. The nominalists, who asserted 'universalia post res', originally understood under *universalia* general concepts, and in that respect justly tried to prove their dependent nature and the lack of content in them; although, in defining them solely as *nomina* or *voces*, they had evidently gone to an extreme. On the other hand, the realists, who affirmed 'universalia ante res', understood by this term real ideas, and therefore justly ascribed to them independent being. Because, however, neither side had properly differentiated between these two meanings of the word *universalia*, or at any rate, had not defined the distinction with sufficient exactness, endless disputes naturally could not but arise between them.

tion: then it is only the extant idea, which reveals itself to mental contemplation, that can constitute the object [of artistic creation].

Because of this direct connection of art with the metaphysical world of ideal beings, we find that the same national genius who first conceived the divine beginning as the ideal cosmos—the same national genius was also the real progenitor of art. Therefore, speaking of Greek idealism, we must understand by that term not only the philosophical idealism of Plato, but also all the rest of the world-view of the Greek people which was expressed in their whole culture and was their true religion. Platonism merely elevated to the level of the philosophical consciousness those ideal foundations which had lain in the artistic religion or the religious art of the Greeks. The Greeks learned from Plato only the philosophical formula of that ideal cosmos which was already known to them as a living reality in the Olympus of Homer and Phidias. If the ancient Greek cognated the divine beginning only as harmony and beauty, he certainly did not perceive its *whole* truth, for it is *more* then harmony and beauty; but, although it did not embrace the *whole* truth of the divine beginning, this idealism obviously represented a certain aspect, a certain side, of Divinity, contained in itself something divine in a positive sense. To assert the opposite, to regard that idealism as merely a pagan deception, means to assert that the truly divine has no need of harmony and beauty of form, that it can dispense with the realization of itself in the ideal cosmos. But (as is obviously the case) if beauty and harmony form a necessary and essential element of Divinity, then we must certainly acknowledge Greek *idealism* as the first positive phase of religious revelation, [the phase] in which the divine beginning, removed from sensual nature, appeared in a new luminous kingdom populated not with poor shadows of the material world, nor with accidental creations of our imagination, but with real beings, which unite with the purity of the idea the whole force of being, and which are simultaneously objects of contemplation [for us] and subjects of existence (in themselves).

As we have seen, all ideas are inwardly interconnected, being equally partakers of the one all-embracing idea of the unconditional *love*, which, by its very nature, inwardly contains in itself all the 'other', is the focused expression of the whole, or is *all as unity*. But in order that this focusing, or this unity, be real, i.e., that it be *unification of something*, a separate existence of what is united, or its existence *for itself*, is obviously necessary in actual distinction from the one; and in order that ideas be separate, they must be independent beings with specific acting forces and specific centres or foci of those forces, i.e., they must be not only ideas, but monads and atoms.

Thus, from the point of view of unity, from the point of view of the one universal idea, we come necessarily to the plurality of ideal beings, for without such plurality that is to say, in the absence of that which has to be united, the unity itself cannot be actual, cannot be manifest but remains potential, unrevealed existence, an empty possibility, or nothing. On the other hand, just as every idea, i.e., every positive content necessarily presupposes a definite subject or bearer [of it], [that which] possesses definite forces for the realization of the idea; so also the all-one or the unconditional idea cannot be only a pure idea or a pure object: in order to become the essential unity of all and to actually connect everything through [the medium of] itself, it itself must obviously possess essentiality and reality, must exist in itself and for itself, and not only in the other one or for 'the other one'—in other words, *the all-one idea must be the self-determination of the single central being.* But what are we to think of that being?

If the objective idea, or the idea as object, i.e., in contemplation or for 'the other one', differs from all other ideas by its essential quality or character, [i.e.,] differs *objectively;* then, on its own part, the bearer of that idea, or its subject (to be more exact—the idea as the subject) must be distinguished from others *subjectively,* or by its existence; i.e., it must possess a separate reality of its own, be an independent centre *for itself;* must, consequently, possess self-consciousness and personality. For otherwise, i.e., if the ideas differed only objectively by the cognizable qualities, but were not self-differentiated in their own inner being, they would really be but representations for him who thinks, would not be real beings—which as we know, cannot be admitted.

Thus, the bearer of the idea, or the idea as a subject, is a *person.* These two terms, person and idea, are correlative as subject and object, and for the fullness of their activity are necessarily requisite to each other. Personality void of idea would be something empty, an external senseless force; there would be nothing for it to actualize; and therefore its existence would be only a striving, an effort to live, but not a real life. On the other hand, the idea without a corresponding subject or bearer to realize it, would be something completely passive and impotent, a pure object, i.e., something that could be only represented, but not anything really existing; for a real, full being the inward unity of personality and idea is necessary, as are heat and light in fire.

Applying what has been said to the unconditional idea, we find that, being defined by its objective substance as all-embracing or the all-one, it is at the same time defined also in its inner subjective existence as a singular and sole person containing in itself the whole in an equal manner and thereby equally differing from all.

Here for the first time we get the idea of the *living God,* and at the same time our former idea about God as the *all* receives a certain new explanation. God is the whole, this means that as every real being has a definite substance or content, of which he is the bearer, in reference to which he says 'I am', which is to say, I am *this* and not another; in the same way the divine being asserts its 'I am', but not in relation to any separate particular content, but in relation to *all*, i.e., in the first place, in relation to the unconditional, all-one, and all-embracing idea, and through it and in it, also in relation to the all separate ideas which constitute the scope and content of the unconditional idea.

In the Bible, when Moses inquires about the name of God, he receives the answer: *ehjeh asher ehieh*, that is to say (literally), 'I will be whom I will be', i.e., *I am I*, or, I am the unconditional (ultimate) person.[4] If in Indian Buddhism the divine beginning was defined negatively as Nirvana or nothingness; if in the Greek idealism it was defined objectively as the ideal whole or the universal essence, then in Jewish monotheism it receives an inner subjective definition as the *pure* I or the unconditional personality. This is the first individual, personal revelation of the divine beginning.

Neither Buddhism nor the platonic idealism assert the divine beginning in itself, express its own reality *for itself*: the ideal whole or unconditional idea can be only an attribute or the content of the unconditional beginning, but not that beginning itself.

If every idea has reality only when it is represented by a definite, specific being, then also the unconditional idea or the ideal whole can possess reality not by itself but as the content of the existant one, which is the subject or the bearer of that idea.

Divinity, understood solely as the ideal cosmos, as the whole or as the harmony of all—such divinity appears to man only as a pure object, consequently, only in ideal contemplation; and a religion which confines itself to that has an intellectual, artistic character, exclusively contemplative, but not active; the divine beginning is revealed here for the imagination and feelings, but says nothing to the will of man. And a really moral element is completely foreign to the whole Greek world view.[5] The whole domain of practical activity was left to the instincts, not to the principles. Although Greek philosophy was engaged in ethical problems, its doctrines came in their final result to a simple denial of the moral principle as such. If Socrates reduced virtue to knowledge, removing thus its substantial particularity, his great

[4]In all probability the future tense *ehjeh*, is here only a substitution for the present tense which does not exist for that verb in the Hebrew language. The interpretations of those words, which assume here the direct meaning of the future tense and visualize in it an indication of the forthcoming revelations of God, seem to us very strained. In any case, the conception of God as a pure 'I' is expressed in the Old Testament with sufficient clarity even outside of this quotation so that the one or the other interpretation of the latter does not have much importance for us.

[5]Therefore, giving to the absolute idea the moral definition of love, we had in mind the full truth of idealism, but not its one-sided expression in the Greek point of view, for which the absolute quality was not grace or love, but only the good—once more, only an object.

disciple recognized with a greater definiteness, as the highest good for man, as the norm and goal of man's life, a state in which all desires and all will disappear. According to Plato, the ideal man was a philosopher, and the characteristic peculiarity of a philosopher, using the expression of Plato himself (the Phaedo), lies in the fact that he continuously *dies* to practical life, i.e., is in a state of pure contemplation of eternal ideas, excluding any practical effort, any actual will. Therefore the ideal state also, according to Plato, should be a kingdom of philosophers; i.e., the supreme goal of the commonwealth also lies in the development of the theoretical sphere and its unconditional domination over practical life. Among the Stoics, likewise, the complete imperturbability of the spirit (ἀταραξία) was accepted as a moral norm, i.e., the pure negation of all definite will. But if, therefore, here (as in Buddhism) the moral goal was the simple extinction of the will, this was true evidently because the unconditional norm, i.e., Divinity, was conceived here only as a pure object, impersonal and without a will, revealed therefore only in pure contemplation, as a state of moral indifference (in so far as good and evil are properties of the will, and not of knowledge); for if it was recognized that Divinity has the element of the will, an active principle of the will, then the moral task of man would be not the simple annihilation of his own will, but the substitution of the divine will for his own will. Therefore only that religion could have a positive moral value, could fill and define by itself the domain of practical life—only that religion in which Divinity was revealed as a willing person, whose will gives a supreme norm to the human will. Herein lies the essential significance of the Old Testament revelation, placing it incommensurately higher than all the other religions of antiquity. That Divinity must be a person exerting its will, a living God, in order that the personal will of man be determined in a positive way—is quite clear. But, it is asked, can Divinity in its unconditional nature, be a person? This question is obscured by misunderstandings born from the one-sidedness of opposing points of view, which, however, both equally contradict the most initial conception of Divinity, as unconditional. Thus, on one hand, those who affirm that Divinity has personality, habitually assert at the same time that Divinity is *only* a personality, i.e., is a certain personal being with such and such attributes. The pantheists rightfully rebel against that (position), pointing out that it implies a limitation of Divinity, deprives it of infinity and unconditionality, makes it one of many. It is obvious, indeed, that Divinity, as the absolute, cannot be *only* a personality, only an 'I', that it is more than a personality. But those who protest against this limitation also fall into an opposite one-sidedness in stating that Divinity is simply *deprived* of personal being, that it is merely an impersonal substance of the all. But if Divinity is substance, i.e., the self-existent, then, as containing all in itself, it must differ from all or assert its own being, for otherwise there would be no subject of the containing, and Divinity, deprived of its inward independence, would become not the substance (of all) but merely an attribute of the whole. Thus, in its capacity of substance, Divinity must possess self-determination and cognizance of itself (reflection), i.e., personality and consciousness.

Thus, obviously, the truth lies in the fact that the divine beginning is not solely a personality, solely in the sense that it is not exhausted by a personal definition, that *it is not only the one but also the whole,* that it is not only the individual but also the all-embracing being; that it is not only the extant one but also essence.

As the unconditional, the subject (of all), it is also substance; being a personality or having personal being (existence), it is also the unconditional content or the idea which fills that personal being (existence). Divinity is greater than personal being, it is free from it, but not because it is deprived of it (that would be a poor freedom), but because, possessing that personal being, it is not exhausted by it, but has also another definition, which makes it free from the first one.

In the historical development of religious consciousness gradually reaching towards the whole truth, the pagan world, the flower of which was expressed in Hellenism, established the Divinity as pre-eminently all (the whole). Of the two necessary momenti of divine reality: the personal or subjective one, and the ideal or objective, this (the Hellenic) world conceived and expressed in a definite manner only the second one. Judaism, on the contrary, forming in this respect a direct opposite to Hellenism, conceived and realized in a definite way the first momentum, that of the personal or subjective reality (of the unconditional); it conceived Divinity as the extant one or (as) the pure Ego.

Of course, this contrast was not and could not be absolute. Plato, the greatest representative of the Hellenic spirit, developed the doctrine of ideas and of Divinity as the supreme idea; but we also find in the same Plato the definition of Divinity as the demiurge, i.e., creative being, which forms the world according to unconditional norms and ideas. But such a view appears in Plato and in the whole of Greek philosophy only in passing; it is overshadowed by another, the dominant view according to which the divine beginning is not a being but is only the ideal whole.

Likewise in Judaism, although Divinity is defined as the extant one or '*I*', we also find a conception of that *I* as possessing unconditional content. But here, too, this second conception is generally engulfed by the first; the dominant understanding of God in Judaism, is, without doubt, the understanding of Him as the pure '*I*', regardless of any content; 'I am that I am'—and that is all.

But the *I* in its unconditional centrality is something absolutely impermeable, is the exclusion from itself of all else, of all that is not *I;* the unconditional *I* must be the sole independent being, which does not admit independent reality in anything else—'I am the consuming fire', says God of Himself in the Old Testament. What can be the relation of human personality to the divine beginning thus affirmed (defined)? If the divine beginning, as the unconditional I, as the one independent being, excludes any other independence, then man's relation to it can be only an unconditional subordination, an unconditional renunciation of all independence (on his part). Man must acknowledge that in his whole being and in his whole life he represents only a consequence, only a product of the unconditional will of that unconditional *I.*

The unconditional *I* is impermeable for another *I;* it appears for him as an external force, the action of this force is for him necessity, and the acknowledgment of necessity is the law. Thus, the religion of the unconditional personal God is a religion of the law, because for the self-asserting human ego, while it remains in (the process of) that self-assertion, the unconditional being must necessarily appear as external, and his will—the external law.

But the revelation of the Old Testament—and herein is its full truth and justification—contains in itself the acknowledgment that the religion of the law is not the normal, true religion, but only a necessary transition to another, non-external relation or bond with the divine beginning. This acknowledgment is expressed by the prophets, and the truth of the Old Testament religion of the Bible consists in the fact that it is not only the religion of the law, but also the religion of the prophets.

In the prophetic books we find clear indications that the law and the legal cult have a purely conditional and transitory importance.

'To what purpose is the multitude of your sacrifices unto me? saith the Lord: I am full of the burnt offerings of rams, and the fat of fed beasts; and I delight not in the blood of bullocks, or of lambs, or of he goats. When ye come to appear before me, who hath required this at your hand, to tread my courts? Bring no more vain oblations; incense is an abomination unto me; the new moons and sabbaths, the calling of assemblies, I cannot away with; it is iniquity, even the solemn meeting. Your new moons and your appointed feasts my soul hateth; they are a trouble unto me; I am weary to bear them' (Isaiah, I, 11-14).

'Thus saith the Lord of hosts, the God of Israel: Put your burnt offerings unto your sacrifices, and eat flesh. For I spake not unto your fathers, nor commanded them in the day that I brought them out of the land of Egypt, concerning burnt offerings or sacrifices: But this thing commanded I them, saying, Obey my voice, and I will be your God, and ye shall be my people; and walk ye in all the ways that

I have commanded you, that it may be well unto you'. (Jeremiah VII, 21-23).

The ceremonies and sacrifices established by the law can in no way by themselves express the will of God: as unconditional, this will cannot be connected with any external object, no external action can satisfy it—before it disappear all differences between the holy and the impure in external objects and acts. Although certain acts are established by the law of Jehovah, yet there cannot be any internal relation between them and Jehovah, and if man thinks to satisfy the absolute will merely by the execution of those acts, these acts thereby become impure and criminal.

'Thus saith the Lord, The heaven is my throne, and the earth is my footstool; where is the house that ye build unto me? and where is the place of my rest? For all those things hath mine hand made, and all those things have been, saith the Lord: but to this man will I look, even to him that is poor and of a contrite spirit, and trembleth at my word. He that killeth an ox is as if he slew a man; he that sacrificeth a lamb, as if he cut off a dog's neck; he that offereth an oblation, as if he offered swine's blood; he that burneth incense, as if he blessed an idol'. (Isaiah LXVI, 1-3).

But if the divine will can have no separate definite object—and yet as a will it must relate to something—then, obviously, its object can only be *all*. The will of God, as absolute, cannot exclude anything from itself, or what is the same thing, desire anything *exclusively:* knowing no privation, it knows no envy; it equally asserts the being and the good of all, and therefore is defined itself as the unconditional grace or love. 'Yea, I have loved thee with an everlasting love; therefore with lovingkindness have I drawn thee'. (Jeremiah XXXI, 3).

But if the will of God is love, then by this is determined the internal law for the human will also.

'Is not this the fast that I have chosen? to loose the bands of wickedness, to undo the heavy burdens, and to let the oppressed go free, and that ye break every yoke? Is it not to deal thy bread to the hungry, and that thou bring the poor that are cast out to thy house? when thou seest the naked, that thou cover him; and that thou hide not thyself from thine own flesh? Then shall thy light break forth as the morning and thine health shall spring forth speedily: and thy righteousness shall go before thee; the glory of the Lord shall be thy rereward. Then shalt thou call, and the Lord shall answer; thou shall cry, and he shall say, here I am. If thou take away from the midst of thee the yoke, the putting forth of the finger, and speaking vanity; And if thou draw out thy soul to the hungry, and satisfy the afflicted soul; then shall thy light rise in obscurity, and thy darkness be as the noonday'. (Isaiah LVIII, 6-10).

The will of God must be the law and norm for the human will not as ratified despotism, but as the cognated (and accepted, chosen) *good*. Upon this internal relationship is to be (established) a new covenant between God and mankind, a new divine-human order ('godman-hood') which is to replace the other, preliminary and transitory, religion which was grounded in the external law.

'Behold, the days come, saith the Lord, that I will make a new covenant with the house of Israel, and with the house of Judah: Not according to the covenant that I made with their fathers in the day that I took them by the hand to bring them out of the land of Egypt; which my covenant they brake, although I was an husband unto them, saith the Lord: But this shall be the covenant that I will make with the house of Israel; After those days, saith the Lord, I will put my law in their inward parts, and write it in their hearts; and will be their God, and they shall be my people. And they shall teach no more every man his neighbour, and every man his brother, saying: Know the Lord: for they shall all know me, from the least of them unto the greatest of them, saith the Lord: for I will forgive their iniquity, and I will remember their sin no more'. (Jeremiah XXXI, 31-34).

That new divine-human covenant, based upon the internal law of love, must be free from all exclusiveness: here there can be no place for any arbitrary choice or condemnation of persons and nations; the new internal covenant is the universal covenant, which restores all humanity, and through it also the whole of nature.

'And it shall come to pass in the last days that the mountain of the Lord's house shall be established in the top of the mountains, and shall be exalted above the hills; and all nations shall flow unto it. And many people shall go and say, Come ye, and let us go up to the mountain of the Lord, to the house of the God of Jacob; and he will teach us of his ways, and we will walk in his paths; for out of Zion shall go forth the law (the law-Giver, Adonai, the Messiah) and the word of the Lord (the Word, Christ) from Jerusalem. And he shall judge among the nations, and shall rebuke many people; and they shall beat their swords into plowshares, and their spears into pruninghooks:' (Isaiah II, 2-4).

'The wolf also shall dwell with the lamb, and the leopard shall lie down with the kid; and the calf and the young lion and the fatling together; and a little child shall lead them. And the cow and the bear shall feed; their young ones shall lie down together: and the lion shall eat straw like the ox. And the sucking child shall play on the hole of the asp, and the weaned child shall put his hand on the cockatrice' den. They shall not hurt nor destroy in all my holy mountain: for the earth shall be full of the knowledge of the Lord, as the waters cover the sea. And in that day there shall be a root of Jesse, which shall stand for an ensign of the people, to it shall the Gentiles seek: and his rest shall be glorious'. (Isaiah XI, 6-10).

LECTURE SIX

We have seen that the essential principle of Judaism—the revelation of God in his unconditional oneness, as the pure *I*—was being set free from its exclusiveness already in the revelation of the prophets of Israel, to whom God appeared not as the pure *I* only, which in its activity has no other basis besides the exclusively-subjective principle of arbitrary will that subjects man to itself by external force, arousing fear in him (as such to the Jew appeared, at first El-Shaddai, the God of force and fear; and as such, mainly, even now, Allah appears to the Mohammedans). To the prophets, God was revealed as possessing a definite, essential, ideal definition, as the all-embracing love—in consequence of which the action of God upon the 'other one', his relation to man, became defined by the *objective* idea of the absolute good, and the law of His being appeared no longer as a purely arbitrary will (in Himself) and an external, forced necessity (for man); but as an internal necessity, or true freedom. In conformity with this broadening of the religious principle, in the prophets the Jewish national consciousness also came to be broader. If the revelation of God as the exclusive *I* was answered in the people of God also with an exclusive assertion of its own national ego among other nations, then the consciousness to which God revealed Himself as the universal idea, as the all-embracing love, necessarily had to be emancipated from national egoism, necessarily had to become pan-human.

Such was, indeed the consciousness of the prophets. Jonah preached the will of Jehovah to the pagans of Nineveh; Isaiah and Jeremiah heralded the coming revelation as the banner of the nations, to which all nations shall flow. Yet the Jewish prophets were at the same time really the greatest patriots, fully permeated with the national idea of Judaism; precisely because they were completely permeated with it, they had to understand it as universal, as predestined for all men—as sufficiently great and broad to be able to unite with itself inwardly all humanity and the whole world. In this regard the example of the Jewish prophets—the greatest patriots and at the same time the greatest representatives of universalism—is in the highest degree instructive for us, for it points to the fact that if true patriotism is necessarily free from national exclusiveness and egoism, then at the same time and thereby, the true pan-human point of view, the true universalism, in order to be something, in order to possess actual force and positive content, must necessarily be an expansion or universalization of a positive national idea, but not an empty and indifferent cosmopolitanism.

Thus, in the prophetic consciousness, the subjective, purely personal element of the Old Testament Jahve [the extant One] was united for the first time with the objective idea of the universal divine essence. But since the prophets were inspired *men of action,* were practical men in the highest sense of that word, and not contemplative thinkers, the synthetic idea of the divine being was for them more of a perception of [their] spiritual sense and the stirring of [their] moral will than an object of mental perception. Yet, in order to fill and define with itself the whole consciousness of man, that idea had to become also an object of thought. If the truth of Divinity consists in unity of God as the extant One, or [the unity of] the unconditional Subject with His absolute essence or objective idea, this unity, this inner relation of the two elements (the personal and the essential) in Divinity, must be conceived of in a certain manner, must be defined. And if one of these divine elements (the unconditional personality of God) was pre-eminently revealed to the genius of the Jewish people, while the other one (the absolute idea of Divinity) was perceived particularly by the genius of Hellenism, it is very easy to understand that the synthesis of these two elements (which is necessary for the full knowledge of God) could come into being the soonest at the time and the place at which the Jewish and Greek nationalities collided.

And, in fact, the realization of this great intellectual task was commenced in Alexandria among Hellenistic Jews (i.e., those [Jews] who had received the Greek education), the outstanding representative of whom was the renowned Philo (who was born sometime before Christ and died in the apostolic era); who, as we know, developed the doctrine of the Logos (the word or reason), as 'the expressor' of the divine universal essence and [as] the mediator between the one God and all that exists. In connection with this doctrine of the Logos, as its further development, also in Alexandria appeared the doctrine of the Neoplatonics concerning the three Divine hypostasies, which effect the absolute content or express in a definite manner the relation of God as the one to the whole, as the extant One to being. This doctrine was developed by the Neoplatonics independently of Christianity; the most important representative of Neoplatonism, Plotinus, lived in the second century A.D., yet knew very little about Christianity. However, it is totally impossible to deny the connection between the doctrine of Philo and Neoplatonism on the one hand and Christianity, i.e., the Christian doctrine of the Holy Trinity, or of the triune God, on the other. If the essence of the divine life was defined by the thinkers of Alexandria in a purely apperceptive way on the basis of the theoretical idea of a Divinity, in Christianity *the same* all-one divine life appeared as a fact, as an historical reality, in the living individuality of an historical personality. Christians alone came to know the divine Logos and the Spirit, not from the point of view of logical or metaphysical categories, under which they appeared in the Alexandrian philosophy, but for the first time recognized the Logos in their crucified and resurrected Saviour, and the Spirit in the living, concretely experienced, beginning force of their own spiritual regeneration. But does it follow from this that these metaphysical and logical definitions of the Trinity were alien to Christianity *as a doctrine,* and did not represent a certain part of the [Christian] truth? Quite on the contrary: as soon as the Christians themselves felt the need of making this divine life which had been revealed to them, *an object of thought,* that is, of explaining it [on the basis of] its internal foundation in Divinity itself—[as soon as the Christians felt] the need of understanding as a universal idea that which they had experienced as a particular fact—they naturally turned toward the intellectual definitions of the Greek and Graeco-Jewish thinkers, who had already perceived the theoretical truth of those principles, the manifestations of which (they) the Christians, experienced as a living actuality. And, in fact, we see that the first writings concerning God and His inner life by the Christian teachers—Justin the Philosopher, Hippolytus, Clement of Alexandria, and especially Origen—reproduced the essential truth of the doctrine of Philo and Neoplatonism, [that truth] appearing [now in the form of] different variations of the same contemplative theme, the self-revelation of the all-One Divinity; and we know also that St. Athanasius the Great, in revealing the true dogma of the Trinity, relied upon the same Origen, who at that time enjoyed in the Church the high authority which he fully deserved.[1]

The assertion of essential kinship between the Christian dogma of the Holy Trinity and the Graeco-Jewish thoughts on the same subject, by no means lessens the original value of Christianity itself as a positive revelation. In fact, the originality of Christianity is not in its general views, but in [its] positive facts; not in the apperceptive content of its idea, but in the personal incarnation of that idea. This originality cannot be taken away from Christianity, and for its assertion it is not necessary to try to prove, in spite of history and common sense, that all the ideas of the Christian dogmatics came as something completely new, that they dropped, so to speak, ready-made from Heaven. Such

[1]As regards, in general, the formulas of this dogma, established by the Church at the Oecumenical Councils against Arius, Eunomius, and Macedonius—fully true, as we shall see, even from the speculative point of view—these formulas, naturally, are limited to the most general definitions and categories, as the 'uni-extant', equality, and so forth; the metaphysical development of these definitions and, consequently, the intellectual content of these formulas, were naturally left by the Church to the free activity of theology and philosophy, and it is undoubted that the whole essential content of the Alexandrian speculations concerning the three hypostasies is covered by these Orthodox formulae, and can be reduced to these definitions—if we consider the thoughts and do not insist on the words only. On the other hand,

was not the opinion of those great fathers of the ancient Church who affirmed that the same divine Reason, which was revealed in Christ, even before His incarnation enlightened with the eternal truth the inspired wise men of paganism, who were, [thus] *Christians before Christ.*[2]

Passing now to the exposition of this doctrine itself, concerning the trinity of Divinity as the all-one—the doctrine which is at once the crown of the pre-Christian religious wisdom and the basic apperceptive beginning of Christianity—I shall not dwell upon the details of the teaching, for they appear in one or another system in the works of Philo or Plotinus, of Origen or Gregory the Theologian; I have in mind only the essential truth of this doctrine, common to all its variations, and shall expound that truth in a form which I deem to be the most logical, the most pertinent in regard to the requirements of contemplative reason.

God is *the extant One,* that is to say, to Him belongs being. He possesses being. But one cannot just *be, only* be; the assertion *I am,* or *this is,* necessarily raises the question, *what* I am, or *what* this is. Being *in general* connotes, obviously, only an abstract conception, while actual being necessarily demands not only a definite extant-one as the subject of which it is said that it is, but also a definite objective content, or essence, as the predicate which answers the question: *What* is this subject, or what does it represent? Thus, if in the grammatical sense the verb 'to be' forms only a link between the subject and the predicate, then logically also *being* can be thought of only *as the relation of the extant one to its objective essence or content*—the relation in which it asserts, posits or manifests this (its) content, this (its) essence, in one

[2]The expression of St. Justine about certain Greek philosophers. Although the close inward connection between the Alexandrian theosophy and the Christian doctrine represents one of the firmly established theses of Western science, yet in our theological literature, for one reason or another, this fully reliable situation does not enjoy common acknowledgment; therefore, I consider it necessary to devote to this question a special appendix at the end of these lectures, where I will have to touch upon the significance of the native Egyptian theosophy (the revelations of Tot and Hemes) in its relation to both the doctrines mentioned.   [Omited in this edition. Tr.]

for a complete logical explanation of this fundamental dogma, an invaluable means can be found for us in those definitions of pure logical thought, which were so perfectly developed in recent German philosophy, which on the formal side have for us the same importance as the doctrines of the Academy and Lyceum had for the ancient theologians; and those who at present rebel against the introduction of this philosophical element into the domain of religion, would have to deny first the whole past history of Christian theology, which, it may be said, was nourished by Plato and Aristotle.

way or another.[3] Indeed, if we supposed a being which *in no way* asserts or established *any* objective content, which does not represent anything, which is not anything either in itself and for itself, or for anyone else, then we would have no logical right to acknowledge the existence of such a being; for in the absence of all actual content, being would become but an empty word, by which nothing would be meant, nothing would be asserted; and the only possible answer to the question: What is this being, would be *nothing*.[4]

If, thus, God as the extant one cannot represent being *in general* only, since that would have meant that He has nothing (in the negative sense), or simply that He did not exist at all; and if, on the other hand, God as the absolute cannot be *merely something*, cannot be limited by any particular definite content: then the only possible answer to the question, What is God, appears to be the one already known to us, namely, that God is all; that is to say, *all* in the positive sense, *or the unity of all comprises the proper content, object, or objective essence of God;* and that being, the actual being of God is the establishment or the positing of this content, of this essence; and in it, the assertion of Him who posits, or the extant One. The logical necessity of this proposition is evident. If the divine essence were not all-one, did not contain all, then something existant could, consequently, be outside of God; but in such a case God would be limited by this being, external to Himself: God would not be absolute, i.e., He would not be God. Thus the assertion of the all-unity of God does away with the dualism which leads to atheism. On the other hand, the same assertion, establishing in God the whole fullness or the totality of all being as His eternal essence, has neither the incentive nor the logical possibility of connecting the divine being with the particular conditional reality of the natural world; con-

[3]Those expressions in which the verb *to be* itself seems to take the part of the predicate, namely when the mere fact of existence of something is asserted, are not in contradiction with the above statement. The fact is, it is but a manner of expression for an abstracting thought, and it is not intended then to express the full truth of the object. Thus, for example, if I simply say: The devil exists, or There is a devil; then, although in this instance I do not say *what* the devil is, yet I do not mean to say that he is not something; also, I by no means assume here that he *only* is, or is only a being, a subject without any objective qualitative definition, without any substance or content; I simply *do not dwell* upon the problem of essence or content, but limit myself only to pointing out the existence of that subject. Such expressions, thus, represent only an *omission* of the real predicate, but in no way its denial or identification with existence as such.

[4]Hereof consists the deeply-correct meaning of the famous paradox of Hegel, with which starts his 'Logic': namely that being, as such, that is to say, a pure, empty being, is identical with its opposite, or nothing.

sequently, that assertion does away with the naturalistic pantheism, which understands under the [term] 'all' not the eternal fullness of the divine being, but only the aggregate of natural phenomena, the unity of which it calls God. Finally, as we shall presently see, our assertion of God as the all-one does away with the idealistic pantheism [also], which identifies God as the extant One with His objective idea.

Indeed, if *all* represents the content or essence of God, then God as the subject or the extant One, i.e., as the one who possesses this content or essence, is necessarily distinguished from it; as we have to distinguish in every being it itself as a subject from that which forms its content, which is asserted or expressed by it or in it—we have to distinguish 'the expressor' from the expressed, or *Himself* [the subject] from *His own* [the subject's attribute]. And a distinction is a *relation*. Thus God, as the existant one, is in a certain relation towards His content or essence; He manifests or asserts it. In order to assert it as *His own*, He must possess it substantially, i.e., [He] must be the whole or the unity of the whole in an eternal inner act. As the unconditional beginning, God must include or contain all in Himself in uninterrupted and immediate substantial unity. In this *first status*, all is contained in God, i.e., in the divine subject or the extant One, as in its common root; all is engulfed or immersed in Him as in its common source; consequently, here, all as *totality* is not distinguished *actually*, but exists only as a possibility, potentially. In other words, in that first status only, as the extant One, is God actual; whereas His content—*all* or the universal essence—exists only in a latent state, potentially; although [it is] also present here, for without it, as we have seen, the extant One Himself would be nothing, i.e., would not exist. In order that it be actual, God not only must contain it in Himself, but must assert it for Himself, i.e., He must assert it as the 'other one' [His antipode], must manifest and actualize it as something distinct from Himself.

Thus we get the *second mode*, or the *second status* of the extant One; that all or the universal content, that proper essence of God, which in the first status or in the first mode (manner) of existence was contained in a latent state, only as potential, here, in this second mode [of being] comes forth as a certain ideal actuality; if in the first state it was hidden in the depth of the subjective, unmanifested being, here it is set forth as an object.

This object cannot, of course, be external to the divine subject. Since the latter, in the capacity of the absolute, cannot have anything outside of Himself, it is only His own inner content, which He through His own internal action distinguishes from Himself as from the extant One, segregates Himself, or objectifies it. Should we wish to find an analogy for this relation in the world of our own experience, then the most fitting one would appear to be the relation of an artist towards the artistic idea in the act of creation. Indeed, the artistic idea is not anything alien, external to the artist; it is his own inner essence, the *essence* [being] of his own spirit and the content of his life, which makes him to be what he is; and in aiming to realize or embody that idea in an actual artistic creation, he wishes merely to have this essence of his, this idea, not only in himself, but also for himself, or before himself as an object; wishes to represent [that which is] his own as his 'other one' [his antipode], [to represent it] in another, objective, mode.[5]

Thus the second state or the second mode of being of the extant One is but a different *expression* if that which is already in the first. But in the first state that which is being expressed, i.e., the absolute content as the totality of all essential forms or the fullness of all ideas, appears only internally, in the positive possibility or power of the absolute subject, and consequently has only the essential, not the actual being, since all actuality belongs here to this unconditional subject, or the extant One in His immediate unity. He, as the one, is here a pure act, pure unconditional actuality, about which we can get a certain knowledge when —abstracting ourselves from all the manifested, already formed content of our external and internal life, abstracting ourselves not only from all the impressions, but also from all the feelings, thoughts, and desires—we gather all our forces in a single concentration of immediate spiritual being, in the positive power of which are found all the acts of our spirit, and by which is defined the entire circumference of our life. When we plunge into that mute and immovable depth from which the muddy stream of our actuality takes its beginning, without violating its chastity and peace—in that generic source of our spiritual life, we inwardly come into contact with the original source of the universal life, come to cognate God essentially, as the primordial beginning or the substance of all: we come to know [then] God the Father. Such is the first image of the extant One, the reality of Him *alone*. In order that not only He Himself as the subject, but also *that of which He* is the subject, i.e., the whole fullness of the absolute content might receive the same actuality and from potential become actual, a certain act of self-determination or self-limitation of the extant One is necessary. Indeed, outside of God, [regarded] as the absolute, there is not, and cannot be, anything unconditionally independent, anything that from the beginning might have been His 'other one', which would have determined the extant One from outside of Him: therefore, every definite being [existence] can be primordially only an *act of self-determination of the absolutely-extant One*. In this act, the extant One on one hand contrasts himself, sets forth Himself in contradistinction with his own con-

[5]This analogy, of course, is not complete, because our artistic creation presupposes a certain passive state of inspiration or an inner perception in which the artist does not possess the idea but is possessed by it. In that respect the words of the poet are well justified: 'In vain thinkest thou, Oh artist, that thou art the creator of thy works . . .'

tent as its 'other one', or as an object—this is the act of self-differentiation of the extant One into two poles, one of which expresses the unconditional oneness, while the other one expresses the 'all', or plurality;
on the other hand, through his own self-determination the extant One
receives a certain active force, becomes energy.

In fact, if the extant One were only in the first states i.e., if it were
only an unlimited and consequently indifferent act, it would not be
able to act; for then it would have no real object *for which* the (being
in itself actuality) would appear as a positive possibility or force.
For every action by its own meaning is a unity of force and actuality,
or a manifestation of its own inner actuality, as force, on its 'other one',
or for the 'other one'. And since outside of God there is nothing, and
His object is contained in Himself, then His action is not a determination of the other by another [of one antipode by another antipode] but
self-determination, i.e., the segregation from Himself of His own
content, or the objectivization of it through self-limitation in its immediate, unlimited, or purely-actual being. As the absolute, Divinity
cannot be only an immediate act, it has to be a potentiality or power
also; but, as contained in the absolute, this power is only its own power
over itself, or over its own immediacy. If a limitation by another contradicts the conception of the absolute, self-limitation not only does
not contradict it, but is directly demanded by it. In fact, in determining
itself and thereby actuating its own content, the extant, obviously, not
only does not lose its own actuality, but on the contrary realized it
fully, becoming actual not only in itself, but also for itself. Since that
which God actualizes in the act of His own self-determination—*all*, or
the fullness of everyone—is His own content or substance; then, also,
its realization is only the full expression or manifestation of that being
to whom this content or substance belongs, and who is expressed in or
by it in the same way as the subject is expressed by the predicate. Thus,
returning to our illustration, the poet who fully gives himself to creation and, so to speak, translates his own inner life into objective artistic
creations, not only does not lose his own individuality through this,
but on the contrary, asserts it in the highest degree and realizes it more
completely.

The absolutely-extant which itself is not subject to any determination, determines itself by manifesting itself as the unconditionally-one
through the positing of its 'other one', or its content, i.e., all: for the
truly one is that which does not exclude plurality, but on the contrary
produces that plurality in itself and yet is by no means changed by it,
but remains what it is, remains one and thereby proves that it is unconditionally one—one, that is to say, by its very being, whose oneness cannot be taken away or destroyed by any plurality. If the one
were such only because of the absence of plurality, i.e., if it represented
a simple lack of plurality, and, consequently, with the appearance of the

latter would have lost its character of oneness—obviously that oneness would be only accidental, and not unconditional; plurality would have had power over it, it would have been subordinate to plurality. The true unconditional oneness is necessarily stronger than plurality, excels it; it can prove or realize this superiority only by generating or positing in itself actually all plurality, and constantly triumphing over it: for everything is tested by its own opposite. In the same way our spirit also is truly single not because it would be deprived of plurality, but, on the contrary, because it manifests in itself an infinite plurality of feelings, thoughts, and desires, and at the same time always remains itself and communicates the character of its spiritual oneness [unity] to the whole natural element of the plurality of [its] manifestations, making it [that plurality] its own, belonging to it [to the spirit of man] alone.

> As the immobile depth in mighty space
> Remains the same as in stormy commotion,
> So the spirit is clear and bright in free repose,
> But in passionate desire, [also] remains the same.
> Freedom, captivity, repose, and commotion
> Pass by and appear again,
> But it [the spirit] is always one, and its elemental
>   striving
> Merely reveals its power.

In its *other one*, the extant remains what it is; in plurality it remains one. But this identity and this unity necessarily differ from that identity, that oneness, which are represented by the first status of the extant: there it is immediate and indifferent—here, it is already asserted, manifested, or mediated, passed through its own antithesis, i.e., through a differentiation, and thereby *strengthened* (potentiated). Thus we here meet a new, the third, state or mode of the absolutely-extant—[one in which it has] the aspect of a finished, completed unity: or the absolute which has asserted itself *as such*.

Thus we have *three relations or three states* of the absolutely-extant [regarded] as determining itself in relation to its content. *In the first* it is posited as possessing this content in an immediate substantial oneness or indifference with [regard to] itself—it is posited as the one substance, essentially containing all in its unconditional power. *In the second*, it is posited as manifesting or realizing its absolute content by contra-posing it to itself, or detaching it from itself by the act of its own self-determination. *In the third*, finally, it is posited as preserving and asserting itself in its own content, or as manifesting itself in the actual, mediated, or differentiated oneness [which is now its unity] with this content or essence, i.e., with *all*—in other words, as the one which finds itself in its 'other one', or [the extant one] eternally returning unto itself and in itself subsisting.

This is only the three-fold nature of *relations*, states, or modes of existence. A similar three-fold character is exemplified by our own spirit, if only we acknowledge it as self-subsisting, i.e., as a real being. If we turn our attention to our inner psychical life, we observe first of all certain complex of definite phenomena of the soul: we find there a series of conditions which we experience—desires, thoughts, feelings, in which or by which, in one way or another, is expressed our inner character, is revealed the qualitative content of our spirit. All these states, which we immediately observe, are experienced by us consciously (for otherwise they would, obviously, not be accessible to direct observation) and in this sense they can be called the states of our consciousness; in them our spirit is the active or self-realizing force, [and] they [the states of our consciousness] comprise its inner reality, or its expressed determined being.

But it is easy to see that the being of our spirit is not exhausted by this psychical actuality, that it constitutes only one periodic phase of our existence, beyond the bright field of which repose the depths of the spiritual being, which does not enter into the actual consciousness of the present moment. It would be illogical, it would contradict experience to limit the being of our spirit solely to its actual, differentiated life, to its revealed, palpable actuality, i.e., to assume that at every moment the spirit is only that of which it is conscious (in itself) at that moment. Indeed, from the logical standpoint it is evident that the spirit as manifesting itself, or in its inner integrity, must always be prior to its given manifestation—while from the empirical standpoint, indubitable experience shows that not only the domain of our *real* consciousness, i.e., of the consciousness of external objects, but even the domain of our inner *actual* consciousness, i.e., of the differentiated awareness of our own states, is only a superficial, or, more precisely, a secondary state of our spirit; and that at a given moment this secondary state may well not be [present] and its absence would not destroy our spiritual being. Here I have in mind all those conditions in which the thread of our differentiated consciousness of the external as well as of the internal world is broken off, although the spirit itself certainly does not disappear, if we admit its existence in general; such are the states of the normal hypnotic sleep, of fainting, and so forth.

Thus, admitting in general the existence of our spirit, we must acknowledge that it has a primordial substantial being independently of its own particular manifestation in a series of separate acts and states—we must acknowledge that it exists on a deeper level than all that inner reality which constitutes our current, present life. In this primordial depth lie the roots of that which we call *ourselves*, or our *I*; otherwise, i.e., if our ego, our personal being, were connected exclusively with the expressed, differentiated acts of the life of our soul, with the so-called conditions of our consciousness, then in the cases mentioned above (of sleep, fainting, and so forth) with the disappearance of consciousness we would also disappear ourselves as spiritual beings, in order to reappear suddenly with the return of consciousness, fully armed with all our spiritual forces—a supposition which is (if one admits the existence of the spirit, of course) completely absurd.

Thus, in the first place, we have our primordial indivisible or integral subject; in it, in a certain manner, is already contained the whole proper content of our spirit, our essence or idea, which determines our individual character; if it were otherwise, i.e., if this idea and this character were but the products of our phenominal (manifested) life, or depended upon our conscious acts and states, then it would be incomprehensible why we do not lose that character and idea together with the loss of our vital consciousness (in the states mentioned above), why our conscious life, in being renewed every day, does not form in us [every day] a new character, a new life-content; whereas the identity of the basic character or personal idea amidst all the changes of conscious life, clearly indicates that this character and idea are contained already in that primordial subject [of our ego] which is deeper and more primary than our conscious life—are contained, of course, only substantially, in an immediate unity with it, as its inner, as yet unrevealed or un-incarnated idea. In the second place, we have our differentiated conscious life—the manifestation or expression of our spirit; here our content or essence exists actually in the multitude of diverse manifestations, to which it communicates a definite character, manifesting in them its own peculiarity. In the third place, finally, since with all their plurality, these manifestations are but the disclosures of one and the same spirit equally present in all of them, we can reflect upon, or return into, ourselves from these manifestations or disclosures and assert ourselves actually, as a single subject, as a definite *I*, the oneness of which is, thus, not only not lost by its self-differentiation in the multitude of states and acts of conscious life but, on the contrary, is established in an increased degree; this return to oneself, this reflection upon oneself or assertion of oneself in one's manifestation, is precisely what is called self-consciousness; it appears whenever we not only experience certain states of feeling, thinking, and so on, but also, pausing at these states in a special inward action, assert ourselves as a subject which experiences them, as one who feels, thinks, and so forth, i.e., when we inwardly say: I feel, I think, etc. If in the second state our spirit manifests or discloses its content i.e., segregates it from itself as something other [than itself], then here, in this third state, our spirit manifests or asserts the content in self-consciousness as *its own*—and, consequently, itself as one who has manifested it.

Thus the three-fold relationship of our subject to its content is the same as the relationship of the unconditional or absolutely-extant subject to its unconditional content or the universal essence, which was pointed out above. But here the equality between our being and that of the absolute [being] ends. Indeed, in the actuality of our spirit the three conditions mentioned [above] are but periodical phases of the inner being, which replace one another; or, to put it more exactly, only the first condition of the spirit as existing in itself is permanent and un-alterably abiding, while the other two may exist or not—they are only phenomena, not substances. The spirit as substance, exists always and necessarily (the first proposition). But then it can either limit itself with this substantial existence, remain in inner inactivity, retaining all its forces and all its content in the depth of the essential and undifferenti-ated being (the first phase); or disclose and manifest its forces and its content in a distinctive conscious life, in a series of the states of the soul which it experiences, and actions which it effects (the second phase); or to reflect, finally, upon these states and these acts as ex-perienced and performed by it, to recognize them as its own, and, be-cause of this, to assert itself, its *I*, as possessing these powers and as re-vealing its content in those definite states and actions (the third phase). Here therefore, one and the same subject of being, one and the same spirit, appears at different moments as only essential or substantial; or over and above this, as active and actual; or, finally, as self-conscious or asserting itself in its own revealed actuality. This change of the three modes takes place *in time,* and it is possible only in so far as we exist in time. Indeed, these three states exclude one another: one cannot be at the same time inactive and active, manifest one's forces and content and keep them hidden; one cannot at one and the same time experience definite states and reflect upon them—one cannot simultaneously think, and think about one's own thought.

Thus, these three states or modes of existence, which cannot be present in a single subject *simultaneously,* can belong to it only *at different moments of time;* their belonging to this subject as distinct phases of its being, is necessarily conditioned by the element of time. But it can refer, thus, only to limited beings, [those] living in time. For the absolute being, which by its very meaning cannot be con-ditioned by the element of time, such an alternation of its three states, or of the three relations of it to its substance or content, appears per-fectly impossible: it must present these three states simultaneously, in one external act. But three states, excluding each other, *in one and the same act of one and the same subject,* are decidedly unthinkable. One and the same eternal subject cannot at the same time conceal *in itself* all its determinants and manifest them *for itself,* segregating them as its 'other one', and remain in them *by itself,* as in its own; or, to use Biblical language, one and the same divine hypostasis cannot be at the same time 'the one who dwells in the inaccessible light, whom no man has ever seen', and be also 'the light which lighteth every man that cometh into the world'—one and the same hypostasis cannot be the Word 'by whom all things were made', as well as be the Spirit who 'trieth all things'.

But if so, if on the one hand, there cannot be in the absolute being three consecutive acts, [at once simultaneous and] succeeding one another; while on the other hand, three eternal acts, by their definition mutually excluding one another, are unthinkable in a *single* subject; then it is necessary to assume for these three eternal acts *three eternal subjects (hypostases), the second* of which, *being immediately begotten by the first,* is the direct image of its hypostasis, expresses by its actuality the essential content of the first, serves for it as the *eternal expression or the Word; while the third, proceeding from the first, as from the one who has already found its expression in the second, asserts the second as expressed or in its expression.*

But it is possible to ask: If God as the first subject already contains the unconditional content or the whole what need is there, then, for the other two subjects? But God, as the absolute or the unconditional, cannot be content with the mere fact that He has all *in Himself;* He must possess all not only in Himself, but also *for Himself* and *by Himself.* Without such fullness of existence Divinity cannot be completed or absolute, i.e., cannot be God; consequently, to ask, What is the need for God to find Himself in this triune positing of Himself, is the same as to ask: What is the need for God to be God?

But, admitting the three divine subjects, how can one escape contradiction with the requirements of monotheism? Do not these three subjects appear as three Gods?

It is necessary to agree, first, what is to be understood by the word 'God'. If we designate by this name any subject which, in one way or another, is participant of the divine essence, then we must necessarily acknowledge not only three but a great multitude of gods, for every being somehow or other participates in the divine essence according to the word of God: 'I have said; *Ye are gods,* and ye are *all* the children of the Most Highest'.[6] If, however, with the name of God one is to unite the total and actual possession of the whole fullness of the divine content in all its aspects, then (not to mention finite beings) even to the three divine subjects (hypostases) the name of God belongs only in so far as they are necessarily in unconditional oneness, in an unbreakable inner unity among themselves. Each of them is the true God, but precisely because each is inseparable from the other two, if one of them could exist separately from the other two, then, obviously, in that separateness He would not be absolute, consequently, He would not be God in the proper sense; but it is precisely such separateness which is impossible. It is true, each divine subject already contains in Himself the whole fullness of Divinity, but that is because He finds in himself

[6]Psalm lxxxii.6. Italics by Solovyev. Translator.

the unbreakable union or unity with the other two, since His relation towards them necessarily is internal, essential, for these can be nothing external in Divinity. God the Father, by His very being, cannot be without the Word, by Whom He is expressed, and without the Holy Spirit, Who asserts Him; in the same way the Word and the Spirit cannot be without the first subject, who is that which is expressed by one and asserted by the other, is their common source and primal beginning. Their separateness exists only for our abstracting thought, and, obviously, it would be completely ideal and uninteresting to try to determine whether the name of God belongs to the divine subjects in such abstract separation, once there is no doubt that this abstract separateness does not correspond to the living truth. In actual truth, although each of the three subjects possesses the divine content or the fullness of Divinity, and, consequently, is God; yet—since He finds himself in possession of that fullness which makes Him God, not by Himself exclusively, but only in the unconditional and indivisible inner and essential unity with the other two—this does not assert three Gods, but only one God who realizes Himself in three indivisible subjects (hypostases) of one substance.

We must note that the general idea of the triunity of God, being as much a truth of contemplative reason as of revelation, never encountered any objections from the most profound representatives of contemplative philosophy; on the contrary, they not only admitted of this idea, but regarded it with enthusiasm, as the greatest attainment of apperceptive thought. Only to the externalist, mechanistic intellect does this idea appear incomprehensible, [only to the point of view] which does not consider the inward connection of things in their integral being, does not discern the one in the many and the self-differentiation in the one, but regards all objects in their one-sided abstract exclusiveness, in their separateness, and [only] in their outward interrelation in terms of space and time. The negative attitude of *such* an intellect towards the idea of the triunity serves only as a confirmation of the truth [of the latter]; for [that negative attitude] is the result of the general inability of mechanistic thinking to conceive the inner truth or meaning (in Greek, logos) of things.

The mechanistic approach is one which takes different concepts in their abstract separateness and, consequently, analyses things under some particular, one-sided definition; and then contrasts them one with another in an external manner, or compares them in some similarly one-sided, although more general relation. In contrast to this, organic thinking regards every object in its many-sided wholeness and, consequently, in its internal bond with all the other [objects], which allows one to deduce from within each concept all the others, or to develop a single concept into the fullness of the whole truth. Therefore, one may say that organic thinking is evolutional, one which [unfolds or] develops, while the mechanistic (rationalist) approach only contrasts and combines. It is easy to see that the organic view which perceives or grasps the whole idea of an object, is really that mental or ideal contemplation which was discussed in the previous lecture. If this contemplation is united with clear consciousness [awareness] and is accompanied by reflection, which gives logical determinations to the contemplated truth, then we have that apperceptive thought which characterizes the philosophical creation; if, however, mental contemplation remains in its immediacy and does not clothe its images with logical forms, it appears as that live thought which is characteristic of the people who have not yet emerged from the unreflective experience in their common tribal or national unity; such thought expresses what is called the folk spirit, manifesting itself in folk-creation in art and religion—in the living development of language, in beliefs, myths, ways of life and traditions, in folk-tales, folk-songs, and so forth.

Thus organic thought (in general) in its two aspects belongs on one hand to the true philosophers, and on the other to (the masses of) the people. What concerns those who stand between these two [groups] i.e., the majority of the so-called educated or enlightened people, who are detached, as a result of a greater formal development of mental activity, from the direct people's view of life, but have not reached the integral philosophic reflection, they are confined to the abstract mechanistic thought which breaks up or differentiates (analyses) immediate reality—and this constitutes its significance and merit—but they are not in a position to give it a new, higher, unity and connection; and herein is its limitation.[7] Certainly it is possible (and in reality it often happens) that persons of this group, influenced in practical life by the ideas of other people's organic thinking in the form of religious beliefs,[8] in their own theoretical activity stand upon the point of view of abstract and mechanistic reason, as a result of which, of course,

[7]This capacity to analyse, which is necessary as a means or as a transition to the integral and *reflective* world-view from the instinctive folk-mind, is absolutely sterile and even harmful if one confines oneself to it. And it is this limitation which conditions the pride of the half-educated people (whose number comprises the majority of the learned specialists, who in our days understand little outside of their own speciality)—pride in relation to the 'unenlightened masses submerged in superstitions', as well as in regard to the philosophers, devoted to 'mystical phantasies'. However, the significance of those groundless negators is as illusory as their knowledge is superficial.

[8]Speaking of religious belief as a product of organic thought, we must remember that this [type] of thought is based upon the contemplation of the ideal, which, as has been pointed out in the previous lecture, is not a subjective process, but the actual relation towards the realm of ideal things, or the interaction [between the actual and the ideal]; consequently, the results

there develops a dualism and contradiction in their general world-view, more or less smoothed out or reconciled in an external manner.

Such dualism naturally appeared in Christianity also, when the Christian doctrine, which belongs entirely to the domain of organic thought in both its aspects, became the universally recognized religion not only for the people and the theosophers but for the whole educated class of those days. Persons of that class naturally appeared in all grades of the Christian hierarchy; they sincerely accepted Christian ideas as the creed of faith, but because of their mechanistic mentality, were unable to conceive those ideas in their contemplative verity.

Hence we see that many Fathers of the Church considered the Christian dogmas, especially the fundamental dogma of the Holy Trinity, as something which cannot be comprehended by human reason. To refer to the authority of these Church teachers against the assertion of the dogma of the Holy Trinity [discussed here] in the sense of the contemplative truth would be completely unfounded, since it is obvious that these teachers, being great in their practical wisdom concerning Church matters, or because of their holiness, might have been weak in the domain of the philosophical understanding; and, of course, they might have been apt to regard the limits of their own thought as the limits of the human mind in general. On the other hand, there were many real philosophers among the great Fathers of the Church who not only acknowledged the deep apperceptive truth in the dogma of the Holy Trinity, but even themselves contributed a good deal to the development and the explication of this truth.[9]

However, there is a certain sense in which we must acknowledge the triunity of God as completely inconceivable by [human] reason, and it is as follows: [the divine] triunity, being the actual and substantial [inter-] relation of the living subjects, the inner life of the extant One, cannot be covered, completely expressed, or exhausted by any definitions of the mind: [definitions] which by their very meaning, always express only the general and the formal but not the essential and material aspect of being; all the definitions and categories of reason are only the expressions of the objectivity or comprehensibility of being, but not of its own inner subjective being and life. But it is obvious that *such* incomprehensibility, derived from the very nature of reason in general as a formal capacity, cannot be ascribed to the limitation of the human reason; for every reason, no matter to whom it

[9]This was asserted also by Hegel in his 'History of Philosophy'.

of this contemplation are not the products of subjective, arbitrary creation, not inventions and phantasies, but are actual *revelations* of the super-human reality, received by man in one form or another.

may belong, as reason is able to perceive only the logical aspect of what exists, its concept (in Greek, logos), or the general relation [of the particular] to the whole, but in no way that [particular] existing [entity] in its direct, unitary, and subjective actuality. Furthermore, from this it is clear that not only the life of the divine being appears *in this sense* to be incomprehensible, but the life of any creature [in general]; for no being [regarded] as such is exhaustively expressed by its formal objective aspect or by its concept; as an extant, it necessarily has its inner subjective side which constitutes the very act of its existence, in which it is something unconditionally unitary and unique, something inexpressible, and from this point of view it always represents something foreign to reason, something that cannot enter its sphere, something irrational.[10]

Thus Divinity in Heaven and a blade of grass on earth are equally inconceivable and equally conceivable by reason: one as well as the other, in its general being, as a concept, constitutes an object of pure thought, is wholly subject to logical definitions, and in this sense is fully intelligible and comprehensible for reason; yet both in their own being, *as existant but not as objects of thought,* are something greater than a concept, lie beyond the limits of the rational as such; and in that sense, [they] are impermeable or incomprehensible for reason.

Returning to the truth of the triunity, we must say that it is not only fully comprehensible in its logical aspect but that it is based upon the general logical form which defines every actual being; and if this form in application to Divinity seems to be more difficult to comprehend than when it is applied to other objects [of thought], this is not because the divine life in its formal, objective aspect is less subject to logical definitions than anything else (there is no ground for such supposition), but only because the domain of the divine being is not an habitual object of our thoughts. Therefore, for a better grasp of the form of the triunity, it is necessary to apply it to a being that is closer, more familiar to us than the divine being; having understood the general form of triunity in a finite being known to us directly, we can then without difficulty develop also those variations of the form [of triunity] which are conditioned by the peculiarities of that new content to which this form must be applied in defining the absolute being. In this respect, the analogies which point to the formula of triunity in the beings and phenomena of the finite world, have an actual value for the truth of the

[10]Irrational not in the sense of being without reason but in the sense of not being subject to reason, incommensurate with it; for senselessness is a contradiction of concepts, [and] consequently belongs to the domain of reason, is judged and condemned by it; while that aspect of being of which we are speaking is outside the limits of reason and, consequently, can be neither reasonable nor senseless; in the same manner as, for example, the taste of lemon cannot be either white or black.

triunity of God, not as proofs of it—for it is proved or deduced in a purely logical way from the very idea of Divinity—but as examples which facilitate its comprehension. But for this purpose it is not enough to indicate merely the presence of a three-fold character coextant with [its] oneness in some object, as has been habitually done by the theologians who maintain the view-point of the mechanistic thinking (and it should be noted that such external analogies merely outlined the supposed incomprehensibility of this truth); for a real analogy it is necessary that triunity appear as an internal law of the very life of a being. It is necessary, in the first place, that triunity have an essential significance for that object, that it be its essential form, and not an external accidental attribute; and, secondly, it is necessary that in this form triunity follow from the unity and the unity from the trinity, so that these two momenti would be in a logical interconnection, would internally condition each other. Therefore the domain of spiritual being alone is suitable for such analogies, as one that bears the law of its life within itself. I have already shown above the general triunity in the life of the human spirit [taken] in its whole scope; deserving of attention are also other, more particular and definite, analogies in the same domain, [and] of these I shall here mention two.

The first was originally pointed out with full clarity by Leibnitz, and later on played a considerable part in German idealism. Our reason, says Leibnitz, necessarily represents an inner triunity when it reflects upon itself, in self-consciousness. Here it appears as three in one and one in three. Indeed, in reason which [in reflecting upon itself] recognizes or understands itself, the knower (subject) and the cognized (object) are one and the same, namely, one and the same reason; but the very act of cognition and consciousness, the act which unites the cognized with the knower (subject and object) is nothing other than the same reason in action; and, as the first two momenti exist only with the third one and in it, so likewise the third exists only in their presence and in them; so that here we actually have a certain indivisible trinity of one essence.

Another analogy, which is less known although it is still keener, is the one pointed out by St. Augustine in his *Confessions*. It seems that for some reason it has attracted much less attention than other examples of triunity in various objects, cited in abundance by the same St. Augustine in his book *de Trinitate*, which belong to the same external and irrelevant analogies of which I spoke above. In the *Confessions*, St. Augustine states the following: In our spirit we must distinguish its simple immediate being (*esse*), its knowing (*scire*), and its willing (*velle*); these three acts are identical not only by their content, in so far as the extant one knows and wills himself, but their unity goes far deeper: each of them contains in itself the other two in their own characteristic quality, and, consequently, each internally contains already the whole fullness of the triune spirit. Indeed, in the first place, I am but not simply am—I am the one who knows and wills (*sum sciens et volens*); consequently, here my being as such already contains in itself both knowledge and will; secondly, if I know then I know, or am conscious of my being as well as of my will, I know or am conscious of the fact that I am and that I will (*scio me esse et velle*); thus here also, in knowledge, as such, or under the form (in the attribute) of knowledge, both being and will are contained; thirdly and finally I wish myself yet not simply myself, but myself as existing and knowing, I will my existence and knowledge (*volo me esse et scire*); consequently, the form of the will also contains in its attribute being and knowledge. In other words, each of these three fundamental acts of the spirit is completed in itself by the other two, and thus becomes individualized into a full triune being.

This consideration approaches the truth of the triunity of God very closely and can serve as a natural transition to the further development of this truth, namely, in regard to the specific individual relations of the three divine subjects to the single essence or idea, which they actualize and in which they themselves become concretely realized.

LECTURE SEVEN

W<small>E</small> have seen that, in acknowledging the divine beginning in general as the extant with [its] unconditional content, it is necessary to admit in that principle the presence of three subjects, inseparable [and] of one substance, each of whom *in his own* way is related to one and the same unconditional essence, in his own way possesses one and the same unconditional content. The first is the unconditional Prime Beginning [First Cause], spirit as self-extant, i.e., the immediately-extant One as the absolute substance. The second is the eternal and adequate manifestation or expression, the essential Word of the first. And the third is the Spirit, returning until himself and thereby completing the circle of the divine being: the Spirit actuated or completed—the Holy Spirit.

Such are these three subjects in their interrelationship. Their distinction, as we have seen, is logically conditioned first of all by the necessary three-fold relation of the extant One to his general essence or content. That relation we were able to present at the start only in a most general logical form (as being-in-itself, being-for-itself, and being-with-itself); but now, when the extant One has already been determined for us as three separate subjects, his three-fold relation to the essence can be represented in a more definite and concrete manner, which, in turn, will lead to a more meaningful definition of the three subjects.

If definite being is a certain relation of the extant One, or the subject [of being] to his essence or content, then the modes of this relationship are the modes of being. Thus, for example, at the present moment my state of being as one who is thinking, is nothing other than the relation of my ego to the object, i.e., to the content, or to the objective essence of my thoughts; that relationship which is called thinking, is what constitutes a certain mode [*modus*] of my being. But if being is a relationship between the extant One as such and its essence, then the latter is not the extant as such, but [is] its 'other one' [antipode]; at the same time it belongs to it as its own inner content: the extant is the positive beginning [even] of its essence, consequently, it is *the beginning of its antipode*. And the beginning of its antipode is the *will* [of the extant one]. In truth, that which I posit by my will is mine, in so far as I posit it; and at the same time it is another, [something] different from me; for otherwise I would not have posited it [forth]. Thus, the first mode of being—when essence is not yet separated from the extant, but differs from it only potentially, or in its tendency—when it is and is not, [when] it is its own and its 'other one'—this mode of being is revealed to us as the *will*.

But positing essence in the primordial act of the will as its own and as its opposite, the extant One distinguishes it (i.e., [His] essence) not only from himself as such, but from his will also. In order that the extant One could desire his opposite, it must, evidently, in a certain way be given to him or in him; it must already exist for him as the 'other', i.e., it must be represented by him or [presented] to him [displayed before Him]. Thus the existence of the extant One is determined not only as the will, but also as representation [perception].

The perceived essence, as the 'other' [of the being], [thus] begets the power of acting upon the perceptor in so far as he is also the one who wills. In this interaction, the object of the will, segregated by perception from [within] the extant One, is united with him again; for in this interaction the extant One finds himself in his essence, and [the] essence in himself. In acting one upon the other, they become *sensible* one for the other. Thus this interaction, to the third mode of being, is nothing other than *sense* [feeling].

Thus the extant One wills his essence or content, represents [perceives] it, feels it; hence his very being, which is nothing other than his relation to [His] essence, is defined as the will, perception, [and] feeling. Of what these three modes of being precisely consist (as actual), we know from our immediate consciousness, in so far as our own inner experience is entirely composed of different states of the will, sensation, and perception. Certainly, these data of our inner experience, with all their accidental properties, cannot be directly transferred into the realm of the divine being, but it is not difficult to detach, by logical analysis, those negative elements which are conditioned by the nature of a finite entity, and thus get a positive conception of this three-fold being as it must appear in the unconditionally-extant.

Thus, in regard to the will, we distinguish in ourselves the active or creative will, which acts in the realization of some ideal beginning that does not [directly] change the external actuality (for example, when an artist wishes to give external being to an artistic image which he contemplates inwardly, or when a thinker endeavours to find and determine the truth, or a public man wants to embody the idea of the good in practical life); from that active and extravertive will, which realizes its own inner content in its opposite, we distinguish the passive, externally excited will (or lust), the object which is not formed by it but exists materially and formally outside of it and independently of it, [which] exists not as a universal idea but as a singular fact—while our will [then] endeavors only to identify itself with that fact and, consequently, loses its universal and ideal character and becomes [itself] but an accidental and material fact. It is obvious that the absolutely-extant, which, first, has nothing external to itself, and, second, in which nothing can exist as a separate and accidental fact, since it contains all in itself as [in] the whole in an internal unity—it is obvious, I say, that the absolutely-extant cannot be subject to a passive will; its will, consequently is always immediately creative, or powerful.

In the same manner, in reference to perception as a state or action of the absolutely-extant, the distinctions which exist in our perceptions, have no meaning; distinctions such as that between the actual (objective) perception and the illusory or fantastic one, or between the contemplative (intuitive) perception and the abstract one, or thinking proper (in [terms of] general concepts); and, in this latter case, between the objective or cognitive thinking and the subjective thinking or opinion. These distinctions take place because every finite entity, as a detached portion of the whole, has outside of itself a whole world of other definite entities, a whole world of external being independent of it; this world determines by its action the representations of each separate being, which (the representations) possess an objective value in relation to this defining cause, while outside of it they only represent subjective conditions of consciousness. The action of other entities, received by us through the external, bodily medium—which is itself a complex relationship, independent of our ego, of similar entities—we call external experience, and in that manner differentiate the objective world, which relates to us in this external experience, but is independent of us by its own existence, from the subjective world of our inner states, which have no direct relationship to any other being except our own. Although that distinction has a relative character and represents many transitional steps, yet for us it undoubtedly exists. For the absolute [on the other hand], as having outside of itself no existence independent of it, the differentiation of the objective from the subjective is determined by its own will. In so far as the perceived essence is not only perceived but is also asserted by the will of the extant one as its 'other one', in so far as it gains the meaning of its own actuality, and as such reacts upon the will [of the extant one] as feeling.

In regard to this last, we must also note that for the finite entities there are two kinds of interaction of objective existence (representation) with the subjective one (the will); first, the interaction of the external empirical reality, or of the represented material objects with our material physical subject, i.e., with our animal organism (which in its total life is nothing other than the manifestation of the unconscious material desiring)—this first interaction produces the external or physical sensuality; secondly, the interaction of our inner objectivity, i.e., of our thoughts[1] with our inner subjective being, i.e., with our personal

[1]If our thinking in reference to external reality is something subjective, then in regard to our will it represents an objective element. Evidently these definitions are perfectly relative.

conscious will—through this are produced our inner sensations, or the so-called perturbations of the soul. It is conceivable that in the absolutely-extant One there can be no such distinctions and that, consequently, the inner and external feelings do not exist in Him separately.

If, thus, the three fundamental modes of being of the extant One are defined as the will, perception, and feeling, then in correspondence with this we must have certain definitions for that antipode [of the extant One] to which the extant One is related in these modes of being; i.e., we must get certain new definitions for the essence or the idea (of the whole).

It is obvious that the idea as such must be differentiated according to the differentiations in the being of the extant One, since this being is only the relationship between the extant One and the idea. The idea as the object, or the content, of the extant One is really that which it desires, what it perceives, what it feels or senses. In the first relationship, i.e., as the content of the extant One or as the object of its desire, the idea is called the good; in the second, as the content of its perception, it is called the truth; in the third, as the content of its feeling, it is called beauty. The general meaning of these terms is given to us in our inner consciousness, while their more definite signification will be indicated later on.

In its unity, the extant One already potentially contains the will, perception, and feeling. But in order that those modes of being would really appear as such, i.e., [that they] be singled out of its undifferentiated oneness, it is necessary that the extant One should assert them in their distinction, or to speak more exactly, that it should assert itself in them as distinct, as a result of which they would appear independent [also] in regard to each other. But as these modes of being by their very nature are indissolubly connected, since one cannot wish without perception or feeling, one cannot perceive without the will and feeling, and so on, the extant One cannot manifest those modes of being in their simple separateness so that these would appear first *only* as the will, secondly, *only* as perception, thirdly *only* as feeling; consequently, they cannot become singled out by themselves, and the separateness necessary for their real existence can consist only in the differentiation within the being itself: as, first, the *pre-eminently willing*, secondly, *pre-eminently representing*, thirdly, the *pre-eminently sensing*. That is to say, manifesting itself in its will, the extant One together with it already has perception and feeling, but as momenti subject to the will; furthermore manifesting itself in perception, it has together with it also the will and feeling, subject to perception; finally, asserting itself in feeling, the extant One has in it the will and perception, but as momenti defined by feeling and dependent upon it. In other words, perception, being detached from the will necessarily receives [begets] its own will, and consequently, also feeling (since this last is conditioned by the reaction of the perceived upon the will); by virtue of which the perceiving as such becomes a subject separate and complete. In the same way feeling, detached from the will and perception, necessarily receives its own will and its own perception, as a result of which that which feels, becomes *per se* an independent and complete subject. Finally, the will, having separated from itself perception and feeling as such, thereby receives its own perception and feeling, and, as the one that wills, is integrated into a separate and whole subject. From what has been said it must be clear that in ascribing to each of the divine subjects a separate will, perception, and feeling, we understand only that each of them is one who wills, one who perceives, and one who feels; i.e., each is an extant subject or hypostasis; while the essence of the will, perception, and feeling of each is one and the same, namely, divine: by virtue of which all three hypostases will one and the same thing, namely, the unconditional good; think one and the same thing, namely, the absolute truth; and so on; and only the *relation* of these three modes of being are different with them.

Thus, we have three separate subjects of being, to each of which belong all three basic modes of being, but in a different relationship. The first subject perceives and feels only in so far as it wills, which follows necessarily from its primeval meaning. In the second, which has the first before it, predominates the objective element of representation, the defining cause of which is first subject; here the will and sensation are subordinate to representation—it wills and feels only in so far as it perceives. Finally, in the third subject, which has behind it both the immediately-creative being of the first and the ideal being of the second, the distinctive or independent significance belongs only to the real or sensory [mode of] being; it represents and wills only in so far as it senses. The first subject is pure *spirit*; the second is the *mind* (in Greek, *nus*); the third, as the spirit manifested or acting in its 'other one', may, in order to differentiate it from the first, be called the *soul*.

The primeval spirit is the extant One as the subject of the will and the bearer of the good, and therefore or because of that, is also the subject of the representation of the truth and of the sense of beauty. The mind is the extant One as the subject of perception and the bearer of truth and, in consequence of that, also the subject of the will of the good, and of the sense of beauty. The soul or the manifested spirit is the extant One as the subject of feeling and the bearer of beauty, and only as the result of this, or in so far as, it is also the subject of the will of the good, and of the representation of the truth.

I will illustrate these relationships by an example taken from our human experience. There are people who, having suddenly fallen in love, form on the basis of this love a general idea about the beloved object, and by the force and degree of this love they also define the force and the value of the sense impressions excited by the beloved creature. But there are also those in whom each given creature evokes from the beginning a certain general theoretical idea about itself, and then their will and feelings in regard to this [or that] creature conform to the idea [about it]. Finally, there are also those who are first of all impressed by the real aspect of the object, and then the effects or emotional states aroused in them determine their mental and moral attitude towards the object. The first in the beginning love or desire, and only afterwards, according to their love or desire, form perceptions and feel; the second in the beginning form perceptions, and only after that deside and feel; the third, first of all feel, and then form perceptions and desire according to [their] feelings. The first are the men of the spiritual type, the second are the men of reason, the third—the men of the soul.

To the three divine subjects (and to the three modes of being) correspond, as we have seen, the three images of essence, or the three ideas, each of which represents the predominant object or content of one of the three subjects. Two questions arise here. First, what do these three ideas really contain, i.e., what is desired as the good, what is perceived as the truth, and what is sensed as beauty. And then, in what relationship are these three ideas to the general definition of the divine essence [when it is regarded] as one, i.e., to its definition as love?

What is desired, perceived, and felt by the absolutely-extant One can only be the *all;* thus, that which is contained in the good, truth and beauty, as the ideas of the absolute, is one and the same *all* [totality], and the difference between them is not a difference in the contained (material [difference]), but only a difference in the image of the content (formal [difference]). The absolute wills as the good the same thing that it represents as the truth and feels as beauty, namely, *all.* But all can be the object of the absolutely-extant One only in its inner unity and integrity. Thus the good, the truth, and beauty are the different images or species of unity, under which for the absolute appears its content, or all—or the three different aspects of it, through which the absolutely extant One reduces all to unity. But generally speaking, every inner unity, every unification of the many—the unification emerging from within—is love (in that broad sense in which this conception coincides with the conception of accord, harmony, and peace, or of the world, cosmos). In that sense goodness, truth, and beauty appear only as different images of love. But these three ideas and the three modes of being corresponding to them, do not represent the inner unity in the same degree. Obviously, this unity appears at its strongest and, so to speak, in a more innermost way, (more intimately, in the will, as the good; for in the act of willing, the object of the will is not yet segregated from the subject even ideally: it remains in a substantial unity with it. Therefore if inner unity in general is denoted by the term love, then the absolute is defined by this term especially in that sphere in which inner unity appears as the primordial and uninterruptable [inviolate], i.e., in the sphere of the will and the good. The will of the good is love in its inner essence, of the primordial source of love. The good is the unity of all or of everyone, that is to say, love as the desired, i.e., as the beloved; consequently, here we have love in a special and pre-eminent sense as the idea of ideas: this is the *essential* unity. The truth is the same love, i.e., the unity of all, but as objectively perceived: this is the *ideal* unity Finally, beauty is the same love (i.e., the unity of all), but as manifested or sensible: that is the *real* unity. In other words, the good is unity in its positive possibility, [in its] force or power (according to which the divine will also may be denoted as the immediately-creative, or *mighty*, beginning); while truth represents the same unity as the necessary, and beauty—unity as the real. In order to express the relationship of those terms in a few words we may say that *the absolute realizes the good through the truth in beauty.* The three ideas, or the three universal unities, representing but different aspects or conditions of one and the same [idea], compose together in their interpenetration a new concrete unity, which represents the complete realization of the divine content, the wholeness of the absolute essence, the realization of God as *the all-One,* 'in whom dwelleth the whole fullness of God bodily'.

In this its full definition, the divine beginning appears to us in Christianity. Here, finally, we enter upon the ground of the Christian revelation proper.

In following the course of the development of the religious consciousness up to the advent of Christianity, I pointed out the main phases of that development; in the first place, pessimism and asceticism (a negative attitude towards nature and life), developed in Buddhism with extraordinary consecutiveness; then idealism (the acknowledgment of another, ideal world beyond the limits of this reality) which reaches full clarity in the mystical perceptions of Plato; then monotheism (the acknowledgment, beyond the boundaries of the visible reality, not only of the realm of ideas but also of the unconditional beginning as the positive subject, or the ego), as the characteristic principle of the religious consciousness in Judaism; finally, the last definition of the divine beginning in the pre-Christian religious consciousness—the definition of it as the triune God, which we find in the Alexandrian [school of] theosophy, and which was founded upon the consciousness of the relationship of God as the existant one to his universal content or substance.

All these phases of religious consciousness are contained in Christianity, became parts of it.

In the first place, Christianity necessarily contains the ascetic principle; it is derived from the recognition, expressed by the Apostle, St. John, that 'the whole world lies in evil'. Secondly, a necessary element in Christianity is idealism—the acknowledgment of another, ideal cosmos, the acknowledgment of the Kingdom of Heaven beyond the limits of the earthly world. Furthermore, Christianity is essentially monotheistic. Finally, the doctrine of the triune God has not only entered into the composition of Christianity, but it is only in Christianity that the teaching became a general and open [manifest] religious dogma.

All these phases of [the] development [of religious thought] thus constitute parts of Christianity; but it is equally evident that neither one of them, nor all of them together, represent the special characteristic content of Christianity. If Christianity were only a combination of those elements, then it would not have represented any new world power; it would have been only an eclectic system of a type which is often found in schools but never works in life, which does not perform any world-wide historical upheaval, does not destroy one world and build another.

Christianity has its own content, independent of all these elements, which enter it; and this content is singularly and exclusively Christ. In Christianity as such we find Christ, and only Christ—here is a truth many times expressed but not very well assimilated.

At the present time in the Christian world, especially in the Protestant world, one meets people who call themselves Christians but maintain that the substance of Christianity is not in the person of Christ, but rather in His teaching. They say: We are Christians because we accept the teaching of Christ. But in what does the teaching of Christ consist? If we take the moral teaching (and this is precisely what they have in mind in this case) developed in the Gospel and all reduced to the rule, 'love thy neighbour as thyself', then it is necessary to admit that this moral rule does not represent the peculiarity of Christianity. Much earlier than Christianity, the Hindu religious teaching—love and compassion, and not only towards men, but towards everything living—was preached in Brahmanism and Buddhism.

In the same way it is impossible to assume as the characteristic content of Christianity the teaching of Christ about God as the Father, concerning God as a being pre-eminently loving and gracious; for neither is this doctrine specifically Christian (not to mention the fact that the name 'father' was always applied to the supreme deities of all religions—in one of them, namely, the Persian, we find the conception of the supreme God not only as a father, but even as a father full of graciousness and loving to all).

If we consider the whole theoretical and the whole moral teaching of Christ, which we find in the Gospel, then the only new doctrine specifically different from all other religions is the teaching of Christ about Himself, the reference to Himself as to the living, incarnate truth 'I am the way, the Truth and the life: he who believeth on Me shall have life eternal'.

Thus, if one is to find the characteristic content of Christianity in the teachings of Christ, even here one must admit that this content means Christ Himself.

What, then, ought we to think [about Him], what is presented to our mind under the name of Christ as the Life and the Truth?

The eternal God eternally realizes Himself by realizing His content, i.e., by realizing all. This 'all', in opposition to the living God as the un-conditionally-one, is a plurality; but a plurality as the content of the unconditionally-one, as overcome by the one, as reduced to unity.

Plurality, reduced to unity, is the whole. The real whole is a living organism. God as the extant One, which has realized its content, as one which contains in itself all plurality, is a living organism.

We have already seen that 'all', as the content of the unconditional beginning cannot be a mere sum of separate indifferent beings, that each of these beings represents its particular idea expressed in an har-monious relationship towards all else, and that, consequently, each is a necessary organ of the whole.

It is on this basis that we may say that 'all' as the content of the un-conditional, or that God as [He who has] realized His content, is an organism.

There is no reason for limiting the conception of an organism solely to material organisms—we may speak of the spiritual organism as we speak of the national organism, of the organism of mankind, and, there-fore, we may speak of the divine organism. The concept of an organ-ism does not by itself exclude such an expansion [of it] since we call an organism anything that is composed of a multitude of elements which are not indifferent to the whole or towards one another, but are defin-itely necessary for the whole as well as for one another, in so far as each represents its definite content, and, consequently, has its own special significance in relationship to all others.

The elements of the divine organism of themselves exhaust the full-ness of being; in this sense it is the universal organism. But not only does that not prevent this universal organism from being at the same time perfectly individual, but on the contrary, with logical necessity demands [of it] such individuality.

We call (relatively) universal that which contains in itself a greater quantity of different particular elements than others [do]. It is evident that the more elements there are in an organism, the more particular entities enter into its composition, the greater the number of combina-tions in which each of these elements finds itself, and the more each of them is conditioned by the others; and as a result of this, the more in-dissoluble, the stronger is the connection of all these elements [among themselves], the stronger and the more unbreakable is the unity of the whole organism.

It is evident, furthermore, that the more elements in the organism and, consequently, the greater the number of combinations into which they enter among themselves—the less possible is such a combination of elements in another being, in another organism—the more this organism has of peculiarity, originality.

Furthermore, since every relationship and every combining [co-ordination] is necessarily at the same time a distinction [differentiation], then the more of these elements there are in an organism, the more distinctions it represents, in its unity the more it is *distinctive* from all others. In other words, the greater the plurality of elements which the principle of unity of this organism reduces to itself, the more this same principle of unity asserts itself; and, consequently, once more, the more individual is that organism. Thus, from this point of view also, we come to the previously stated proposition, that the universality of a being is in direct relationship to its individuality: the more universal it is, the more individual it is; and therefore, the absolutely universal is the absolutely individual.

Thus the universal organism, which expresses the unconditional content of the divine beginning, is pre-eminently a peculiar individual being. This individual being, or the realized expression of the unconditionally-extant God, is Christ.

In every organism we necessarily have two unities; on one hand, the unity of the active beginning which reduces the plurality of the elements to itself as to one; on the other hand, that plurality as reduced to unity, as the definite image of this beginning. We have the producing unity and the produced one, or unity as the beginning (in itself) and unity in phenomena.

In the divine organism of Christ, the acting, unifying beginning, the beginning which expresses the unity of the unconditionally-extant one, obviously is the Word of Logos. The unity of the second kind, the produced unity, in Christian theosophy bears the name of Sophia. If in the absolute we differentiate in general the absolute as such, i.e., as the unconditionally-extant One, from its content, essence or idea, then we find the direct expression of the first in the Logos, and of the second in Sophia, which is thus the expressed, realized idea. And as the extant One, differing from its own idea is at the same time one with it, so Logos, too, differing from Sophia, is eternally connected with her. Sophia is God's body, the matter of Divinity,[2] permeated with the beginning of divine unity. Christ, who realized that unity in Himself or is the bearer of it, as the integral divine organism—universal and at the same time individual—is both Logos and Sophia.

To speak about Sophia as an essential element of Divinity does not

[2]Such expressions as 'body' and 'matter' we use here in the most general sense, as relative categories, not connecting with them those particular conceptions which can have place only in application to our material world but are absolutely unthinkable in relation to Divinity.

mean, from the Christian point of view, to introduce new gods. The thought of Sophia was always present in Christianity; more than that, it existed even before Christianity. There is in the Old Testament a whole Book ascribed to Solomon which bears the title of Sophia. This book is not canonical, but, as is known, even in the canonical book of the 'Proverbs of Solomon' we find the development of this idea of Sophia (under the corresponding Hebrew name of Hohma). 'Wisdom', it is stated here, 'existed before the creation of the world' (i.e., of the natural world); 'God possessed her in the beginning of His ways', i.e., it is the idea which God had before Him in His [work of] creation and which He, consequently, realizes. We find this term in the New Testament as well, now in a direct relation to Christ (in St. Paul).

The representation of God as the integral being, as the universal organism, which presupposes a plurality of essential elements comprising this organism—this representation may seem to violate the absoluteness of Divinity, to bring Nature into God. But it is precisely in order that God be unconditionally distinguished from our world, from our Nature, from this visible reality, that it is necessary to acknowledge in Him His particular eternal nature. His special eternal world. Otherwise our idea of Divinity will be poorer, more abstract, than our conception of the visible world.

The negative course in the [evolution of] religious consciousness was always such that Divinity was first, so to speak, cleared of all actual definition, was reduced to a pure abstraction, and then religious consciousness easily dispensed with this abstract Divinity and passed into irreligious consciousness, into atheism.

If we do not acknowledge in Divinity the whole fullness of reality, and consequently, of necessity, plurality also, then, inevitably, the positive significance [it has] passes to the plurality and to the reality of *this* world. Then Divinity retains only a negative significance and little by little is denied; for if there is no other reality, [if] the unconditional one [does not exist], [and if there is no] other plurality, [no] other fullness of being, then our present reality is the only one; and then Divinity is left without any positive content: it is either merged with this world, with this nature—this world, this nature are acknowledged [then] as the direct, immediate content of Divinity [so that] we pass into a naturalistic pantheism, where this finite nature is all, and God is an empty word only; or, and this is more logical, Divinity, as an empty abstraction, is simply denied, and consciousness appears [to be] frankly atheistic.

Thus to God, as the integral being, together with unity belongs plurality—the plurality of substantial ideas, i.e., of potencies or forces with definite special content.

These forces, each possessing its own particular definite content, [and] related in a different manner to the content of the others, neces-

sarily represent different secondary wholes or spheres. They all constitute one divine world, but this world is necessarily differentiated into
a plurality of spheres.

If the divine whole is composed of essential elements, of living forces
with definite individual content, then these entities must represent
[certain] fundamental traits, which necessarily belong to every individual being—certain traits of a psychical character, common to all
living forces.

If each of them realizes a definite content or idea, and if the force
realizing them can, as we have seen, be related to a definite content or
idea in three ways, i.e., can possess this content as an object of the will,
can enclose it in itself as the desired, then represent it, and, finally, feel
it; if it [the force] can be related to it [to the content] substantially,
ideally, and really or sensuously [sensorially?]: then it is easy to see that
the sensory elements of the divine whole must differ among themselves
according to the predominance of this or that relationship: if the will
predominates, [it is the sphere of] the moral principle; if perception
[predominates], it is that of the theoretical principle; or, finally, [in the
case of] feeling, the principle of aesthetics.

Thus we have three classes of the living forces which form three
spheres of the divine realm.

The individual forces of the first class, in which the principle of the
will predominates, may be called pure spirits; the forces of the second
class may be called the minds; those of the third class, the souls.

Thus the divine world is composed of three main spheres: the sphere
of pure spirits, the sphere of the minds, and the sphere of the souls.
These spheres are [united] in a close and unbreakable bond among
themselves, represent complete inner unity or solidarity, for each
among them fulfils the other, each is necessary to the other, is affirmed
by the other. Each separate force and each sphere posits as its object,
as its goal, all the others; they form the content of its life: and each
separate force and separate sphere, likewise, is the goal and object of all
the others, for it possesses its own special property which they lack; and
thus a single, unbreakable bond of love unites all the countless elements
which form the divine world.

The reality of this world, which is necessarily infinitely richer than
our visible world, the reality of this divine world, obviously, can be
completely accessible only to him who really belongs to that world.
But since the natural world also is necessarily in close union with this
divine world (what this bond is, we shall see further on), since there
is not and cannot be between them any impassable abyss, the separate
rays and reflections of the divine world must penetrate also into our
reality and [must] constitute all the ideal content, all the beauty and
truth, we find in it. And man, as belonging to both worlds, by an act
of mental contemplation can and must touch the divine world, and

even while still in the world of struggle and confused disquietude [can and must] enter into communion with the clear images from the kingdom of glory and eternal beauty. In particular, this positive although incomplete knowledge of, or penetration into, the reality of the divine world is open to creation in poetry. Every true poet must necessarily penetrate into 'the fatherland of the flame and the word' in order to gather from there the prototypes of his creations as well as inner enlightenment, which is called inspiration, and by means of which our natural reality finds sounds and colours for the embodiment of the ideal types, as one of the poets says:

> Mine dark sight became enlightened,
> And I could see the world unseen;
> Mine ear can hear since then
> What is inaudible to others.
> I came down from the mountain height,
> Knit through with its rays.
> The agitated dale below
> With new eyes I behold,
> An endless chatter hear
> Everywhere.
> I hear the mountains' stone heart
> Beat in dark cliffs with love;
> With love the clouds roll
> In the blue firmament above;
> Under the tree-bark, the living sap
> With love climbs up into the leaves
> In singing streams.
> Then with foreknowing heart I understood
> That all, born of the Word,
> Shedding about rays of love
> Yearns to return to Him;
> That every stream of life,
> Love's law subject, to the divine bosom strives
> Irresistibly.
> All is alive with sound, athrob with light,
> With love all nature breathes—
> And all the worlds are of one Beginning.

LECTURE EIGHT

THE eternal or divine world, which was the subject of my last lecture, is not a puzzle for the mind. That world, as the ideal fullness of all as well as the realization of the good, truth, and beauty, presents itself to the mind as that which by itself ought to be, as *the normal*. That world as the unconditional norm is *logically* necessary for the mind, and if the mind by itself cannot certify to us the *factual* existence of that world, then it is only because the mind by its nature, in general, is not an organ of cognition of any factual reality. Factual reality, obviously, can be cognated only through actual experience; whereas the ideal necessity of the divine world and of Christ, as the unconditionally-universal and at the same time and because of that—the unconditionally-individual centre of this world, in possession of its whole fullness—this ideal necessity is evident to the contemplative reason, which can find that unconditional measure [norm] in relation to which or in comparison with which it recognizes the given natural world, our reality, as something conditional, abnormal, and transitory, only in the eternal sphere.

Thus, not the eternal divine world, but on the contrary, our nature, our factually given world, constitutes a puzzle for the mind; the explanation of this factually-indubitable, but for reason, obscure, reality, constitutes its task.

This task is, thus, the deduction of the conditional from the unconditional; the deduction of what by itself ought not to be from the unconditional norm; the deduction of the accidental reality from the absolute idea, of the natural world of phenomena from the world of the divine essence.

This deduction would be an impossible task if between the two opposite terms, one of which must be deduced from the other, i.e., from its opposite, there would not be a bond, belonging equally to one and to the other sphere, and therefore serving as a transition between them. This uniting link between the divine and natural worlds is *man*.

Man combines in himself all possible opposites which can all be reduced to one great polarity between the unconditional and the conditional, between the absolute and eternal essence and the transitory phenomenon or appearance. Man is at once divinity and nothingness.

There is no need to dwell on the assertion of this undoubted contrast in man, because it has of long represented the common theme of poets as well as of psychologists and moralists.

Our task is not the description of man, but the pointing out of his significance in the general connection of the truly-extant.

In the past lecture I spoke about the necessity of distinguishing two unities in the divine being: the acting or producing one, the unity of the divine creation of the Word (Logos); and the unity produced, realized. As in a particular organism of the natural world we distinguish the active unity, the beginning [element] which produces and supports its organic wholeness—the beginning which comprises the living and active *soul* of this organism—and then also the unity of that which is produced and realized by that soul, the unity of the organic *body*.

If in the divine being, in Christ, the first or the producing unity is properly the Divinity—God, as the acting force, or Logos—and if, thus, in this first unity we have Christ as the divine being proper; then the second unity, the produced one, to which we have given the mystical name of Sophia, is the principle of humanity, is the ideal or normal man. And Christ, as participant in this unity of the human being, is a man, or to use the expression of the Holy Scripture, the second Adam.

Thus, Sophia is the ideal or perfect humanity, eternally contained in the integral divine being or Christ. Since it is indubitable that God, in order to exist actually and really must manifest Himself, His being, i.e., must act in the 'other' [in that which is not He], the existence of this 'other' [this antipode] is thereby established as necessary; and, since in speaking of God we cannot have in mind any form of time, because all that is said about God presumes eternity, then the existence of this 'other', in relation to which God is manifested, must necessarily be acknowledged as eternal. This 'other' is not *unconditionally* alien to God (that is unthinkable), but is [rather] His own expression or manifestation; and it is in regard to this antipode of His that God is called the Word.

But this unfolding or the inner revelation of Divinity, and consequently also the distinction of God as Logos from God as the primordial substance for the Father, this revelation and this distinction necessarily presupposes that in which Divinity is revealed, or in which it acts, and which in the first (in the Father) exists substantially, or in a latent form, and is manifested through the second (i.e., through Logos).

Consequently, in order that God exist eternally as Logos, or as the active God, it is necessary to assume the eternal existence of real elements which receive [as objects of it] the divine action; it is necessary to assume the existence of the world as subject to divine action, as giving in itself place to divine unity. The proper unity of that world, i.e., the produced unity—the world's centre and at the same time the circumference of Divinity—is humanity. Every actuality presupposes action, and every action presupposes a real object of [that] action:— a subject which receives that action; consequently, the actuality of God, based upon the action of God, presupposes a subject receiving this action, presupposes man—and presupposes him eternally, since the action of God is eternal. This [proposition] may not be countered [with a statement] that God already has such an eternal object for [His] action, in Logos; for Logos is the same God made manifest, and manifestation presupposes that 'other' for which or in relation to which God is manifested, i.e., presupposes man.

It is obvious that in speaking of the eternity of man or mankind, we do not understand the natural man, or man as a phenomenon—this would be a contradiction of terms as well as of the empirical data of science.

Science, namely, geology, shows that our natural or earthly man appeared on earth at a definite period of time, as the final link of the organic development of a terrestrial globe. But man as an empirical phenomenon presupposes man as a mentally conceivable being, and it is of him that we are speaking. But, on the other hand, in speaking of the essential and eternal man, we do not mean by that term either the conception of man as human genus, or mankind as a collective name. For those who accept the given actuality of nature as something unconditional and the only positive and real [universe]—for those, of course, all that is not this given reality, can only be a general conception or an abstraction. When they speak about an actual man, they understand this or that individual man, who exists in a definite space and time as a physical material organism. Beyond this, man for them is only an abstraction, and mankind is only a collective name. Such is the viewpoint of empirical realism; we will not argue against it, but rather will attempt to develop it with full logical consistency, which will reveal its insolvency better than anything else, as we shall presently see. Admitting that only a single real fact has true existence, we, being logically consistent, cannot acknowledge even a separate individual man to be a real actual being; even he, from this point of view, must be regarded only as an abstraction. Indeed, let us take a definite human specimen: what do we find in it as in an [empirical] reality? First of all it is a physical organism; but every physical organism is an aggregate of a plurality of organic elements—[i.e., it] is a group in space. Our body consists of a great many organs and tissues, which can all be reduced to a varied association of minutest organic elements, the so-called cells, and from the empirical point of view there is no ground for regarding this association as a real rather than merely a collective unit. The unity of the physical organism, i.e., of all this multiplicity of elements appears empirically only as a connection, as a relationship, but not as a real unit.

Thus, if we find the organism to be empirically an aggregate of a multitude of elementary entities, then a specific physical man from this point of view cannot be called a real indivisible [unit] or a specimen in the proper sense [of the word]; with as much foundation we could acknowledge each separate organ as a real unit, and with far more reason—a separate organic element, the *cell*. But even here one may not stop, for the cell also is a complex being; from the standpoint of empirical reality it is but a physico-chemical association of material particles, i.e., in the end, only an association of a great many homogeneous atoms. But the atom, as a material [unit] and, consequently, a unit of extension [space] (and only in this sense may atoms be acknowledged on the part of empirical realism) cannot be ultimately indivisible; matter as such is divisible to infinity, and, consequently, the atom is only a conditional [conventional] unit of division and nothing more. Thus, not only a separate man as an organic specimen, but even the very last elements of which he is composed, do not represent any real unit; and it appears to be absolutely impossible to find such [a unit] in external reality in general.

But perhaps the real unity of the human specimen, not found in his physical being, in [him as] an external phenomenon, is to be found in his psychical being—in [man as] an internal phenomenon? But here, too, what do we find from the empirical point of view?

We find, from this point of view, a succession of separate states in the life of man's soul—a series of thoughts, desires, and feelings. It is true, this series is connected in self-consciousness by the fact that all these conditions relate to one ego; but this very reference of different conditions to a single psychic focus, which we call *I*, is, from the empirical point of view, only one psychical phenomenon among others. The consciousness of oneself is only one of the acts of the psychical life— the *I* of which we are aware is a *result* produced or conditioned by a long series of processes, but not a real being. The *I*, as a mere act of self-consciousness, by itself is deprived of all content, is but a bright point in the confused stream of psychic states.

As in the physical organism, because of the continuous changes of matter, there cannot be any real identity of that organism at two different moments of time (as is known, any human body was materially quite different a month ago from what it is at present; in the latter there may not be a single material particle left from the first); so also in the psychical life of man [regarded] as a phenomenon, every act represents something new: every thought, every sensation is a new phenomenon, bound with all the rest of his psychic content solely by the laws of association. From this point of view we do not find [any] unconditional unity—any real unit—either in the external, physical, or in the inner, psychical organism of man.

Man, i.e., this separate specimen, appears here [from the empirical point of view] on one hand as an aggregate of an infinite number of elements, continuously changing their material composition and retaining only a formal, abstract unity; and on the other hand, as a series of psychical states following one after another according to an external, accidental association, and connected among themselves only through a formal, devoid of content, and even not contiguous, act of reflection or self-consciousness, expressed in our *I*; and this *I* itself is different in each separate act of one's awareness of oneself (when I say *I* at the present moment, and when I say later on the same thing in the following moments of time, these are different acts or states which do not represent any real unity [among themselves]). If thus, as a phenomenon, the individual man represents in his physical aspect only a spatial group of elements, and in the psychical sense, only a time series of separate states or events: then, from this point of view, not only man in general, or mankind, but even a separate human specimen, is only an abstraction, and not a real unit. As it has been pointed out, it is impossible to find any real unit from this point of view in general. For, as every material element entering into the composition of the organism can, as extended in space, be divided ad infinitum; similarly, every psychical event, occurring in a definite time, can be divided ad infinitum into infinitely short moments of time. There is no ultimate unit in either case: all assumed units prove to be conditional and arbitrary. But if there are no real units, then there is no real whole; if there are no really definite parts, then there is no actual whole. The result, of this point of view, is a complete nothingness, the negation of all reality—a result which, obviously, proves the inadequacy of the point of view itself. If, in fact, empirical realism which acknowledges the given phenomenon as the sole reality, cannot find any ground for any ultimate reality, for any real units; then we have the right to conclude that these real units, without which nothing can exist, have their own independent essence beyond the limits of the given phenomena, and that the latter are only the manifestations of the true essences and not [the essences] themselves.

Thus, we must acknowledge that full actuality belongs to the ideal beings, which are not given in the direct external experience—[that full actuality belongs] to the beings which themselves are neither the elements materially existing in our space, nor the events (or states) psychically taking place in time.

From this point of view, when we speak of man, we have no need or right to limit man to the data of visible reality; we speak of the ideal man, [who is] nevertheless altogether essential and real—much more, incommensurably more essential and real than the visible manifestation of human beings. There is an unlimited wealth of forces and content in us which are hidden behind the threshold of our present consciousness; only a certain part of those forces or of that content crosses the threshold of [and into] our consciousness at a time, never exhausting the whole.

'It is in ourselves', an ancient poet states, 'and not in the stars of heaven, nor in the depths of Tartarus, that the eternal powers of the whole universe reside'.

If a man as a phenomenon is a transitory fact, then as essence he is necessarily eternal and all-embracing; what is, then, the ideal man? In order to be actual he must be one and [at the same time] many; consequently, he is not only the universal general essence of all human specimens, abstracted from them; he is a universal, and at the same time, an individual being, containing in himself all these specimens actually. Every one of us, every human being, is essentially and actually rooted, and takes part, in the universal or absolute man.

As the divine forces comprise a single, whole, unconditionally universal and unconditionally individual, organism of the living Logos, so all human elements form a similarly whole simultaneously universal and individual organism—the necessary realization and receptory [receptacle] of the first—the pan-human organism, as the eternal body of God and the eternal soul of the world. As this latter organism, that is to say, Sophia, in its eternal being necessarily consists of a multiplicity of elements, of which it is the real unity: it follows that each of the elements, as a necessary new part of eternal Godmanhood, must be acknowledged *eternal* in the absolute, or the ideal, order.

Thus, when we speak of the eternity of mankind, we implicitly understand the eternity of each separate human being.[1] Without this eternity [of its constituent parts], mankind itself would be illusory.

Only in the recognition [of the truth] that every man is rooted in his deepest essence in the eternal divine world, that he is not only a visible phenomenon, i.e., a series of events and a group of facts, but an eternal and particular being, a necessary and irreplaceable link in the absolute whole, only with the recognition of that [truth], I say, is it possible to admit rationally of the two great truths unconditionally necessary not only for theology, i.e., for religious knowledge, but for human life in general: I mean the truths of human freedom and human immortality.

To begin with the latter: it is perfectly obvious that if man be regarded as a being produced in time, created at a certain moment, and non-existent prior to his physical birth, then man is really reduced to his phenomenal appearance, to his manifested existence, which does start with the physical birth only. But such existence also ends with the physical death. That which appeared in time must also disappear in time; an infinite existence *after death* is in no way logically compatible with nothingness *before birth*.

As a natural being, as a phenomenon, man exists only in between physical birth and physical death. To admit that he exists after physical death is possible only with the admission that he is not merely an entity

[1]In speaking of the eternity of every human being in the sense here indicated, we do not assert anything new or contradictory to the established religious positions. Christian theologians and philosophers always distinguished between the finite phenomenon of the world in space and time, and the eternal existence of the idea of the world in the thought of God, i.e., in Logos; and it must be remembered that in God, as in the eternal reality, the idea of the world is not to be regarded as anything abstract, but appears necessarily as something real.

living in the natural world—merely a phenomenon—but that, besides, he is an eternal, apperceptive essence. But in such a case it is logically necessary to recognize that he exists not only after death, but also before birth, because an apperceptive essence, by its very meaning, is not subject to the form of our [the empirical] time, which is only a phenomenal form.

Passing to the second truth mentioned above, the freedom of man, it is easy to see that by regarding man as a being created in time, [created] out of nothing, and, consequently, as a sort of chance creation of God—for it is [thereby] assumed that God can exist without man, and that He really had so existed before the creation of man—by regarding man, I repeat, as determined unconditionally by the peremptory will of God and, therefore, in relation to God a creature absolutely passive, we decidedly leave no room for his freedom.

How the problem of freedom can be solved from the point of view which regards man as eternal—i.e., the point of view of Godmanhood —we shall try to demonstrate in the next lecture.

LECTURE NINE

THE religious consciousness, starting with the divine, all-perfect beginning, finds the actual natural world out of accord with this beginning, i.e., [finds it] imperfect or not normal, and because of that, mysterious and incomprehensible. It appears to be something untrue, something that ought not to be, and therefore it is necessary *to explain* it from [the point of view of] the true and that which ought to be [the norm], i.e., [to deduce it] from the other, the supernatural or divine world, which is revealed to the religious consciousness as its positive content. The middle term or the uniting link through the medium of which the natural being is explained or deduced from the divine being is, as we know, mankind [understood] as a concrete unity of all beginnings.

First of all, we have to determine what, precisely, is abnormal or imperfect in the natural world, what in it requires explanation or justification from the religious point of view.

It is obvious that the constant forms of natural phenomena, their harmonious relationships and their immutable laws, the whole ideal content of this world, which presents itself to objective contemplation and study—all this contains nothing abnormal or imperfect, nothing that would be in contradiction or contrast to the character of the divine world. With a purely theoretical approach to nature, as to something merely contemplated and cognized, the mind cannot find anything that would evoke condemnation or require eulogy; regarding nature in its general forms and laws, it can discern in the phenomena of nature only a clear reflection of eternal ideas. In regarding the actuality of nature ideally, i.e., contemplating it in its general aspect, in its idea, we thereby absolve it of everything accidental and transitory, and as the poet says: 'gaze directly from within time into eternity, and see the flame of the universal sun'.

> *Immovable upon fiery roses,*
> *Fumes the living altar of universal creation;*
> *As in creative reveries, amidst the fume*
> *Vibrates all power, all eternity comes in a dream.*
> *And all that rushes over the chasms of ether,*
> *And every ray corporeal or incorporeal*
> *Is only thy reflection, O sun of the world,*
> *And only a dream, only a passing dream.*

And, in truth, in ideal contemplation (as well as in purely scientific knowledge) every individual separateness, every particularity of a real phenomenon, is only 'a passing dream', only an indifferent and transitory case or example of the universal and the one; what matters here is not the real existence of the object but its ideal content, which is something in itself perfect and fully clear to the mind. But if in pure contemplation and in theory, (in its objective aspect) the individual existence is deprived in its separateness of all self-sustained significance, then in practical *life*, for our active will, (in its subjective aspect) this separate egoistic existence of the individual is of primary significance, is what really matters; here we have to take it into consideration, at any rate; and if this egoistic existence is a dream, it is a heavy and torturous dream, from the spell of which we are not able to free ourselves—a dream that oppresses us, regardless of our awareness of the fact that it is illusory (if such an awareness does appear). It is this heavy and torturous dream of the separate egoistic existence, and not the objective character of nature in its general forms, what from the religious point of view is mysterious, what requires explanation.

In the light of the ideal contemplation we do not feel and do not assert ourselves in our separateness: here the tormenting flame of our personal will is extinguished, and we recognize our essential unity with all else. But such an ideal state lasts in us but a moment; outside of these bright moments, in the course of all the rest of our life, our ideal unity with everything else appears to us illusory, unessential; as actual reality [in our experience] we acknowledge only our own separate, particular *I*: we are locked in our own selves, impermeable for the 'other', and, therefore, the 'other' is also impermeable for us. Admitting in general, in theory, that all else has the same inner subjective being as we have, [that it also] exists for itself, we nevertheless completely forget that in actual practical relations, and here all other beings appear to us not as living persons but as empty masks.

It is this abnormal attitude towards all [around us], this exclusive self-assertion or egoism, all-powerful in practical life even if it is rejected in theory—this contra-position of self to all others and the practical negation of these others—it is this which constitutes the fundamental *evil* of our nature. And, since it is common to all living creatures—since every being in nature, every animal, every insect, and every blade of grass, in its own personal being detaches itself from all else, endeavours to be the whole in itself by absorbing or by repulsing the others (and that is the origin of the external material being)—therefore, evil is the general property of all nature. Being on one hand, namely, in its ideal content or in its objective forms and laws, but a *reflection of the all-one idea*, nature appears, on the other hand—namely, in its real, segregated, and disjunct existence—as something alien and inimical to that idea, as something that ought not to be, something evil, and evil in a double sense: for if egoism, i.e., the striving to establish one's exclusive ego in place of all [else], or to annul all by oneself, is evil par excellence (the moral evil)—then the fatal impossibility of actual realization of egoism, i.e., the impossibility of being all while remaining in one's own exclusiveness, is the root of *suffering*, in relation to which all other sufferings are particular cases of the general law. Indeed, the common basis of all suffering, both moral and physical, is reducible to the dependence of the subject upon something external to it, some external fact which coercively binds and oppresses it; but such an external dependence would be obviously impossible if the given subject was in an inner and actual unity with all else, if it sensed [found] itself in all: then nothing would be completely foreign or external to it, nothing could coercively limit or oppress it; sensing itself in accord with all else, it would feel the action of all [around it] upon itself also as concordant with its own will, as agreeable to itself; and, consequently, it would not be able to experience [any] actual suffering.

It will be clear from what has been said that evil and suffering have the inner, subjective significance; they exist in us and for us, i.e., in every being and for it. They are the *states* of individual being; namely, evil is an exerted condition of his will which asserts itself exclusively and denies all else, and suffering is the necessary reaction of the other one to that will, a reaction to which the self-asserting being is subjected involuntarily and inevitably, and which it feels as suffering. Thus suffering, which constitutes one of the characteristic marks of natural being, appears to be a necessary result of moral evil.

We have seen that the actual being of the natural world is something that ought not to be, or something abnormal, in so far as it is contraposed to the being of the divine world (as the unconditional norm); but this contraposition and, consequently, evil itself is, as it has been demonstrated, only a condition of individual beings and their certain relationship to one another (namely, a negative relationship), but not any independent essence or separate principle. The world, which according to the apostle, lieth in sin, is not any new world, completely separate from the divine world and composed of some special essential elements of its own; it is rather but the wrong *interrelationship* of the same elements which constitute the being of the divine world as well. The improper [such as it ought not to be] actuality [reality] of the natural world is the disjunct and inimical *position*, in relation to one another, of the same elements which in their normal relationship, namely, in their internal unity and accord, enter into the composition of the divine world. For if God, as the absolute or the all-perfect, contains in Himself all being, or all beings, then, consequently, there cannot be any beings which would have the foundation of their existence outside of God or were substantially outside of the divine world; and, consequently, nature in its contraposition to Divinity, can be only another position or a *transposition* of certain elements which substantially abide in the divine world.

Thus these two worlds differ one from the other not in essence but only in position [of the elements]: one of them represents the unity of all beings, or such an arrangement of them wherein each finds itself in all, and all in each—while the other [world], on the contrary, represents that position [condition] of entities in which each, in itself or in its own will, asserts itself without regard to the others, as well as against the others (which is evil), and thereby experiences the external actuality of the others as contrary to its will (which is suffering).

This raises a question: how can such an improper situation of the natural world, this exclusive self-assertion of entities be explained? We know that self-assertion is an exerted condition of the will which centres in itself, segregates from, and contraposes itself to, all else. But the will is an inner action of the subject the direct expression and manifestation of its own being. The will is an *extravertive* action, an internal motion proceeding from within the subject itself; therefore every act of the will is, by its nature, free; every good volition is arbitrary [unrestrained, free] volition (as in language, at least in the Russian language, the will and freedom are synonyms).[1]

Thus, if evil or egoism is a certain actual exerted condition of an individual will which opposes itself to the whole, and every act of the will, by its definition, is free; then it follows that evil is a free product of individual beings.

But individual beings cannot be the free causes of evil in their capacity of *physical* beings, which they are in the natural material world; because this world, as well as they themselves in so far as they belong to it, are but consequences or manifestations of evil. Indeed, the external material separateness and particularity—which characterize the natural life and comprise the natural world in its contraposition to the divine world—the external apartness of the physical being is, as we know, a direct result of the internal discord and self-assertion or egoism; the latter, therefore, itself lies deeper than any materially segregated being, beyond the limits of the physical existence of the subjects in their external separateness and plurality. In other words, the

---

[1]This in no way contradicts the undoubted truth that all acts of the will are determined by some motives. In fact, every motive stimulates a definite act of the will only because it acts upon this definite being: it is only a *stimulus*, which *incites* a certain being to independent action, according to the peculiar character of that being. Were it otherwise, were the motive the sole determinant, then it would have affected every will alike; but in reality we do not see that, for the same motive—for example, sensual pleasure—under certain conditions instigates one being to action, while another under the same conditions does not react at all, or opposes and rejects the motivation: i.e., for one will it is an actual, positive motive, while for another will it is not. Consequently, the effectiveness of the motives, i.e., their ability to stimulate in the subject a certain act of the will, depends first of all *upon* the subject *itself*. The acting force belongs not to the motive itself, but to that will upon

individual being as a physical phenomenon, that is itself conditioned by external necessity, cannot be the original free cause of evil.

Universal experience shows that every physical being is born in evil; an evil will together with egoism appear in each specific being at the very beginning of his physical existence, when his free rational or personal beginning does not yet function; so that that incipient evil is for him something already given, fatal, and involuntary, and in no manner his own free production. Unconditional will cannot belong to a physical being as such, for it is conditioned by another and does not act directly of itself.

Thus, evil, having no physical origin, must have a *metaphysical* beginning; the producing cause of evil may be the individual being not in his capacity as a natural, already conditioned, phenomenon, but in his unconditional eternal essence, to which belongs the original and immediate will of that being. If our natural world, lying in evil, as the land of curse and banishment, bringing forth wolves and thorns, is the inevitable consequence of sin and the fall; then, obviously, the *origin* of sin and of the fall lies not here but in that garden of God in which had been planted not only the tree of life, but also the tree of the knowledge of good and evil—in other words, the *primordial* origin of evil may have had place only in the domain of the eternal prenatural world.

In the pre-natural world we distinguish Divinity itself as the all-one, i.e., as the positive (independent, personal, oneness of all—and this 'all', which is contained in the divine unity and originally has its real being only in it, in itself is only a potency of being, the first matter, or the non-existent (*yn ov*). As Divinity is the eternal and absolute *self-determination*—for as the fullness of the whole, as the unity of all, it cannot have anything external to itself and, consequently, is fully determined by itself; therefore, although as *the extant one*, Divinity has in itself an unlimited and immeasurable potentiality or force of being

---

which it acts and which, thus, is really the direct cause and the essential basis of the [ensuing] action. If I act well under the influence of good motives, then those good motives as such can influence me only because I am in general inclined to act well; otherwise they would have no power over me. Thus the motives determine not the acting will, in its character and the direction of its action, (which themselves condition the effectiveness of a given motive), but rather, *the fact of the manifestation* of this will at the given moment; in other words, the motives are only the stimuli for the action of the will; the effective cause of every action is the will itself, or, more correctly, the subject as the one who wills, i.e., as he who starts the action out of himself or from himself. Every act of the will is not the action of the motive, but the *reaction* of the subject to the motive, determined by the character of the subject.

(without which nothing can exist), as *the all-one* it eternally *actualizes* this potentiality (possibility), always fills the unlimitedness of being by a similarly unlimited, absolute content, always quenches the infinite thirst of being, natural to all that exists. [But] it is not so in those particular essences which in their totality or all-unity form the content of the all-one Divinity. Each of these essences, precisely as 'each', i.e., as 'one out of all', is not and cannot be immediately, in itself, 'the whole'. Thus, for 'each' is opened the possibility of 'the other': the 'all', the absolute fullness of being in it (in 'each') is opened as an endless striving, as the unquenchable thirst of being, as a dark fire of life eternally seeking light. It (each) is 'this', but it desires, being 'this', to be 'all'—but the 'all' does not actually exist for it as for merely 'this'; and therefore the striving towards all (to be all) is in it something totally indefinite and immeasurable, in itself without any limits. Thus that unlimitedness (in Greek, to apiron), which in Divinity is only a possibility, which never reaches actuality (because always satisfyable, or satisfied from all eternity), here—in the particular entities—receives the significance of the fundamental element of their being, is the centre and basis of the whole created life.

But this centre of nature is not revealed directly even in particular beings, in so far as they are all originally contained in the unity of God and do not exist for themselves separately, are not aware of themselves as outside the divine all-unity, do not centre in themselves, and therefore the (in Greek, to apiron) in them remains hidden, potential although not in the same sense as in God, in whom it is always *potentia post actum*, whereas in them it is only *potentia ante actum.*

In that their original unity with Divinity, all beings formed one divine world in three major spheres, depending on which of the three basic modes of being—the substantial, the mental (ideal), or the sensual (real)—predominated in them; or by which of the three divine acts (will, representation, feeling) they were chiefly determined.

The first sphere of the divine world is characterized by a decisive predominance of the deepest, most inward and spiritual element of being—the will. Here all beings are in a simple unity of their will with Divinity in the oneness of the pure, immediate love; they are essentially determined by the divine prime-beginning, abiding 'in the bosom of the Father.' In so far as they belong to this first sphere, these beings are pure spirits, and the whole being of these pure spirits is directly determined by their will, because their will is identical with the all-one will of God. Here, then, the predominant tone of being is the unconditional love, in which all are one.

In the second sphere the fullness of the divine being unfolds in a multiplicity of images bound together by an ideal unity; here predominates representation or mental activity defined by the divine mind; entities in that sphere can be called, therefore, minds. Here all beings

have their being not only in God and for God, but also for one another
—in representation or contemplation; here, although only in an ideal
manner, definiteness and distinction appear; all essences (ideas) are
in a certain relation (ratio, in Greek: logos) one to another, and thus
that sphere is pre-eminently the domain of the divine Word (Logos)
who ideally expresses the rational fullness of the divine determinants.
Here every 'mental' being is a definite idea, which has its definite place
in the ideas cosmos.

   In these two spheres (spiritual and mental) of the divine world,
everything that exists is determined directly by the divine beginning in
the first two forms of its being. But if in general the actuality of the
divine world consists in the interaction between the one and all, that
is to say, between the divine beginning itself and the multitude of beings contained in it, then the divine world cannot have its full actuality
in these two first spheres [taken] by themselves, for there is not real
interaction here—because entities, as pure spirits and pure minds,
abiding in immediate unity with Divinity, do not have any separate,
segregated, or self-centred existence, and as such cannot, of themselves, (internally) act upon the divine beginning. Indeed, entities as
pure spirits, in the first sphere, where they are in the immediate unity
with the divine love and will, have by themselves only potential existence; in the second sphere, although these multiple beings are, really,
segregated by the divine Logos as definite objective forms, in a constant
definite relationship one to another, and consequently receive here a
certain individuality; yet it is a purely ideal individuality, for all being
of this sphere is determined by contemplation or pure representation.
But such ideal particularization of its elements is insufficient for the
divine beginning as the one; it is necessary for it that the many beings
receive their own real individualization, for otherwise the force of the
divine unity or love would have no object upon which it could manifest
itself or realize itself in its whole fullness. Therefore, the divine being
cannot content itself with the eternal contemplation of the ideal essences (to behold them and to be beheld by them); it is not sufficient for
it to possess them as its object, its idea, and to be for them only an idea;
but, 'free from envy', i.e., from exclusiveness, it desires their own real
life—i.e., [the divine being] brings its will out of that unconditional
substantial unity, by which the first sphere of divine being is defined,
directs this will upon the whole multitude of the ideal objects contemplated in the second sphere, and stops [rests] upon each of them
separately; through an act of its will, it espouses each one of them, and
thereby asserts, seals its [that entity's] own independent being, which
then may act upon the divine beginning. By that real action [of Divin-
ity] the third sphere of the divine being is formed. This act (or acts) of
the divine will, uniting with the ideal objects or images of the divine
mind, and thereby giving them their real being, is, properly speaking,

the act of divine creation. The following consideration may serve as an explanation of it. Although the ideal beings (or minds) which constitute the object of the divine action, do not really have in themselves, separately, substantial being or unconditional self-subsistence—that would contradict the oneness of the extant One—yet each one of them represents a certain ideal particularity, a certain characteristic property which makes this object to be what it is and distinguishes it from all others, so that it always has been a completely independent significance, if not by [its] being, then by its essence or idea (*non quoad existentiam, sed quad essentiam*), i.e., by that inner property by which is defined its ideal relationship with all else, the relationship perceived in thought or contemplation, or its concept [meaning] (in Greek, logos), independent of its real existence. But Divinity, as inwardly all-one and all-good, fully asserts *all other*, i.e., posits its own will as an unlimited potency of being (in Greek, to apiron) into all else, without retaining it in itself as *in the one*, but actualizing or objectifying it for itself as *the all-one*. By virtue of the essential particularity (by which it is *this* [and not anything else]), belonging to all else, i.e., to every divine idea, or to every objective image, every such image, every idea with which the divine will unites itself, is not indifferent to that will, but necessarily changes its action in accordance with its peculiarity, gives its own specific character, so to speak, moulds it into its own form; for it is obvious that the property of actual will is necessarily determined not only by the one who wills, but also by the object of its will. Every objective image, receiving the unlimited divine will *in its own manner*, by virtue of its own particularity, thereby assimilates it, i.e., makes it to be its own; thus this will ceases to be God's will only; assimilated in a certain way (as idea) and having received from it its own particular definite character, it becomes as much a property of that objective image in its particularity as an action of the divine being. Thus, the unlimited power of being (in Greek, to apiron), which in Divinity is always covered by an act, for God always (*eternally*) desires or loves all, and has all in himself and for himself this unlimited potentiality in each particular being ceases to be covered by His actuality, for this actuality is not *all*, but only one out of *all, something particular*. That is to say, each entity loses its own immediate unity with Divinity, and the act of the divine will—which in Divinity, never separated from all others, has no limits—receives such a limit in a particular being. But in individualizing itself, that being begets the possibility of acting upon the unitary Divine will, determining that will in its own particular way. The particular idea, with which is united the act of divine will, impressing upon that act its own particular character, detaches it from the absolute immediate oneness of the divine will, receives it *for itself* and acquires in it the living force of actuality, which enables it to exist and to act of itself, in the capacity of an individual entity, or an independent subject. Thus we have now not only ideal beings which have their being only in the contemplation of Divinity, but living beings which have their own actuality and of themselves act upon the divine beginning. Such beings we call souls.

Thus, the eternal objects of divine contemplation, becoming the objects of particular divine will (more exactly, particularizing, by virtue of their inherent particularity, the divine will which acts in them), become the 'living souls'; in other words, entities which substantially are contained in the bosom of God the Father, which are ideally contemplated in the light of the divine Logos and themselves contemplate Him, by the power of the quickening Spirit receive their own real being and action.

The oneness of the divine beginning, substantially abiding in the first sphere of being and ideally manifested in the second, can receive its real actualization only in the third. In all the three spheres we distinguish the acting divine beginning of unity or Logos as the direct manifestation of Divinity, and the 'many' or the 'all' which are unified by the action of that One, [which] assimilate it [the One] into themselves, and actualize it. But in the first sphere this 'all' exists by itself only potentially, in the second only ideally; only in the third does it receive its own real existence; and therefore the unity of this sphere, produced by the divine Logos, appears [here], for the first time, as an actual independent being, which is able of itself to act on the divine beginning. Only here the object of divine action becomes a real, actual subject, and the action itself becomes a real interaction. This second [or] produced unity, as opposed to the original oneness of the divine Logos, is, as we know, the soul of the world or the ideal mankind (Sophia), which contains in itself and binds with itself all the particular living beings or souls. Representing the realization of the divine beginning, being its image and likeness, the protoform humanity or the soul of the world is, simultaneously, one and all; she occupies the mediating position between the multiplicity of living beings, which comprise the real content of her life, and the unconditional unity of Divinity, which is the ideal beginning and the norm of that life. As the living focus or the soul of all creatures, and at the same time the real form of Divinity—the extant [living] subject of the created being and the extant [living] object of the divine action—participant of the oneness of God, and at the same time embracing the whole multiplicity of the living souls, the all-one humanity, or the soul of the world, is a dual being: containing in herself both the divine beginning and the created being, she is not defined exclusively by either one or the other and, consequently, remains free; the divine beginning, inherent in her, liberates her from her created nature, while the latter makes her free in regard to Divinity. In embracing all living beings (souls) and in them also all ideas, she is not exclusively bound to any one among them, is free from all of them—but, being the immediate centre and the real unity of all these beings, she receives in them, in their particularity, independence from the divine beginning [and] the possibility of acting upon it in the capacity of a free subject. In so far as she receives unto herself the divine Logos and is determined by Him, the soul of the world is humanity—the divine manhood of Christ—the body of Christ, or Sophia. Conceiving the unitary divine beginning and binding by this unity the entire multiplicity of beings, the soul of the world thereby gives the divine beginning [its] complete actual realization in everything; by means of her [through her as the medium] God is manifested in all creation as the living, active force, or as the Holy Spirit. In other words: in being determined or formed by the divine Logos, the soul of the world enables the Holy Spirit to actualize Himself in all; for that which in the light of Logos is revealed in ideal images, is realized by the Holy Spirit in real action. Hence it is clear that the soul of the world contains in unity all the elements of the world only in so far as she is herself subjected to the divine beginning which she receives, in so far as she retains that divine beginning as the sole object of her will of life, as the unconditional aim and focus of her being; for only in so far as she herself is permeated by the divine all-unity can she transmit it into the whole creation, uniting and subjecting to herself and the whole multitude of beings through the power of Divinity, resident in her. In so far as she is possessed by Divinity, in that measure she possesses all; for in Divinity everything is in unity; and asserting herself in the all-unity [of Divinity] she is thereby free from everything in particular, free in the positive sense, as possessing all. But the soul of the world receives the divine beginning and is determined by it not because of any external necessity, but by her own action; for as we know, she has in herself by her own position, the principle of independent action or the will, i.e., the capacity to initiate from within herself an inner motion (striving). In other words, the world soul can herself choose the object of the striving of her life.

What could be the object, besides the divine beginning, to which the world soul would strive? She possesses all; the unlimited potentiality of being (in Greek, to apiron) is satisfied in her. But it is satisfied not unconditionally and, therefore, not finally. The world soul possesses 'all', as the content of her own being (her own idea) not immediately in herself, but from the divine beginning, which is essentially prior to her, is presupposed by her and defines her. Only as she is open in her inner being to the activity of the divine Logos does the world soul receive in Him and from Him power over all, and possesses all. Therefore, although possessing all, the world soul can still desire to possess it in a manner *different* from the way she does possess it, i.e., she can desire to possess it *of herself*, as God [desires anything]: she may wish to add to the fullness of being which belongs to her, also the

absolute *self-substancy* of her being in the possession of that fullness—
something that does not belong to her. By virtue of this, the soul can
detach the relative centre of her life from the absolute centre of the
divine life, can assert herself outside of God. But thereby the soul
necessarily loses her central position, falls from the all-one focus of the
divine being to the circumference of multiple creation, losing her freedom and her power over this creation: for she possesses such power not
of herself, but only as a mediatrix between creation and Divinity, from
which in her self-assertion she becomes separated. In resting her will
upon herself, centring in herself, she takes herself away from all, becomes but one among many. But when the world soul ceases to unite
all with herself, then all lose their common bond, and the unity of cosmic creation breaks up into a multitude of separated elements, the
universal organism becomes transformed into a mechanical aggregate
of atoms. Because all the particular specific elements of the universal
organism by themselves, i.e., as specific (each as 'something' but not as
the whole, as 'this' but not as the other), are not [connected] in immediate unity one with the other, but have this unity only through the
medium of the world soul, as their common focus which contains or
encompasses all in itself. With the segregation of the world soul, however, when she, arousing in herself her own will, thereby detaches herself from the whole, the particular elements of the universal organism
lose their common tie [which they had] in her, and, left to themselves,
are doomed to the particularized, egoistic existence, the root of which
is evil, and the fruit, suffering. Thus, the whole creature is subjected
to the vanity and slavery of corruption not by its own will, but by the
will of him[2] who has [so] subjected it, i.e., the world soul, as the one
free beginning of natural life.

[2]Solovyev uses here the words of St. Paul but attributes that will to the
'world soul', instead of to God.   Translator.

LECTURE TEN

T H E natural world, which has fallen away from the divine unity, appears as a chaos of disjointed elements. The plurality of disintegrated elements, foreign one to another, impermeable for each other, is expressed in real *space*. Real space does not consist only of the form of extension—every being and every representation has such form for another [being or representation]; even all the content of the inner psychic world, when we represent it concretely, appears as extended or as occupying space in that respect, i.e., in the formal sense[1]; but this is only the ideal space, which does not set any permanent and independent limit to our action; the real space or externality necessarily proceeds from the disintegration and mutual alienation of all that exists, by virtue of which every being has in all others [in all other beings] a constant and coercive boundary to his actions. In this condition of externality every single being, every element, is excluded or pushed out by all others; and, by resisting this external action, occupies a certain definite place, which it strives to retain exclusively for itself, demonstrating the force of inertia and impermeability. The complex system of external forces, shocks, and motions, which results from that mechanical interaction of elements, forms the world of *matter*. *But* this world is not a world of unconditionally homogeneous elements; we know that every real element, every single being (atom) has its own particular individual essence (idea); and if in the divine order all those elements, positively completing one another, form a whole and harmonious organism, then in the natural order we have this same organism only disintegrated in actuality (*actu*); it retains its ideal unity in a latent potentiality and in its tendency [striving, desire]. The gradual actualization of this striving, the gradual realization of the ideal all-oneness, constitutes the meaning and goal of the world process. As in the divine order all *eternally is* the absolute organism; so by the law of natural being, all gradually *becomes* such organism in time.[2]

The soul of this nascent organism—the soul of the world—at the

[1]For example, in a dream we see ourselves in a certain space, and all that happens in a dream, all the images and pictures of dreams, appear in a spatial form.

[2]If space is a form of the external unity of the natural world and a condition of the mechanical interaction of beings, time is a form of the internal unification and a condition for the restoration of the organic union of what exists; which, not *given* in nature, necessarily becomes something *attained* [reached for], in a *process*.

beginning of the world-process is deprived, in actuality, of that unifying, organizing force which it has only in union with the divine beginning, as [the conductor or medium] receiving and transmitting it into the world; but separated from it, by itself, it is only an indefinite tendency towards the unity of all, an indefinite passive possibility (potentiality) of the all-unity. As an indefinite tendency, which as yet has no definite content, the world soul or nature[3] cannot by itself reach that point to which it strives, i.e., all-unity; it is unable to generate it from its own self. In order to bring to unity and accord the disjointed and [mutually] hostile elements, it is necessary to determine for each [element] its specific function, to place it in a definite positive relationship towards all others—in other words, it is necessary not merely to unite everything, but to effect that unification in a definite, positive *form*. This definite form of all-unity or of the universal organism is contained in Divinity as an eternal idea. In the world, on the other hand—i.e., in the aggregate of the elements (of all that exists) which came out of unity—in this world, or rather, in this chaotic state of the existence of all (which had constituted the primordial fact) the eternal idea of the absolute organism had to be gradually realized; and the effort towards that realization, the striving towards the incarnation of Divinity in the world—this striving is universal, one in all, and therefore transcends the limits of each—it is this striving which, representing the inner life and beginning of movement in all that exists, is the world soul, properly speaking. And if, as it has been stated, the world soul by herself cannot realize herself because she lacks a definite positive form [necessary] for that purpose; then, it is obvious that in her impetus towards the realization [of the striving] she must look for that form in another [one]; and she can find it only in the one who eternally contains that form, i.e., in the divine beginning: which thus appears as the active, formative, and determining principle of the world-process.

In itself, the divine beginning is the eternal all-one, abiding in absolute repose and immutability; but in relation to the plurality of finite being, which has emerged from it, the divine beginning appears as the *active* force of unity—Logos *ad extra*. The multiple being rises in its discord against the divine unity, denies it; but Divinity, being by its essence the principle of all-unity, is only stimulated by that negative action of disintegrated being to a positive counteraction, to the revelation of its unifying force—at first in the form of an external law, setting the limit to the disintegration and strife of the elements, and then gradually actualizing a new, positive unification of these elements in the form of the absolute organism or the internal all-unity.

[3]The Latin word *natura* (that which is to be born) is very expressive as a designation of the world soul; for it does not yet exist, in fact, as actual subject of all-oneness; in that capacity it has yet to be born.

And so the divine beginning appears here (in the world process) as the active force of the absolute idea which endeavours to embody itself in the [midst of the] chaos of the disjointed elements. The divine beginning thus strives towards the same aim as the world soul—towards the incarnation of the divine idea or the deification (*theosis*) of all that exists, by means of bringing all into the form of the absolute organism —but with this difference, that the world soul as a passive force, as a pure aspiration, does not know originally towards what it should aim, i.e., does not possess the idea of all-unity; whereas the divine Logos as the positive beginning, as the active and formative force, has the idea of all-unity in Himself, and bestows it upon the world soul as the determining form. In the world process both, the divine beginning and the world soul, appear as the striving; but the striving of the divine beginning is the effort to realize, to incarnate in another that which it already has in itself, which it already knows and possesses, i.e., the idea of all-unity, the idea of the absolute organism; while the striving of the world soul is to receive from another that which she does not yet have in herself, and to incarnate what she will receive in what she has, in that to which she is bound, i.e., in the material being, in the chaos of the disjointed elements. But since the aim of their strivings is the same— the incarnation of the divine idea—and since the actualization of this aim is possible only with the concomitant action of the divine beginning and the world soul (because the divine beginning cannot directly realize its idea in the disjunct elements of the material being, as something alien and opposite to itself, and the world soul cannot immediately unite these elements, not having in herself the definite form of unity), therefore the striving of the divine beginning for the incarnation of the idea becomes the striving for *union* with the world soul, as the one in possession of *the material* [necessary] for that incarnation; and, in her turn, the striving of the world soul towards the realization of unity in its material elements, becomes the striving towards the divine beginning, as the one containing the absolute *form* [necessary] for that unity.

Thus the incarnation of the divine idea in the world, which constitutes the goal of the whole world movement, is conditioned by the union of the divine beginning with the world soul, in which the first represents the active determining, formative, or fertilizing element, while the world soul appears as the passive force which receives the ideal beginning and endues the received with matter [requisite] for its development, with the encasement [shell, frame] [which it needs] for its complete manifestation. But now a question may arise. Why does not this union of the divine beginning with the world soul, and the resultant birth of the world organism as the incarnated divine idea (the Sophia)—why does not this union and this birth take place at once, in one act of divine creation? Why are these labours and efforts necessary in the life of the world, why must nature experience the pains of birth, and why, before it can generate the perfect and eternal organism, must it produce so many ugly, monstrous broods which are unable to endure the struggle for existence and perish without a trace? Why all these abortions and miscarriages of nature? Why does God leave nature to reach her goal so slowly and by such ill means? Why in general, is the realization of the divine idea in the world a gradual and complex process, and not a single, simple act? The full answer to this question is contained in one word, which expresses something without which neither God nor nature can be conceived: that word is *freedom*. By a free act of the world soul, the world united by it, fell away from Divinity and fell apart within itself into the multitude of elements warring among themselves; by a long series of free acts that whole rebellious multitude must make peace among themselves and be reconciled with God, and be reborn in the form of the absolute organism. If all that exists (in nature, or in the world soul) must be united with Divinity—and this constitutes the aim [purpose] of all being—then that unity, in order to be actual unity, must, obviously, be reciprocal, i.e., [must] proceed not only from God but also from nature, be nature's own task. But all-unity cannot be achieved in one immediate act by nature, as it is, eternally, in God; in nature, on the contrary, as immediately detaching itself from God, the actual being belongs not to the ideal all-oneness but to the material discord, while the all-unity appears in it as a pure striving, originally quite indefinite and empty; all is in chaos, nothing is yet in unity; consequently, being without unity, all can only *pass* to unity by virtue of its striving, and do so [only] gradually: because originally the world soul does not know [the idea of] all-unity at all, she strives towards it unconsciously, as a blind force—she strives towards it as towards something 'other'; the content of that 'other' is for her something completely foreign and unknown; and if this content, i.e., all-unity, were suddenly communicated or transmitted to her in its whole fullness, it would have appeared to her only as an external *fact*, as something fatal and coercive; whereas, in order to have it as a free idea, she must herself assimilate or master it, i.e., [must] pass from its indefiniteness and emptiness to more and more complete determinations of all-unity. Such is the general basis of the world process.

After a series of external connections of the divine beginning with the world soul, and external manifestations of the divine idea (all-unity) in the natural world—beginning with the simplest, general, and external one, expressed in the cosmic law of gravitation, according to which all that exists is mutually attracted through an unconscious blind attraction; passing on to more complex means of unification, expressed, for example, in the laws of chemical affinity, according to which not every [molecule] is united with every [other molecule] with equal attraction, differing only according to external spatial relationships (distances) [as in physics], but only definitely specified relationships obtain for each definite molecule; passing, further on, to a still more complex and at the same time more individual form of unity, which we find in the structure and life of the vegetative and animal organisms, where the principle of natural unity or the world soul is realized openly, although not yet fully and visibly, in definite and permanent formations, binding the material element into certain solid and stable wholes, which in itself have the form and law of their own lives—the cosmogonic process is [finally] concluded with the creation of the perfect organism, that of man. The progressive course of this process is explained in the following manner. The world soul in its original state of pure striving for the unity of the whole, itself void of content, could receive unity at first only in the most general and indefinite form (in the law of universal gravitation). That was already an actual form of unity, although as yet completely general and empty; there the world soul was already realized in a certain way. But that form of unity was not sufficient for the world soul, for she was the potentiality not of that but of the absolute unity. Therefore she strove again, now not as a pure potentiality but as one in a certain degree realized (in the first general form of unity), and consequently strives not for unity in general, but for a new one, still unknown to her, which could satisfy her more than that which she already attained. For its part, the active beginning of the world process (the divine Logos) having now before it the world soul not only as a pure potentiality but as a potentiality already realized in a certain manner, namely, as the actual unity of elementary forces, gravitating towards each other, can unite with her in a new, more definite manner, and generate through her a new, a more complex and a deeper connection of world elements, for which their former, already realized connection [will] serve as a real basis or a material medium. On this new level of the process, the world soul appears, thus, clad in a more perfect form of unity, appears more fully realized; but in so far as this new form does not yet express the absolute unity, a new striving arises in the realization of which the previously achieved form of unity serves in its turn, as a material basis; and so on. One can discern a great number of such consequent levels in the world process, but we shall point out three main epochs of that process: The first, when the cosmic matter is drawn by the dominating action of the force of gravitation into large cosmic bodies—the stellar or astral epoch; the second, when these bodies become a basis for the development of more complex forces, (i.e., of the forms of the world unity)—heat, light, magnetism, chemism, and at the same time are concretely differentiated into the complex harmonious system of bodies, such as our solar system; and, finally, the third epoch, during which within the limits of such a system, an already segregated individual member of it (such is our globe) becomes the material basis for new formations, in which the previously dominant contraposition of the ponderable, inert, impermeable matter and the imponderable, eternally mobile, and all-permeating *ether* as a pure medium of unity, is replaced with a concrete confluence of the unifying form with the material elements overcome by it, in the *organic life.*

After all this cosmogonic process, in which the divine beginning, uniting ever more closely with the world soul, overcomes the chaotic matter more and more, and finally brings it into the perfect form of the human organism. When, thus in nature was evolved the external receptacle for the divine idea, a new process began—that of the development of this idea as the momentum of the internal all-unity in the form of *consciousness* and free activity.

In man the world soul for the first time is internally united with the divine Logos in consciousness, as in the pure form of all-unity. Man, in reality but one of the many beings of nature, having in his consciousness the faculty of comprehending the reason or the inner connection and meaning (in Greek, logos) of all that exists, appears, in the idea [ideally], as *all,* and in this sense is the second all-one, the image and likeness of God. In man, nature outgrows itself and passes (in [human] consciousness) into the domain of the absolute being. Man, conceiving and bearing in his consciousness the eternal divine idea, and at the same time by his factual origin and existence inseparably connected with the nature of the external world, appears as the natural mediator between God and the material being, the conductor of the all-uniting divine beginning into the elemental plurality—[is] the organizer and manager of the universe. This rôle, which from the beginning belonged to the world soul (as the eternal humanity) receives in the natural man, i.e., one that was produced in the world process, the first opportunity of being factually realized in the order of nature. For all other beings produced in the cosmic process have in themselves *actu,* actually, only the natural beginning, the material one; the divine idea in the action of Logos is for them but an external law, an external form of being, to which they are subjected by natural necessity, but which they do not sense [know] as their own; here, there is no inner reconciliation between the particular finite being and the universal essence, 'all' [the universal] is only an external law for 'this', [the particular]: of the whole creation only man finding himself factually as [a particular] 'this', is aware of himself in the idea as [the universal] 'all'. Thus man is not limited by one beginning, but, having in himself, first, the elements of material being which bind him to the natural world; secondly, having the ideal consciousness of all-unity which unites him to God; and thirdly, not being exclusively limited by the one or the other; appears as a free 'ego', able to determine himself in one manner or another, in relation to the two sides of his being, free to incline to this side or to the other, to affirm himself in one or another sphere. If in his ideal consciousness man bears the *image* of God, then his unconditional freedom from the idea as well as from the fact, this formal limitlessness of the human 'ego', represents in him a *likeness* of God. Man not only has the same inner essence of life—all-oneness—as God: he is also free to desire to have it as God, i.e., he may of himself wish to be like God. Originally he has this essence from God, in so far as he is determined by it in the immediate perception, in so far as his mind inwardly coincides with the divine Logos. But he (or the world soul in him) by virtue of his limitlessness, is not satisfied with that passive unity. He wishes to have that divine essence of himself, he wishes to take possession of it by himself, to assimilate it. In order to have it of himself and not only from God, he asserts himself apart from God, outside of God, he falls away or separates himself from God in his consciousness in the same manner as the world soul originally seceded from Him in all her being.

But, rebelling against the divine beginning of all-unity, excluding it from his consciousness, man thereby falls under the power of the material beginning, for he was free from this latter only in so far as he kept a counterbalance in the former—he was free from the dominion of the natural fact only through the power of the divine idea; excluding it from himself, he becomes himself but a fact [loosing his former position] of the commanding centre of the natural world, becomes one of the multitude of natural beings: no longer the focus of 'all', he becomes a mere 'this'. If before, as the spiritual centre of the universal creation, he embraced in his soul all nature and lived one life with it, loved and understood and therefore governed it; so now, having asserted himself in his separateness, having shut his soul off from everything, he finds himself in an alien and hostile world, which no longer speaks with him in any intelligible language, and which does not understand or obey his word. If previously man had in his consciousness a direct expression of the universal organic connection of [all] that exists, and that connection (the idea of the all-unity) determined the whole content of his consciousness; then now, no longer having this connection in himself, man loses with it the organizing beginning of his inner world—the world of [his] consciousness is transformed into chaos. The formative principles, which were acting in external nature and which reached in the human consciousness their internal unity, lose it [the unity] afresh. Consciousness appears as a simple form, seeking its content. This content appears here, therefore, as external [to consciousness], as something that consciousness must yet make its own, must yet assimilate. This internal assimilation by the consciousness of the absolute content (necessarily gradual) forms a new process, the subject of which is the world soul in the form of humanity subjected to the natural order. The element of evil, i.e., the exclusive self-assertion which had thrown all that exists into [the state of the] primordial chaos, and which was overpowered externally in the cosmic process, emerges once more in a new aspect, as a free conscious act of the individual man; and the newly arising process has as its aim the inner, moral overcoming of that evil principle.

The world soul, which in man reached an inner union with the divine beginning, transcended the limits of the external natural being and focused all nature in the ideal unity of the free human spirit—by a free act of the same spirit once more loses its inner bond with the absolute being; in the capacity of natural humanity it falls under the dominion of the material element, into the enslavement to 'corruption'; and only in the unconditional form of consciousness preserves the possibility (potentiality) of a new inner union with Divinity. As in the beginning of the general universal (cosmogonic) process, the world soul appeared as a pure potentiality of unity, without any definite form or real content (since all actuality belonged to chaos): so here also, in the beginning of the human or historical process, the human consciousness, i.e., the world soul [which] attained the form of consciousness, appears as a pure potentiality of the ideal all-unity; while all actuality is reduced to the chaos of external natural phenomena which arise (for consciousness) in the external order of space, time, and mechanical casualty, but without any internal unity or connection. For consciousness, which has lost the inner unity of the whole in the divine Spirit, only that external unity becomes accessible then which is generated by the cosmic action of the divine Logos upon the world soul as the matter of the world process. The consciousness of humanity strives to reproduce in itself those definite forms of unity which had been already evolved by the cosmogonic process in the material nature, and the unifying forces of this latter (the offspring of the Demiurge and the world soul) appear now in consciousness as determining it, giving it the content of the natural elements, gradually manifest themselves and reign in it as lords not only of the external world but even of consciousness itself, as real *gods*. This new process is thus, first of all, a theogonic process; not, of course, in the sense that these dominant elements were created in the [course of that] process, [not in the sense] that mankind invented its own gods—we know that these elements existed prior to man as cosmic forces, although in that capacity they were not gods (for there are no gods without worshippers)—they become gods only for the human consciousness which acknowledges them to be such, after it has fallen under their dominion as the result of its separation from the one divine centre.

Since both the starting point and the determining principles of the theogonic process are the same as in the cosmogonic process, and the distinction [between them] is only in the form of consciousness,[4] it is natural to expect a substantial analogy between those two processes. And indeed, even the insufficient and poorly worked out information which we have about the theogonic process (i.e. the development of ancient mythology) allows us to establish such an analogy between this development and the cosmogonic process. As this latter, when analysed as a whole, represents three main epochs—the astral, in which the chaos of material elements, obedient to the force of gravitation, is differentiated into a multitude of cosmic bodies; the solar, in which these bodies are integrated into complex and harmonious systems (of which, for us, there is but one, our solar system); and, finally, the tellurian epoch, when within the limits of the solar system an already detached body (for us our globe) becomes the basis for the development of more complex and differentiated forms of unity which clothe the [evolving] organic life of the world soul—so also in the theogonic process we discern three corresponding epochs. First, when the world unity is revealed to the natural consciousness of mankind in the astral form and the divine beginning is worshipped as the fiery lord of the heavenly legions—the epoch of star-worship or Sabaism. The dominant god of this epoch appears to the consciousness alienated from the divine sphere as a being immeasurably high, incommensurate with man, [and] therefore alien to him, incomprehensible, and terrible; in its infinite supremacy it demands unconditional subordination, does not admit anything by the side of itself, is exclusive and despotic—it is the god of unconditional seclusion and inertness, who is hostile to movement [progress] and to live creation—it is Chronos, who devours his own children, it is Moloch, who burns the children of men; a thousand years later, we recognize this despot of the skies in a somewhat modified form as the Allah of the Moslems. Possessed by that 'divine' force, [human] consciousness strives to eliminate all free movement of human forces, the diversity of living forms, all cultural progress. But human consciousness could not long be satisfied with that grandiose but poor and desolate unity, and soon after the immobile and immutable god of the starry skies, there comes forward an eternally moving and changing, suffering and triumphing, gracious and luminous god—the sun. The astral religion is everywhere followed by the solar religion; among all the peoples of antiquity we meet at a certain epoch of their religious

---

[4]Speaking more definitely, the formative principles of material nature, the forces of unity which are present and act in it, which the human spirit originally had in itself and under itself, as its own basis (in so far as the human consciousness arose, genetically, from the same universal process)—these forces (as a result of the fall of man) appear outside of him and over him; and, gradually, entering his consciousness (in the theogonic process), take possession of him as forces superior or divine.

consciousness the predominant image of the bright solar god, who at first struggles, performs glorious exploits (Krishna, Melcarte, Hercules), then suffers, is vanquished by his enemies and dies (Osiris, Attis, Adonis); and finally rises again and triumphs over his enemies (Mithras, Perseus, Apollo). But, as in the physical world the sun is not only the source of light, but also the source of all organic life upon earth; so the religious consciousness naturally passes from [the worship of] the god of light to [that of] the god of the earthly organic life (Shiva, Dionysus). Here the divine beginning appears as the element of the natural organic process outside of man and in him; the idea of unity (the constant content of religion) takes on the form of the generic unity of organic life, and the natural act through which that unity is preserved receives a special religious significance: after the solar cult everywhere in the ancient world at a certain epoch arose, fighting for supremacy, the cult of the phallus—the religion of the genetic process, the deification of those acts and those organs which serve the genetic unity.

Subjected at first to the distant forces of the celestial lights, mistaking the [seemingly] all-embracing vastness of the stellar dome for the divine infinity and unity, the human soul's [attention] shifted then to the closer and more active force of the sunlight, finding a clear image of Divinity in that beneficent light as the central active principle [power] of the physical world around her. And in the phallic religions, finally, the soul['s attention] returns directly to its own material element, wherein the complex unity of the genetic organic life she finds the supreme natural manifestation of the universal unity. Here individual human soul subjects itself to and adores the common natural life of the humankind—the life of the genus. But that genetic life, this unity of the genus, maintained only by the constantly renewed process of birth—this unity is never realized for the individual soul (because the life of the race is preserved here at the expense of the individual life, by absorbing, not by completing it, so that the life of the race is the death of the individual); this ill, negative unity of the genetic life cannot satisfy the world soul, which by now has reached in man the capacity for an inner, positive unity.

As the cosmogonic process terminated in the birth of the human being endowed with consciousness, so the result of the theogonic process is [the appearance of] the self-consciousness of the human soul [or its awareness of itself] as the spiritual beginning, free from the domination of natural gods and able to conceive the divine beginning in itself and not through a medium of cosmic forces. This liberation of human self-consciousness and the gradual spiritualization of man through the inner assimilation and development of the divine beginning constitutes the proper historical process of mankind. Three great peoples of antiquity appear as the prime movers of this historical process: the Hindus, the Greeks, and the Jews. Their relative significance in religious history has been pointed out before.[5] But the conceptions which we have now reached about the world soul and the world process throw a new light upon the historico-religious character of these three peoples.

In India the human soul was for the first time emancipated from the domination of the cosmic forces, and was as if intoxicated by its freedom, by the consciousness of its unity and unconditionality: its inner action is not bound by anything, it freely gives way to reveries, and in these reveries all the ideal creations of humanity are already complete as in embryo—all the religious and philosophical doctrines, poetry and science—but all in an undifferentiated indefiniteness and confusion, as in a dream all things are entangled, merged, everything is the same and, therefore, all is nothing. Buddhism said the last word of the Hindu consciousness; all the existant and non-existant is alike an illusion and dream. This point of view of the primitive unity and indifference is the awareness of the soul of itself within itself, because in itself, as a pure potentiality in separation from the active divine beginning which [alone] can give it content and reality, the soul, of course, is nothing.

But freed from the material content of life, and at the same time aware of it as nothingness in itself, the soul must either renounce existence or seek new immaterial content. The Indian, and the Eastern consciousness generally, had taken the first course, while classical humanity went along the second path. In the Graeco-Roman world the human soul appears free not only from the external cosmic forces but even from its own self, from its inner, purely subjective contemplation of itself, in which we find it engrossed in India. Now it is again open to the action of the divine Logos, no longer as an external cosmic or demiurgic force, but as a purely ideal, inner force; here the soul of man yearns to find its true content, i.e., the unitary and the universal, not in the empty indifference of its [original] potential being, but in the objective creations which realize beauty and reason—in pure art, in scientific philosophy, and in the state based on government of [by] law.

The creation of this ideal sphere, of this 'world without blood or tears', is the great triumph of the supreme Reason, the actual beginning of the true unification of mankind and the universe. But this unification [so far] takes place only in the [realm of the] idea; it is the revelation of the idea as the truth above the factual being, but not the actualization of it in the latter. The divine idea appears here to the soul as its object and supreme norm, but does not penetrate into the very being [nature] of the soul, does not take possession of its concrete actuality. In knowledge, in art, in pure law, the soul contemplates the ideal cosmos, and in that contemplation egoism and struggle, the power of the material

[5]In the third, fourth, and fifth lectures.

chaotic principle over the human soul, disappear. But the soul cannot for ever remain in a state of contemplation; it lives in factual reality, and this life of it remains outside of the ideal sphere, is not absorbed by it; the idea does exist for the soul, but does not cover [extend over] its actuality. With the unfolding of the ideal world there appear for men two orders of being—the material, factual existence (in Greek, i genesis), the evil [existence], one which ought not to be, the root of which is the wicked personal will; and the impersonal world of pure isead (in Greek, to ontos on), the domain of the true and the perfect. But these two spheres continue to remain so contraposed one to another; they do not find reconciliation in the classical world view. The world of ideas, the ideal cosmos, which forms the truth of this world view in its highest expression—Platonism—represents [a realm of] being absolutely unknown, remains in the undisturbed peace of eternity, leaving the world of material phenomena beneath itself, being reflected in it as the sun in a muddy stream, but leaving it unchanged, neither purifying nor enlightening it. Such a world view demands of man only that he should *leave* this world, dive out of this muddy stream into the light of the ideal sun, that he should free himself from the chains of bodily existence as if from a prison or grave. Thus, the duality and contraposition of the ideal and the material worlds, of the truth and the fact, remains here unsolved; there is no reconciliation. If the truly-extant is revealed only to contemplation, as a realm of ideas, then the personal life of man, the domain of his will and action, remains outside of the truth, in the world of false material being; but in that case man is unable, in fact, to leave this false world entirely, for [in order] to do so he would have to desert himself, his own soul, which lives and suffers in this world. The ideal sphere with all of its wealth can, as an object of contemplation, merely *divert* man from his evil and suffering will, [it can-] not quench it. This wicked and suffering will is a fundamental fact, which cannot be done away with either by the Hindu consciousness [to which] this fact [appears] as an illusion (for even here the fact appears as an illusion for consciousness only, while for the whole life it remains a fact as before); or by the idea that man can for a time get away from this fact into the realm of ideal contemplation, since he will have to return from that bright realm to this wicked life again.

The divine beginning can act upon the human element which separated itself from [God] and asserted itself in its evil will, in a threefold manner.

It [Divinity] can *suppress* it [the human element] externally, but [in doing so] it will suppress only the manifestation of the evil will, not that will itself; the latter, as an inner subjective force, cannot be destroyed by any external action. It is for this reason that the external action of the divine Logos upon man, which we found in the theogonic process, appeared insufficient, inconsistent with the purpose of the inner reunion of mankind with Divinity. The cult of natural religion limited the self-assertion of the human element, compelled it to submit perforce to the higher powers acting in nature, compelled it to bring sacrifices to these forces; but the root of man's life, his evil will, the material principle which had arisen within him, remained untouched, as something alien and inaccessible to these external natural gods.

Closer to the aim, although still insufficient, appears the second kind of action of the divine beginning upon man: the ideal or *enlightening* action. This action can take place because the human soul is something greater than its given factual state. If in this latter it is an irrational element, a blind force of self-assertion, then in its potentiality it is rational, a striving towards inner unity with the whole. And if in the external, suppressive action (in natural religion) the divine Logos is related to the irrational element of the soul as a force to force, then in provoking the rational potentiality of man, it can act within the soul as reason or inner word; namely, He can divert the soul from its factual reality, present this latter as an object, and demonstrate to the soul the illusiveness of its material being, the evil of its natural will, by unfolding before the soul the truth of another being, one which corresponds to reason. This is the ideal action of the divine Logos which we find pre-eminently among the cultured nations of the ancient world in the highest epoch of their development. But this action, too, is not complete, [merely] one-sided, although [it is] internal. To recognize the nothingness [worthlessness] of one's own factual reality [beheld] as an object in contemplation, does not mean to make it insignificant in actuality, does not mean to remove it in fact [from experience]. As long as the truth is opposed to the personal will and life, immersed in the untruth, solely as an idea, life [experience] remains essentially unchanged; the abstract idea cannot overcome it because the personal will of life, although evil, is nevertheless an actual force; whereas the idea, not incarnate in living personal forces, appears only as a light shadow.

Thus, in order that the divine beginning could really overcome the evil will and life of man, it is necessary that it appear for the soul a living personal force, able to penetrate into the soul and to take possession of it; it is necessary that the divine Logos should not only influence the soul externally, but [that He should] be born within the soul not [only] limiting or enlightening it, but *regenerating* it. And as the soul in the natural mankind appears actually only in a plurality of the individual souls, the actual union of the divine beginning with the soul also necessarily assumes an individual form, i.e., the divine Logos is born as an actual individual man. As in the physical world the divine beginning of unity is first manifested as the force of gravitation, binding bodies together by blind attraction; then as the force of light, disclosing their mutual properties; and finally, as the force of organic life, in which the formative principle penetrates matter and after a long series of formations generates the perfect physical organism of man: so in the following process, the divine beginning at first binds together the separate human beings into a generic unity by the power of spiritual gravitation; then it enlightens them with the ideal light of reason; and, finally, penetrating into the soul and uniting with it organically, concretely, gives birth to a new, spiritual man. And as in the physical world a long series of imperfect forms (which were, nevertheless, organic, living forms) preceded the appearance of the perfect human organism, so in history the birth of the perfect spiritual man was preceded by a series of incomplete yet living, personal revelations of the divine beginning to the human soul. These living revelations of the living God we find (preeminently) in the Jewish people.

Every manifestation of the divine beginning, every theophany, is determined by the character of the milieu receiving it; in history it was conditioned first of all by the peculiarity of a national character, by the particular traits of the nation in which the given manifestation of Divinity took place. If the divine beginning was manifested to the Hindu spirit as the nirvana, to the Greeks as the idea and the ideal cosmos, then it was to appear among the Jews as a personality, as a living subject, as an 'I': because their national character consisted precisely of the predominance of the personal, subjective factor. This character is manifested in the whole historical life of the Jews, in all that this nation has created or is creating. Thus, we see that in poetry the Jews have created something specifically their own only in that form which represents the subjective, personal element: they created the masterly lyrics of the Psalms, the lyric idyl of the Song of Songs, but they could not create real epic or drama, such as we find in Hindu and Greek literature—not only during their independent existence but even later on—we can point to Heine, the genius lyrical writer among the Jews, but we cannot find among them a single outstanding dramatist, precisely because drama is an objective form of poesy. It is also remarkable that the Jews distinguish themselves in music, i.e., in that art which expresses preeminently the inner subjective motions of the soul, and have not produced anything worth while in the plastic arts. In the domain of philosophy, during their flourishing epoch, the Jews never went further than moral didactics, i.e., that field in which the practical interests of the moral personality predominate over the objective contemplation and the reasoning of the mind. Correspondingly in religion the Jews were the first fully to conceive of God as a person, as a subject, as the living 'I'; they could not content themselves with the representation of Divinity as an impersonal force and as the impersonal idea.

The character which asserts in everything the subjective element, can be the bearer of the greatest evil as well as the greatest good. For, if the force of the personality in asserting itself in its own separateness is evil and the root of evil, then the same force, having subjected itself to the highest beginning—the same flame [but] permeated with the divine light—appears as the force of the world-wide, all-embracing love. Without the force of the self-asserting personality, without the force of egoism, the good itself in man appears impotent and cold, appears only as an abstract idea. Every actively moral character presupposes the subjugated force of evil, i.e., of egoism. As in the physical world a certain force, in order to manifest itself actually, [in order] to, become energy, must consume or transform (into its own form) a corresponding amount of energy which previously existed [in another form] (thus light is a transformation of heat; heat, of mechanical motion; and so forth); in the same manner, in the moral world, the potentiality of the good in the soul of a man who was subjected to natural order, can be manifested actively only with the consummation or transformation of the energy of the soul already in its possession—which in the natural man is the energy of the self-asserting will, the energy of evil, which must be reduced to the potential state in order that the new force of the good might be actualized from [its heretofore] potential [state] into action. The essence of the good is given by an act of God, but the energy of its manifestation in man can be had only with the transformation of the conquered force of the self-asserting personal will, after it was subjugated into the potential state. Thus, in a holy man the actual good presupposes potential evil; he is great in his holiness because he might be great in evil as well; he overcame the force of evil, has subjected it to the highest beginning, and it has become the basis and carrier of the good. That is why the Jewish people, demonstrating the worst aspects of human nature, 'a stiff-necked people' and with a stony heart, this same people is the people of the saints and the prophets of God, the nation in which was to be born the new spiritual man.

The whole Old Testament represents the history of personal relations of God (Logos or Jehovah) manifesting Himself to the representatives of the Jewish nation—its patriarchs, leaders, and prophets. In these personal relations, which form the religion of the Old Testament, a succession of three grades is noticed. The first mediators between the Jewish nation and its God, the ancient patriarchs Abraham, Isaac, and Jacob, *believe* in the personal God and live by that faith. The representatives of Judaism that follow them—Moses, who saw God, David, 'the man after the heart of Jehovah', and Solomon, the builder of the great temple—receive clear revelations of the personal God and try to carry [the message, the practical bearings of] these revelations into social life and the religious cult of their people; in their person Jehovah concludes a certain external covenant or pact with Israel, as person with person. The last series of Jewish representatives, the prophets, cognizant of the insufficiency of that external union, forefeel and announce another, inner unification of Divinity with the human soul in the person of the Messiah, the son of David and the son of God; and they fore-feel and herald this Messiah not only as a supreme representative of Judaism, but as the 'ensign of the nations', as the representative and the head of all regenerated humanity.

If, thus, the milieu for the incarnation of the divine beginning was determined by the national character of the Jews, its time was contin-gent upon the general course of history. When the ideal revelation of the Word in the Hellenic-Roman world was exhausted and proved to be insufficient for the living soul; when man, regardless of the enor-mous, never seen before, riches of culture, found himself alone in a poor and empty world; when everywhere appeared doubt of the truth and an aversion to life, and the best men passed from despair to suicide; when, on the other hand—precisely because the reigning ideal prin-ciples proved to be radically insolvent—then there appeared an aware-ness of the fact that ideas in general are insufficient for the struggle against the evil of life; then there appeared a demand that the truth should become incarnated in a living personal force. And when the ex-ternal truth, that of the people, of the state, became in fact centred in one living person—the person of a deified man, the Roman Caesar—then appeared also the divine truth in the living person of the incarnate God, Jesus Christ.

THE incarnation of the divine Logos in the person of Jesus Christ is the manifestation of the new spiritual man, the second Adam. As under the first, natural, Adam we must understand not only a separate person among other persons, but the all-one personality, including in himself all natural humanity, so the second Adam is not only *this* individual being, but at the same time also the universal being, embracing all the regenerated, spiritual humanity. In the sphere of the eternal divine being, Christ is the eternal spiritual centre of the universal organism. But since this organism, or the universal humanity, falling into the stream of phenomena becomes subjected to the law of external being, and must through labour and suffering restore in time that which was lost by it in eternity, i.e., its internal unity with God and nature—then Christ also, as the active principle of that unity, for the real restoration of it has to descend into the same stream of phenomena, has to be subjected to the same law of external being, and from the centre of eternity, become the centre of history, appearing at a certain moment of it [namely], 'in the fullness of time'. The evil spirit of discord and enmity, eternally powerless against God, at the beginning of time had overpowered man; in the middle of time it had to be overpowered by the Son of God and the Son of man, as the first-born of the whole creation, in order to be driven out of the whole creation at the end of time—this is the essential meaning of the incarnation. The Latin theologians of the Middle Ages, who transferred the juridical character of ancient Rome into Christianity, built the well known legalistic theory of redemption as the vicarious satisfaction of the violated divine right [law]. This theory, worked out with especial finesse by Anselm of Canterbury and preserved in later ages in different variants, found its way also into the Protestant theology. It is not altogether devoid of correct meaning, but this meaning has been fully obscured in it by certain coarse and unworthy ideas about Divinity and its relation to the world and man which are equally repugnant to philosophic understanding and to truly Christian feeling. Christ's cause is not a juridical fiction, a casuistic solution of an impossible law suit—it is an actual exploit, a real struggle with and victory over evil. The second Adam was born on earth not in order to complete a formal juridical process, but for the real salvation of mankind, for its actual deliverance from the power of the evil force, for pragmatic revelation of the Kingdom of God in humanity.

But before one would speak of the cause of Christ, for which He was incarnated, one must necessarily answer two questions: (1) as to the possibility of the incarnation, i.e., of the real union of Divinity with humanity; and (2) as to the manner of that union.

As regards the first question, certainly the incarnation is *impossible* if we look upon God as only a separate being, abiding somewhere outside of the world and man. With such a view (deism) the inhumanization of Divinity would be a direct violation of the logical law of identity, i.e., a perfectly unthinkable case. But the incarnation is equally impossible from the other point of view according to which (pantheism), God is but the universal substance of the world phenomena, the universal 'all', and man is only one of these phenomena. According to this view, the inhumanization would contradict the axiom that the whole [all] cannot be equal to one of its parts: God could not become man any more than the waters of an entire ocean could remain all its waters and be at the same time only one of its drops. But is it necessary to conceive of God either as only a separate being, or as only the common substance of cosmic phenomena? On the contrary, the very conception of God as the full integrity or perfection (the absolute) removes both one-sided definitions and clears the way for another view, according to which the world as material, as the aggregate of limitations, being outside of God (in these its limits) is at the same time essentially united with God in its internal life[1] or soul [the world-soul]; and God, being at once transcendental *in himself* (abiding beyond the limits of the world), at the same time *in relation* to the world *appears* as the active creative force which becomes incarnate in order to communicate to the world-soul what it seeks and yearns for—(namely) the fullness of being in the form of all-unity—[the active creative force] which wills to unite with the soul and to generate out of it the living image of Divinity. The above determines the cosmic process in material nature which terminated in the birth of the natural man, as well as the following historical process which prepared the birth of the spiritual man. Thus, this latter, i.e., the incarnation of Divinity, was not anything miraculous in the proper sense [of that word], i.e., was not anything *alien* to the general order of being, but, on the contrary, was essentially bound with the whole history of the world and humanity, something prepared in, and logically following from, this history. In Jesus was incarnated not the transcendent God, not the absolute self-enclosed fullness of being (that would be impossible), but God-the-Word, i.e., the [divine] beginning manifested outwardly, [one] acting on the per-

[1]Characterized by the fact that *every* being, asserting itself within its own limit [as a particular] *this*, *outside* of God, at the same time is not satisfied with this limit, endeavours to become also *the whole*, i.e., strives for inner union with God.

(This qualifying clause was taken out of the long sentence as a footnote for clarity. Translator).

iphery of being; and His *personal* incarnation in an individual man was but the final link in a long series of other incarnations, physical and historical—this appearance of God in the human flesh was only a more complete, a more perfect theophany in a series of other, imperfect, pre-paratory, and transformative theophanies. From this point of view the appearance of the spiritual man, the birth of the second Adam, was not any more incomprehensible than the appearance of the natural man on the earth, the birth of the first Adam. Both were new, unprecedented facts in world life; both, in this sense, appear miraculous. But this new and unprecedented phenomenon was prepared in advance by all that had happened before, (it) constituted that which the former life desired, towards which it strove and proceeded: all nature strove and gravitated towards man, the whole history of mankind was directed towards the God-man. In any event, in the discussion of the possibility or im-possibility of the inhumanization of Divinity, the main point consists in the understanding of Divinity and humanity; according to the con-ception of Divinity and humanity presented in these lectures, the in-carnation of Divinity is not only possible but is essentially a part of the general plan of creation. But although the fact of the incarnation, i.e., of the personal union of God with man, is grounded in the general meaning of the universal process and in the order of divine action, that does not yet solve the question as to the form [nature, character] of this union, i.e., as to the relationship and interaction of the divine [begin-ning] and the natural human element in the personality of the God-man, or as to what is the spiritual man, the second Adam.

In general, man is a certain union of Divinity with material nature; and that presupposes in man three constituent elements: the divine, the material, and that which binds both together, the properly human. The conjunction of these three elements is what really forms the actual man, and the properly-human element is the mind (*ratio*), i.e. the relation-ship of the two others. When this relation consisted of a direct and im-mediate subjection of the natural element to the divine [beginning] we had the primordial man, the prototype of humanity, not yet de-tached from but enclosed within, the eternal unity of the divine life; here the natural human element was contained in the actuality of the divine being as an embryo, *potentia*. When, on the contrary, the actu-ality of man belongs to his material element, when he knows himself [only] as a fact or as a phenomenon of nature, and [regards] the divine beginning in himself only as a possibility of a different being, then we have the natural man. The third possible relationship takes place when Divinity and nature are of equal actuality in man, and his human life, properly so called, consists in an active co-ordination of the natural element with the divine, or in a free subjection of the former to the latter. Such relationship forms the *spiritual man*. From this general con-ception of the spiritual man certain conclusions follow. First: in order that concordance of the natural element with the divine beginning in man be an actuality, it is necessary that it take place in a single person—otherwise there would be only a real or ideal interaction between God and the natural man, but there would be no new spiritual man—in order to have an actual union of Divinity with nature, a person is necessary in whom this union might take place. Second, in order that this union be an actual union of the *two* beginnings, the actual presence of both of these beginnings is necessary; it is necessary that this personality be God as well as the actual, natural man—both natures are necessary. Third, in order that the concordance of the two natures in the personality of the God-man be a free spiritual act, it is necessary that the human will take part in it, [a will] distinct from the divine will; it is necessary that, rejecting any possible contradiction with the divine will, the human will would freely submit to it and bring human nature into complete inner harmony with Divinity. Thus, the conception of the spiritual man presupposes a *single God-man personality, uniting in itself two natures and possessing two wills.*[2]

The original immediate union of the two beginnings in man—the unity represented by the first Adam in his state of innocence in the Garden of Eden, which was destroyed in his fall, could not be simply restored. A new unity could not be immediate, [could not be] innocence; it had to be *attained.* It can only be the result of a free act, of an exploit, and a double exploit—[that] of the divine and human self-denial; because for the true union or concordance of the two principles, free participation and action of both are necessary. We have seen previously how the interaction of the divine and natural beginnings defines the whole life of the world and humanity, and (how) the whole course of this life consists in the gradual coming together and interpenetration of these two beginnings, which were at first far apart and external to each other, then came more and more closely together, permeating each other deeper and deeper until nature appeared in Christ as the human soul ready for total self-denial, and God [appears] as the spirit of love and mercy communicating to this soul the whole fullness of divine life—not suppressing it [the soul] by force, not illuminating its understanding, but in His graciousness quickening it. Here we have an actual divine-human personality, able to accomplish the double exploit of the divine and human self-abnegation. To a certain extent such a self-abnegation had already taken place in the whole

[2]This definition, which follows from our conception of the 'spiritual man', or the second Adam, is unconditionally identical with the dogmatic definitions of the Oecumenical Councils of the fifth to the seventh centuries, which were developed in refutation of the Nestorian, Monophysite, and Monothelite heresies, each of which represented a direct contradiction to one of the three essential logical conditions of the true idea of Christ.

cosmic as well as historical process. For here, on one hand, the divine Logos, by a free act of His divine will or love, abnegated His divine dignity (the glory of God) refraining from any manifestation of it; [in the cosmic process] He left the peace of eternity, entered upon the struggle with the evil beginning, and subjected Himself to the anxieties of the world process, appearing in the chains of external being, in the limits of space and time; and then [in history] He appeared to the natural humanity, acting upon it in different finite forms of the world life, which concealed rather than revealed the true being of God. On the other hand, the nature of the world and humanity, in its constant yearning and striving for the ever fuller reception of the divine image, continuously negates itself in its given, actual forms. But here (i.e., in the cosmic and historic process) this self-denial is not perfect on either side because the boundaries of the cosmic and historic theophanies are external limits for Divinity, determining Its manifestation for the 'other' (for nature and humanity) but in no manner affecting its inner being or awareness of Itself.[3] Nature and natural humanity, on the other hand, in their perpetual progress abnegate themselves not by a free act, but only by an instinctive tendency. In the personality of the God-man, however, the divine beginning, precisely as a consequence of the fact that it is related to its antipode not through an external act, which would limit the antipode (without changing itself [i.e., the divine beginning]) but through an inner self-limitation [by] which [it] gives room in itself to the 'other one'—such an inner union with the antipode is the real self-denial on the part of the divine beginning, here it actually descends, annihilates itself, takes on itself the likeness of a slave. The divine beginning here is not hidden from man by the limits of human consciousness, as was the case in the previous, incomplete theophanies: here it itself adopts these limitations. Not that it wholly enters into the limits of natural consciousness (that is impossible) but it actually *feels* these limits as *its own at the given moment;* and this self-limitation of Divinity in Christ liberates His humanity, allowing its natural will to abnegate itself freely in favour of the divine beginning—[to abnegate it] not as an external force (in that case His denial would not be free) but as an inner good—and thereby to acquire that good actually. Christ, as God, freely renounces the glory of God and thereby as man acquires the possibility of *attaining* that glory. On the way to this attainment the human nature and [the human] will of the Saviour unavoidably en-

[3]This may be explained [by a] comparison [taken] from the natural world: man, as a comparatively higher being, acting upon some lower animal, cannot appear to it in all the fullness of his human life; but those limited forms in which, for example, a dog perceives the appearance of its master, belong only to the mind of the animal, by no means limiting or changing the proper being of the man himself.

counter the *temptation* of evil. The divine-human personality represents a dual consciousness: the consciousness of the limits of natural existence, and the consciousness of its divine essence and power. And so, experiencing the limitations of a natural being, the God-man may be subjected to the temptation to make His divine power a means for the aims which develop as the result of those limitations.

First, to a being subjected to the conditions of material existence is presented the temptation to make material welfare the goal, and his divine power, the means for attaining it: 'if thou be the Son of God, command that these stones be made bread'. Here the divine nature— 'if thou be the Son of God'—and the manifestation of that nature, the word 'command', are to serve as means for the satisfaction of a material need. Christ in answer to this temptation asserts that the Word of God is not an instrument of material life, but itself is the source of the true life for man: 'Man shall not live by bread alone but by every word that proceedeth out of the mouth of God'. Having overcome this temptation of the flesh, the Son of Man receives authority over all flesh.

Second, to the God-man, free from the material motives, is presented a new temptation—to make His divine power an instrument for the self-assertion of His human personality, to fall into the sin of the intellect—that of pride: 'if thou be the Son of God, cast thyself down: for it is written, He shall give his angels charge over thee: and in their hands they shall bear thee up, lest at any time thou dash thy foot against a stone'. This act ('cast thyself down') would be a proud call of man to God, a temptation of God by man, and Christ answers: 'it is written again, Thou shalt not tempt the Lord thy God'.[4] Having conquered the sin of the mind, the Son of Man receives authority over the minds.

The third temptation was the last and the strongest one. The enslavement to the flesh and the pride of the mind have been removed: the human will finds itself now on a high moral level, is conscious of being higher than the rest of creation; in the name of this moral height, man can wish for the mastery over the world in order to lead the latter to perfection; but the world lieth in sin and will not voluntarily submit to moral superiority: [it may seem] therefore that the world should be forced into subjection, that it is necessary [for Christ] to use His divine power to force the world into subjection. But such a use of coercion, i.e., of evil, for the attainment of a good would be [equivalent to] a con-

---

[4]Sometimes these words are understood as if Christ says to the temptor: Do not tempt Me, for I am the Lord thy God. But this would have no sense, because Christ was subjected to temptations not as God but as man. In fact, the second reply of Christ, as well as the first one, represents a direct answer to what is presented by the temptor: it is offered to tempt God by a daring deed, and against this as against the first proposition, Christ refers to the Scriptures, which forbid tempting God.

fession that evil is stronger than the good, that the good by itself has no force. It would be [equivalent to] *falling down* before that *element of evil* which dominates the world: 'and [he] sheweth Him all the kingdoms of the world, and the glory of them; and saith unto Him, All these things will I give Thee, if Thou wilt fall down and worship me'. Here the human will is directly challenged with the fateful question: what does it believe, and what does it wish to serve—the invisible might of God or the force of evil that openly reigns in the world? And the human will of Christ, having overcome the temptation of a plausible desire for power, freely subjected itself to the true good, denying any agreement with the evil which reigns in the world: 'Then saith Jesus unto him: Get thee hence, Satan: for it is written, Thou shalt worship the Lord thy God and Him *only* shalt thou serve'. Having conquered the sin of the spirit, the Son of Man received supreme authority in the realm of the spirit; refusing to submit to the earthly power for the sake of dominion over the earth, He acquired for Himself the service of the powers of heaven: 'and, behold, angels came and ministered unto Him'.

Thus, having overcome the temptations of the evil beginning which were trying to incline His human will to self-assertion, Christ subjected and co-ordinated this human will with the divine will, [thereby] deifying His manhood after the inhumanization[5] of His Divinity. But the high deed of Christ was not exhausted by the inner self-denial of His human will. Fully man, Christ had in Himself not only the purely human element (the rational will), but also the natural material element: He not only was inhumanized, but also incarnated (in Greek, Sarx egeneto). The spiritual exploit—the overcoming of the internal temptation—had to be completed with the exploit of the flesh, i.e., of the sensual soul, in the experience of His passion and death: therefore it is that in the Gospel, after the narrative about the temptations in the wilderness, it is stated that the devil departed from Christ *for a season*. The evil beginning, inwardly conquered by the self-denial of the will, [and] not being admitted into the centre of the human being, yet retained power over its periphery—over the sensual nature; and this latter could be delivered from it also by the process of self-denial—[which in the case of the human body meant] suffering and death. After the human will of Christ freely subjected itself to His Divinity, and thereby subjected to itself the sensual nature of man in Him; and, regardless of the infirmity of the latter (the prayer for the passing of the cup), [the human will of Christ] forced it [the human body] to realize

[5]The term 'inhumanization' is used in the Orthodox Church even more frequently than the term 'incarnation', and signifies a much fuller meaning of the incarnation than the mere 'taking on of human flesh'—'And the Word was made man', it would mean, rather than 'And the Word was made flesh'. Translator.

in itself the divine will to the end—in the physical process of suffering and death. Thus in the second Adam has been restored the normal relationship of all the three principles which had been violated by the first Adam. The human beginning, having placed itself in the proper relationship of voluntary subjection to, or accord with, the divine beginning, as its inner good, thereby once more received the significance of the intermediary [or] uniting element between God and nature; and the latter, purified by the death on the cross, lost its material separateness and weight, became a direct expression and instrument of the divine spirit, a true *spiritual body*. It was with that body that Christ arose [from the dead] and appeared to His Church.

The due relationship between Divinity and nature in humanity, which was reached by the person of Jesus Christ as the spiritual centre or head of mankind, must be assimilated by all of mankind as His body.

The humanity which has been reunited with its divine beginning through the mediation of Jesus Christ, is the *Church;* and if in the eternal primordial world the ideal humanity had been the body of the divine Logos, so in the natural world, that has come into existence, the Church appears as the body of the same Logos, only [One who has become] incarnate, i.e., historically individualized in the divine-human personality of Jesus Christ.

This body of Christ, which first appeared as a small embryo in the form of the not very numerous community of the early Christians, gradually grows and develops so as to embrace, at the end of time, all humanity and the whole of nature in one universal organism of God-manhood; because the rest of nature, in the words of the Apostle, is awaiting, with hope, the manifestation of the sons of God; for the creature became subjected to vanity not voluntarily, but by the will of Him who had so subjected it, in the hope, that the creature itself was to be liberated from the enslavement to corruption into the freedom of the glory of the sons of God; for we know that the whole creation groaneth travailing together until now.

This manifestation and glory of the sons of God, hopefully awaited by all creation, is the full realization of the free God-man union in the whole of mankind in all the spheres of its life and activity; all these spheres must be brought into concordant divine-human unity, must become parts of the free theocracy in which the Universal Church will reach the full measure of the stature of Christ.

Thus, starting from the conception of the Church as the body of Christ (not in the sense of a metaphor, but [in that of] a metaphysical formula), we must remember that this body necessarily grows and develops, consequently changes and becomes perfected. Being the body of Christ, the Church until now is not yet His glorified, fully deified body. The present terrestrial existence of the Church corresponds to the [life of the] body of Jesus on earth (before the resurrection)—of the body which, manifesting in some particular cases miraculous properties (which even at present are manifested in the Church also), yet generally speaking [was] material and subject to death, not free from the infirmities and sufferings of the flesh—for all the infirmities and sufferings of human nature were taken on by Christ, But, as in Christ, all that is weak and earthly was 'swallowed up' in the resurrection of the spiritual body, thus must it be also in the Church, His universal body, when it will have reached its fullness.

The attainment of that state in mankind is conditioned, as in the personality of the God-man, by the self-negation of the human will and a free subjection of it to Divinity.

But if in Christ, as in a single person, the moral exploit of victory over the temptations of evil and of the voluntary subjection to the divine beginning, was pre-eminently an internal action, as a subjective phychological process, then in the aggregate of mankind it has been an objective, historical process—and the objects of temptation, which in the psychological process [were primarily subjective] receive an objective reality, so that a part of mankind actually becomes subject to the temptations of evil and only through their personal experience becomes convinced of the falsity of the ways which were previously rejected by the conscience of the God-man.

Since the whole of mankind represents the same three substantial elements as a single man—the spirit, the mind, and the sensual soul—the temptations of evil appear for all humanity also to be threefold, but in a sequence different from that [in which they appeared] to the personality of Christ. Humanity has already received the revelation of the divine truth in Christ, it possesses this truth as an actual *fact*—the first temptation, therefore, is that of a misuse of this truth as such in the name of this same truth, an evil in the name of the good, [which is] the sin of the spirit: a pre-eminently moral evil, i.e., that which was with Christ the last temptation (according to the Gospel of St. Matthew).

Historically, the Christian Church has been composed of all people who have accepted Christ, but Christ can be accepted either inwardly or outwardly.

The inner acceptance of Christ, i.e., of the new spiritual man, consists in the spiritual regeneration, in that birth from above or of the spirit which was spoken of in the discourse with Nicodemus; [it starts] when man, having become aware of the untruth of the fleshly, material life, feels in himself the positive source of the other true life (independent of the flesh as well as of the mind of man), [accepts] the law which was given in the revelation of Christ, and, having acknowledged this new life opened [to man] by Christ as that which unconditionally ought to be [the true life of man], as the good and the truth, voluntarily subjects to it his fleshly and human life, inwardly uniting with Christ as the parent of this new spiritual life [and] the head of the new spiritual kingdom. Such an acceptance of the truth of Christ liberates [man] from sin (although not from sins) and forms [moulds] the new spiritual man.

But there can be [also] a merely outward acceptance of Christ, a mere acknowledgment of the miraculous incarnation of the Divine Being for the salvation of men, and the acceptance of His commandments in the letter, as an outward, obligatory law. Such external Christianity contains the danger of falling into the first temptation of the evil beginning. That is to say, the historical appearance of Christianity has divided all mankind into two groups: the Christian Church which possesses the divine truth and represents the will of God upon earth—and the world which remains outside of Christianity, has no knowledge of the true God, lieth in evil. Such external Christians, believing in the truth of Christ but not regenerated by it, can feel the need and even assume it to be their duty, to subjugate to Christ and to His Church all that outside and hostile world; and, since the world lying in evil will not voluntarily submit to the sons of God, [they may resolve] to subjugate it *by force*. Part of the Church, led by the Roman hierarchy, succumbed to that temptation—and dragged with it the majority of Western humanity in the first great period of its historical life, the Middle Ages. The essential falsity of this path [of this type of Christianity] is contained in that hidden unbelief which lies at its root. Indeed, the actual faith in the truth of Christ presupposes that this truth is stronger than the evil which reigns in the world, that it can by its own spiritual [and] moral force subjugate evil, i.e. bring it to [convert it into] the good; [whereas] to assume that the truth of Christ, i.e. the truth of the eternal love and of the unconditional good, for its realization needs alien and even directly opposite means of coercion and deceit, is to profess this truth to be powerless, to profess that evil is stronger than the good; it means not to believe in the good, not to believe in God. And this unbelief, which at first was hidden in Roman Catholicism as an unperceivable embryo was later on clearly revealed. Thus in Jesuitism—that extreme, purest expression of the Catholic principle—the moving force was an outright lust for power, and not the Christian zeal; nations were being brought into subjection not to Christ, but to the Church authority; the people were not asked for a real confession of the Christian faith—the acknowledgment of the Pope [as the head of the Church]—and obedience to the Church authorities, were sufficient.[6] Here the Chris-

[6]Several years ago in Paris I heard a French Jesuit give the following reasoning: 'Of course, at present no one can believe the greater part of the Christian dogmas, for example, the Divinity of Christ. But you will agree that civilized human society cannot exist without a strong authority and a firmly organized hierarchy; only the Catholic Church possesses such an authority and such a hierarchy; therefore, every enlightened man who values the interest of mankind must side with the Catholic Church, that is to say, must be a Catholic.'

tian faith is but a chance form, the essence and the aim is posited in the sovereignty of the hierarchy; but this is a direct self-conviction and self-annihilation [on the part] of the false principle, for here is lost the very foundation of that authority for which [in the name of which] they act.

The falsity of the Catholic way was early recognized in the West, and finally this realization found its full expression in Protestantism. Protestantism rebels against the Catholic way of salvation [regarded and practised] as an external act, and demands a personal religious relation of man to God, a personal faith without any traditional ecclesiastical mediation. But personal faith, as such, i.e., as a merely subjective fact, does not contain in itself any guarantee of its verity—such faith requires a criterion. In the beginning, the Holy Scriptures, i.e., a book, appeared as such a criterion for Protestantism. But a book requires [proper] understanding; for the establishment of the *correct* understanding, analysis and reasoning are necessary, i.e., the activity of a personal [individual] *reason*, which, thus, becomes the actual source of the religious truth, so that Protestantism naturally passes into rationalism—a transition which is logically inevitable, and which historically, indubitably has been going on. It would be out of place to present here the momenti of this transition; we shall dwell only upon the general result of this path, i.e., on pure rationalism. It consists essentially in the belief that the human mind is not only a law unto itself but gives laws to all that exists in the practical and social spheres. This principle is expressed in the demand that all life, all political and social relations, be organized and directed exclusively on the foundations worked out by the personal [individual] human mind, regardless of any tradition, of any immediate faith—a demand which permeated all of the so-called enlightenment of the eighteenth century and served as the guiding idea of the first French Revolution. Theoretically, the principle of rationalism is expressed in the claim that the whole content of knowledge can be deduced from pure reason (*a priori*) or that all branches of science can be construed apperceptively. This claim formed the essence of German philosophy—it was assumed in a naïve way by Leibnitz and Wolf, [later on] consciously (although in a modest form and with limitations) set forth by Kant, [then] resolutely declared by Fichte, and finally, with a complete self-confidence and awareness [of what was being asserted], but resulting in a just as complete a failure, [was fully] carried out by Hegel.

This self-confidence and self-assertion of human reason in life and knowledge is an abnormal phenomenon, it is the pride of the mind: in Protestantism, and in rationalism which issued from it, Western humanity fell into the second temptation. But the falsity of this path was soon manifested in the sharp contradiction between the excessive claims of the reason and its actual impotence. In the practical domain, reason found itself impotent against the passions and [the lower] interests [of the people], and the kingdom of reason proclaimed by the French Revolution ended in a wild chaos of insanity and violence; in the domain of theory, reason found itself impotent against the empirical fact, and the pretention to build a universal science on the principles of pure reason, ended in the construction of a system of empty abstract concepts.

Of course, the failures of the French Revolution and of German philosophy would not in themselves prove the insolvency of rationalism. The point is, however, that the historical downfall of rationalism was only the expression of its inner, logical contradiction, of the contradiction between the relative nature of reason and its unconditional [absolute] claims. Reason is a certain relation (*ratio*) of things that gives them a certain form. But relationship presupposes the related parties, the form presupposes content; rationalism, however, positing human reason, as such, as the supreme principle, abstracts it thereby from all content, and [therefore] has in reason only an empty form; but at the same time, by virtue of such an abstraction of reason from all content, from all that is given in life and knowledge, all this datum remains for it unreasonable [irrational]. Therefore, when reason comes forth against the actuality of life and knowledge with a consciousness of its own supreme rights, it finds in life everything strange to itself, dark, impermeable, and cannot do anything with it; for, abstracted from all content, changed into an empty concept, reason naturally cannot have any power over actuality. Thus the self-elevation of human reason, the pride of the mind, at the end inevitably leads to its downfall and abasement.

The falsity of this path, cognated through experience, was acknowledged by Western humanity; but it freed itself from it only to fall into the third and last temptation.

Human reason could master neither the passions and the lower human interests in life, nor the facts of the empirical reality, in science; i.e., in life and in science it found itself opposed by the *material* beginning; was it not right to conclude from this that the material element in life and knowledge—the animal nature of man, the material mechanism of the world—[is precisely what] forms the true essence of all, [and] that the aims of life and science really consist of the maximum possible satisfaction of material needs and the greatest possible knowledge of empirical facts? And, behold, indeed, the dominion of rationalism in European politics and science is replaced with the preponderance of materialism and empiricism. This path has not been traversed to the end as yet, but its falsity has been already recognized by the leading minds in the West itself. Just as the previous path, this one also falls the victim of its inner contradiction. Starting from the material element, the element of discord and chance, they wish to reach unity and integrity, to organize a right human society and a universal science. At the same time the material aspect of existence, the cravings and passions of human nature, the facts of external experience, all these comprise only a general foundation of life and knowledge, the material of which they are formed; but in order that anything might be really created out of this material, a formative, uniting principle and a form of unity are necessary. And if it has already been shown that human reason cannot serve as such a formative principle, and [that] in its abstractness, [it] contains no real form of unity; if it has been shown that the principle of rationalism cannot form either a right commonwealth or a true science: it follows that it is necessary to have recourse to another, more powerful principle of unity—but by no means that it is necessary to be content with the material side of life and knowledge, which by itself cannot form either the human society or science. Therefore, when we see that economic socialism wishes to place the material interests at the foundation of the whole society, and positivism, the empirical knowledge as the basis of all science: then we can foretell in advance the failure of both of these systems with the same certitude with which we should assert that a pile of stones by itself, without an architect and a plan, will not compose itself into a correct[ly built] purposeful building.

An attempt actually to place the material beginning alone at the foundation of life and knowledge, an attempt to realize, in fact and in full, the lie that man shall live by bread alone, such an attempt would perforce lead to the disintegration of mankind, to the destruction of society and science, to a universal chaos. To what extent Western humanity, which has fallen into the last temptation of the evil beginning, is destined to experience all those consequences—cannot be said in advance. In any event, having learned by experience the falsehood of the three 'broad ways', having experienced the deceitfulness of the three great temptations, Western humanity sooner or later must turn to the truth of Godmanhood. From whence, then, and in what form will this truth now appear? And, first of all, is this conscious but involuntary conversion to the truth, through actual experience of every falsehood, the only possible path for mankind?

As a matter of fact, not all Christian humanity has followed that path. It was chosen by Rome and the Germano-Romanic nations which accepted the Roman culture. The East, i.e., Byzantium and the nations (with Russia at their head) which received the Byzantine culture, remained aside.

The East did not fall into the three temptations of the evil beginning—it preserved the truth of Christ; but keeping it in the *soul* of her nations, the Eastern Church has not realized it in external actuality, has not given it expression in factual reality, has not created a *Christian culture* in the same manner as the West has created an anti-Christian culture. And it [the Eastern Church] could not have created it, it could not have realized the Christian truth. For what must we understand under such a realization, what is a truly Christian culture? The establishment in the whole of human society and in all its activities, of such a relationship among the three elements of the human being as was realized individually in the person of Christ. This relationship, as we know, consists of the free co-ordination of the two lower elements (the rational and the material) with the higher, the divine beginning, by their voluntary subjection to it; not as to [a coercive] force but as to the good. For such a *free* subjection of the lower elements to the higher beginning, in order that they may *of themselves* come to the recognition of the higher beginning as the good, it is necessary they be independent. Otherwise the truth would not have anything on which it could manifest its action, in which it could become actualized. But in the Orthodox Church the enormous majority of its members were captivated into obedience to the truth through an immediate [direct] inclination, not through a conscious [reflective] process in their inner lives. The really human element, in consequence, proved in the [Eastern] Christian society to be too weak and insufficient for a free and rational carrying out of the divine beginning into the external actuality—and as a result of this, the latter (i.e., the material actuality) remained outside of the divine beginning, and the Christian consciousness was not free from a certain *dualism* between [its attitude towards] God and [towards] the world. Thus the Christian truth, mutilated and finally repudiated by Western man, remained imperfect in the man of the East. This imperfection, conditioned by the weakness of the human element (reason and personality), could be removed only with the full development of the latter—the task which fell to the lot of the West. Thus, the great Western development, negative in its direct results, indirectly has had a positive value and purpose.

If the true society of Godmanhood, created in the image and likeness of the God-man Himself, ought to represent a free concordance of the divine and human beginnings, then, obviously, it is conditioned by the active force of the first as well as by the co-operative force of the second. Consequently, it is required that society would, first, preserve the divine beginning (the truth of Christ) in all of its purity and, second, develop the principle of human initiative in all its fullness. But by the law of the development or of the growth of the body of Christ, a concomitant fulfilment of these two demands—as the highest ideal of society—could not be given all at once, but had to be attained [gradually]. That is to say, before the perfect unity [is reached], appears disunity, the disunity which, with the [general] solidarity of mankind, and the law of the division of historical functions following from it, was expressed as a partition of the Christian world into two halves, in which the East with all the forces of its spirit was attached to the divine [beginning] and preserved it, working out in itself the conservative and ascetic attitude necessary for that [function]; while the West applied its whole energy to the development of the human element, which was necessarily detrimental to the [conservation] of the divine truth, which was at first mutilated and then altogether repudiated. The above makes it clear that the two historical trends, far from excluding each other, have been absolutely necessary to each other and for the 'fullness of the stature of Christ' in all humanity; for if history were limited to the Western development only, if the immovable and unconditional principle of the Christian truth did not stand behind this uninterrupted stream of movements [which were] replacing one another, and of principles [which were] mutually destructive, the whole Western development would have been devoid of any positive sense, and modern history would have ended in decadence and chaos. On the other hand, had history included only the Byzantine Christianity, the truth of Christ (Godmanhood) would have remained imperfect, in the absence of a [developed] human element of free initiative and activity necessary for its perfection. As it is, however, the divine element of Christianity, preserved by the East, can now reach its perfection in mankind, for now it has the material upon which it can act, in which it can manifest its internal force: namely, the human element which has been emancipated and developed in the West. And this has not only an historical, but also a mystical, meaning.

If the overshadowing that descended upon the human Mother with the active power of God, produced the incarnation of Divinity; then the fertilization of the divine Mother (the Church) by the active human beginning must produce a free deification of humanity. Before Christianity, the natural principle in humanity represented the datum (the fact), Divinity represented the unknown (the ideal), and as the unknown, acted (ideally) on man. In Christ the unknown was given, the ideal became a fact, became an event, the active divine beginning became material. The Word became flesh, and this new flesh is the divine substance of the Church. Before Christianity, the immovable basis of life was human nature (the ancient Adam), while the divine was the principle of change, motion, progress; after Christianity, on the contrary, the divine, as incarnate, becomes the immovable foundation the stratum of the life of humanity, while humanity appears as the unknown—[that part of humanity] which would correspond to the divine, i.e., which is capable of uniting with it of itself, [and] assimilating it. As the sought [the ideal], this ideal humanity appears as the active beginning [force] of history, the element of motion, of progress. And, as in the pre-Christian course of history, human nature or the natural element of mankind represented the basis, matter; the divine mind, (in Greek, O logos tu Feu), represented the active and formative principle; and God-man, i.e., God who has adopted human nature, was the result (the offspring): so in the process of Christianity the divine nature or the divine stratum (the Word which became flesh, as well as the body of Christ, the Sophia) appears as the foundation or matter, while human reason appears as the active and formative principle; and the man-God, i.e., man who adopted Divinity, appears as the result. And, since man can receive Divinity only in his absolute totality, i.e., in union with *all*, the man-God is necessarily collective and universal, i.e., [it is] the all-humanity [the whole of mankind] or the Universal Church [that receives Divinity]; the God-man is individual, the man-God is universal. Thus the radius is one and the same for the whole circumference at any one of its points, and consequently it is itself the beginning of a circle; while the points on the periphery form the circle only in their totality. In the history of Christianity, the immovable divine foundation in humanity is represented by the Eastern Church, while the Western world is the representative of the human element. And here also, before reason could become the fertilizing principle of the Church, it had to move away from it in order that it might be at liberty to develop all its powers; after the human element was completely segregated, and then in that separateness became aware of its helplessness, it will be able to enter into a free union with the divine foundation of Christianity, which has been preserved in the Eastern Church—and, in consequence of that free union, to give birth to the spiritual mankind.

BIBLIOGRAPHY

SOLOVYEV, S. VLADIMIR: *Sobranie Sochinenij* Pod redaktsiej S. M. Solovieva i E. L. Radlova. St. Peterburg, Knigoizdatelstvo Prosveshtchenia, 1911 goda. Tom 1, 2, 3, 4, 5, 6, 7, 8 i 9 dopolnitelnij.

SOLOVYEV, S. VLADIMIR: *La Russie et l'Eglise Universelle*, Paris.

SOLOVYEV, S. VLADIMIR: *Stikhotvorenia* (Poems).

SOLOVYEV, S. VLADIMIR: *Pisma* (Letters) Tom, 1, 2, 3.

ALIS, ADHEMAR: *The Russian Newman Wladimir Soloviev*, New York 1933, *Thought* v. 8.

AMBROZAITIS, K.: *Die Staatslehre W. S. Soloview*, 1927.

AMFITEATROFF, A.: *V. S. Soloviev, Nekrolog, Dwe Vstrechi, Tri Vstrechi, Zametchaniya i Lektsii*, Literaturnij Albom, 1907.

ANDREYEVITCH: *Ocherki Tekoutschei Russkoi Literatoury*, Zhizn, Peterburg 1900.

ANICHKOFF, E. V.: *Ocherki Razvitia Esteticheskich Outenij.* Voprosy Teorii i Psychologii Tvorchestva, T. I. Kharkov, 1915.

ASTAFJEV, K.: *K. Sporou s V. S. Solovievim*, Russkij Vestnik, St. Peterburg, 1890, v. 210.

BALASHOV, V.: *Vsled za Solovievym*, Slovo Istiny, 1913, January 1.

BEGOUEN, COMTE: *Chez les Yougoslaves il y a trente deux ans.* Paris, 1919.

BELOTSVETOV, N.: *Das Raetsel von Vladimir Soloviev*, Das Goetheanum 1933.

BELYI, A. (B. BOUGAEFF): *Pervoie Svidanie*, Berlin, 1922.

BELYI, A. (B. BOUGAEFF): *Vospominania o Bloke*, Epopeia, Berlin, 1922.

BELYI, A. (B. BOUGAEFF): *Na Roubezhe dvoukh Stoletij*, Moskva, 1930.

BERDYAEV, N.: *O Kharaktere Rouskoi Religioznoi Mysli 19-go Veka*, Sovremennyia Zapiski, 1930, T. X211.

BERG, L. (DR.): *Die Roemisch-katolischme Kirche und die Orthodoxen Russen.*

BEZOBRAZOVA, S. M.: *Byl li V. S. Soloviev Katolikom*, Rousskaya Mysl, Moskva, 1915. *Vospominania o Brate V. Solovieve*, Minouvshie Gody, St. Peterburg, 1908.

BLOK, A.: *Pisma Aleksandra Bloka*, Leningrad, 1925.

BLOK, A.: *S. Predisloviem i Primetchaniami M. A. Beketovoy*, Leningrad, 1927.

BOKOVNEFF, PAVEL: *Die Erkenntnisstheorie Solovievs*, Der Russische Gedanke, Bonn, 1934, Ergenzungsbau, N.3.

BOSFOROFF, M. S.: *Neskolko Slov o Znatchenii V. S. Solovieva*, Vera i Rodina, 1925, Nos 20-22 Avgust i Sentiabr.

BULGAKOV, N. S.: *Chto Daet Sovremennomu Soznaniu Filosofia V. Solovieva*, Voprosy Filosofii i Psichologii, Moskva, 1907.

BULGAKOV, OTETS SERGEI: *Agnets Bojiy*, Parizh, 1936.

BULGAKOV, OTETS SERGEI: *Uteshitel*, Parizh, 1938.
BULGAKOV, OTETS SERGEI: *Sophia*, Parizh, 1938.
BULGAKOV, OTETS SERGEI: *Lestvitza Iakovleva*, Parizh, 1928.
BULGAKOV, S. N.: *Tikhiya Doumy*, Sbornik Statei.
BUTLER, CHR.: *Solovief*, Downside Review, Exeter 1932, v. 50.
CHALUPNY, E.: *Pravny Filosofie V. S. Solovieva*, Vys Myto (s.d.)
CHULKOFF: *Poezia V. Solovieva*, Voprosy Zhizni, St. Peterburg, 1905.
CHULMAKOFF, V.: *Sviastchenaya Kniga Tota*, Velikie Arkanytura, Moskva, 1916.
DAVIDOFF, N.: *Iz Vospominanij o Vl. Solovieva*, Golos Minuvshego, Moskva, 1916, T. 12.
DEINER, I.: *Prorok Sv. Edinstva*, Slovo Istiny, 1914, Janvaria 1-go.
DELLA SETA: *Nationalismo e Cosmopolitanismo nell Etica di Vladimiro Soloviev*, Conferenze e Prolusioni, 1914.
DOSTOEVSKY, M. F.: *Pisma F. M. Dostoevskago k Zhene*, Moskva-Leningrad, 1926.
DUDDINGTON, N.: *The Religious Philosophy of Vl. Solovieff*, Hibbert Journal, Boston, 1917, v. 15.
ENGELGHARDT, N.: *Idealy Vl. Solovieva*, Rousskij Vestnik, St. Peterburg, 1902.
FLORINSKY, O. P.: *Stolp i Outverzhdenie Istiny*, Moskva, 1914.
FLOROVSKY, OTETS GEORGII: *Puti Russkago Bogosloviya.* Parizh, 1937.
FLOROVSKY, OTETS GEORGII: *Novya Knigi o Vladimire Solovieve*, Izvestia Odesskago Biograficheskago Obschestva, Odessa, 1913.
GERRARD, TH.: *Vl. Soloviev the Russian Newman*, Catholic World, New York, 1927.
GIZETTI, A.: *O Mirosozertzanii Vl. Solovieva*, Zavety, St. Peterburg, 1914.
GOETZ, F.: *Ob Otnosheniakh Vl. Solovieva k Evreiskomu Voprosou*, Voprosy Filosofii i Psychologii, Moskva, 1904.
HERBIGNY, M.: *Vladimir Soloviev a Russian Newman*, 1918.
HERBIGNY, M.: *L'unité dans le Christ.*
HESSEN, S. J.: *Borba Outopii i Avtonomii Dobra v Mirovozrenii Dostoevskago i Vl. Solovieva*, Sovremenniya Zapiski, Parizh, 1931, T. 45, 46.
Iz Literatournago Proshlago, Saltykoff—Vl. Soloviev, Bulleteni Literatoury i Zhizni, Moskva, 1913.
Iz Literaturnago Proshlago Buleteni Literatoury i Zhizni, Moskva, 1913, T. 12.
Iz Vospominanij Koni Buleteni Literatoury i Zhizni, Moskva, 1912, T. 6.
Iz Vospominanij o Vl. Solovieve, Vestnik Evropy, St. Peterburg, 1913.
JANKELEVITCH, J.: *Quelques tendances de la pensée philosophique Russe, Wl. Soloviev philosophe spiritualiste et mystique*, Revue de Synthèse Historique, Paris, 1912, v. 24.

KIREYEFF, A.: *Neskolko Zametchanij na Statyu Vl. Solovieva 'Velikji Spor'*, Moskva, 1883, Journal Rous.

KOCHEVNIKOFF, A.: *Die Geschichtsphilosophie Vl. Solovievs*, Russische Gedanke, Bonn 1930, Jahrgang I.

KOCHEVNIKOFF, A.: *La Metaphysique religieuse de Vladimir Soloviev*, Revue d'Histoire et de la Philosophie Religieuse, 1934 et 1935.

KONI, A.: *Vl. S. Soloviev*, Vestnik Evropy, T. I.

KONI, A.: *Vl. S. Soloviev v Ego 'Na Zhiznenom Puti.'*, Revel, 1923, T. 4.

KOUSMIN-KARAVAIEFF: *Iz Vospominanij o V. S. Solovieve*, Vestnik Evropy, St. Peterburg, 1900, T. 206.

KOZLOFF, A.: *Vl. S. Soloviev Kak Filosof*, Znanie, St. Peterburg, 1875.

KRUKOVSKY, A. V.: *Vladimir Soloviev Kak Myslitel i Tchelovek*, 1905, Rousskij Pochin.

LANZ HENRI: Slavonic Review.

LAVRIN, JANKO: *Vladimir Solovyev*. Slavonic and East European Revue, London, 1930-1931, December 9th, June 10th.

LESSEVICH, V.: *Kak Inogda Pishutsia Dissertatsii*, Otechestvenyia Zapiski, St. Peterburg, 1875.

LEVITSKI, S.: *Pravoslavie i Narodnostj*, Moskva, 1888.

LOPATIN, L. N.: *Filosofskoye Mirosozertzanie Vl. Solovieva*, Voprosy Filosofii i Psychologii, Moskva, 1901.

LOSSKI, N.: *Die Lehre Wl. Solovievs von der Evolution*, Bonn, 1930, T. I.

LOSSKI, N.: *The Philosophy of Vl. Soloviev*, Slavonic Revue, V. 2, London, 1923-1924.

LOURIE, OSSIP: *Vladimir Soloviev*, Revue Philosophique, Paris, 1914, v. S.

LUKJANOFF, S. M.: *O Vl. S. Solovieve*, Petrograd, Gosud. Tipofrafia, 1921.

LUKJANOFF, S. M.: *Yunosheskij Roman Vl. S. Solovieva v Dvoinom Osvestchenii*, Journal Ministerstva Narodnago Prosvestchenia, Petrograd, 1914.

LUKJANOFF, S. M.: *Zametki o Teoreticheskoi Filosofii Vl. S. Solovieva*, Journal N. Prosvestchenia, St. Peterburg, 1909.

MAKSHEYEVA, N.: *Vospominania o V. S. Solovieve*, Vestnik Evropy, St. Peterburg, 1910, T. 264.

MATVEIEFF, P.: *V. S. Soloviev*, Rousskij Vestnik, St. Peterburg, 1903, T. 288.

MEDVEDSKY, K.: *Pamiati Vl. S. Solovieva*, Istoritcheskij Vestnik, Dekabr 1903.

MILIOUKOFF, P. N.: *Ocherki po Istorii Rousskoj Koultoury*, T. 11, Parizh, 1931.

MILIOUKOFF, P. N.: *Po Povodu Zametchanij Vl. Solovieva*, Voprosy Filosofii i Psychologii, Moskva, 1893.

MOCHOULSKI, K.: *Vladimir Soloviev*, Zhizn i Outchenie, Y.M.C.A. Press, Paris, 1936.

MOKIEVSKI, P. V.: *Dobro Vl. Solovieva* Rousskoye Bogatstvo, St. Peterburg, 1897.

MOROZOFF, F. (ARCHIMANDRITE): *Religiosno-Filisofskoie Mirovozrenia Vl. S. Solovieva*, Warszawa, 1928.

MOSKOFF, EUGENE: *The Russian Philosopher Chaadayev, His Ideas and His Epoch*, New York, 1937.

MUCKERMANN, F8.: *Abendland und Morgenland bei Soloviev*, in: Stimmen der Zeit, Freiburg, Breisgau, 1924, Jahrgang 54.

MUCKERMANN, R. P.: *Soloviev und das Abendland*, Grünewald, Mainz, 1926.

NEUMANN, O.: *Wladimir S. Soloviev*, Deutsche Monatsschrift, fuer Russland, Reval, 1913.

NIKIFOROFF, N.: *Peterburgskoye Studentchestvo i Vlad. S. Solovyev*, Vestnik Evropy, St. Peterburg, 1912, God 47, T. I.

NOVGORODZEFF, P.: *Ideia Prava v Filosofii Vl. S. Solovieva*, Voprosy Filosofii i Psychologii, Moskva, 1901.

OBOLENSKY, A.: *Opyty Postroyenija Naouchno-Filosofskoj Religii*, Mysl, St. Peterburg, 1880.

OSTROGORSKI: *Afonskie Isichasty i Ikh Protivniki*, Zapiski Rousskago Nauchnago-Instituta, v Belgrade, 1931, Vypusk 5.

PETROVSKI, A.: *Pamiati Vl. Solovieva*, Voprosy Filosofii i Psychologii, Moskva, 1901.

POGODIN, A. L.: *Vl. S. Soloviev i Episkop Strosmajer*, Rousskaya Mysl, Praga, 1923-1924, Kniga 9-12.

PYPINA-LYATSKAYA, V.: *V. S. Soloviev Stranitchka iz Vospominanij*, Golos Minouvshago, Moskva, 1914.

R. G.: *V. S. Soloviev*, Rousskij, Vestnik, St. Peterburg, 1900, T. 268.

RACHINSKI, G. A.: *Vzgliad V. S. Solovieva na Krasotou*, Moskva, 1901.

RADLOV, E.: *Estetika Vl. Solovieva*, Vestnik Evropy, St. Peterburg, 1907, T. 243.

RADLOV, E.: *Charakter Tvortchestva Vl. S. Solovieva*, Journal Min. Nar. Prosv., St. Peterburg, 1909.

RADLOV, E.: *Mistizism Vl. S. Solovieva*, Vestnik Evropy, T. 236, St. Peterburg, 1905.

RADLOV, E.: *Sobranie Sotchinenij V. S. Solovieva*, Journal Min. Nar. Prosv. St. Peterburg, 1905, T. 6.

RADLOV, E.: *Vl. S. Soloviev Nekrolog*, Journal Min. Nar. Prosv. St. Peterburg, 1900.

RADLOV, E.: *Vl. S. Soloviev Zhizn i Outchenie* St. Peterburg, Obrazovanie, 1913.

RAPPOPORT, S. J.: *The Russian Philosopher V. Solovyev*, Contemporary Review, New York, 1913, v. 108.

RONAN, M. V.: *Vl. Soloviev, a Russian Newman,* Irish Ecclesiastical Record, Dublin, 1916, Series 5, v. 8.

ROSANOFF, V.: *Iz Starykh Pisem,* Pisma Vl. S. Solovieva, Zolotoe Rouno, Moskva, 1907.

ROSANOFF, V. V.: *Ob Odnoi Osobennoi Zaslouge V. S. Solovieva,* Novy Puti, St. Peterburg, 1904.

ROSANOFF, V. V.: *Otvet Vl. Solovievou,* Rousskij Vestnik, St. Peterburg, 1894, T. 231.

ROSANOFF, V. V.: *Pamiati Vl. Solovieva,* Mir Isskoustva, St. Peterburg, 1900, T. 4.

ROSANOFF, V. V.: *Svoboda i Vera,* Rousskij Vestnik, St. Peterburg, 1894, T. 230.

SACKE, GEORG: *W. S. Solovievs Geschichtsphilosophie,* Ost-Europa Verlag, 1929.

SBORIK-PERVY: *O Vl. Solovieve,* Moskva, Puti, 1911.

Sbornik Statei Pamiati Vl. S. Solovieva, Izdanie Pouti, Moskva, 1910.

SCYKARSKY, WLADIMIR: *Solovievs Philosophie der All-Einheit,* Humanitariniu Mokslu Fakultetas, Kaunas, Lietuvos Universitetas. Humanitariniu Mokslu Fakulteto Rastai, Kaunas, 1932, vol. 9. Anhang: Wl. Solovievs religioese und philosophische Lyrik.

SETNITSKI, N. A.: *Rousskie Mysliteli o Kitae,* Kharbin, 1926.

SIKORSKI, J. A.: *Nravstvennoe Znatchenie Litchnosti Vl. Solovieva,* Rechj, 1900. Otcherk iz Voprossov Nervno-Psicho-logicheskoi-Meditdiny, T. 6.

SKESTOV, L.: *Oumozrenie i Apokalipsis,* Sovrenennye Zapiski, Parizh, 1927, T. 33.

SKOBTZOVA, VL.: *Mirosozertzanie Vl. Solovieva,* Parizh, Y.M.C.A. Press, 1929.

SLONIMSKI, L.: *Vl. Soloviev,* Vestnik Evropy, St. Peterburg, 1900, T. 205.

SPASSOVICH, V. D.: *Vl. S. Soloviev Kak Poublitzist,* Vestnik Evropy, St. Peterburg, 1901, T. 207.

STANKEVITCH, ALEXANDER VL.: *Tri Bezsilia Tri Sily,* Vestnik Evropy, St. Peterburg, 1877, T. 2.

STRAKHOFF, H. N.: *Nasha Koultoura i Vsemirnoe Yedinstvo,* Rousskij Vestnik, St. Peterburg, 1888, T. 198.

STRAKHOFF, H. N.: *Poslednij Otvet Vl. Solovievou,* Rousskij Vestnik, St. Peterburg, 1889, T. 200.

STRAKHOV, P.: *Istoria i Kritika Filosofii,* Journal Min. Narodnago Prosvestchenia, St. Peterburg, 1891.

STREMOOUKHOFF, D.: *Vl. Soloviev et Son Oeuvre Messianique,* Paris, 1935.

STRUVE, P.: *Pamiati Vl. Solovieva,* Mir Bozhiy, St. Peterburg, 1900.

TAVERNIER, E.: *A Great Russian Philosopher,* The Nineteenth Century, 1916.

TIKHOMIROV, D. C.: *Letopis Petchati po Voprossou o Terpimostt.* Rousskoye Obozrenie, Moskva, 1893.

TIKHOMIROV, L. A.: *Letopis Petchati, Dva Obyasnenia,* Rousskoe Obozrenie, Moskva, 1894.

TIKHOMIROV, L. A.: *Letopis Petchati, Soustchestvouet-li Svoboda?* Rousskoe Obozrenie, Moskva, 1894.

TROUBETSKOY, S. N.: *Osnovnoye Natchalo Outchenia V. S. Solovieva,* Voprossi Filosofii i Psychologii, Moskva, 1901.

TROUBETSKOY, S. N.: *Smertj Vl. Solovieva,* Vestnik Evropy, St. Peterburg, 1900, T. 205.

TROUBETSKOY, S. N.: *Tri Razgovora,* Voprossy Filosofii i Psychologii, Moskva, 1900.

TROUBETSKOY, E.: *K. Voprossou o Mirosozertzanii Vl. S. Solovieva,* Voprossy Filosofii i Psychologii, Moskva, 1913.

TROUBETSKOY, E.: *Kroushenie Teokratii v Tvoreniakh Vl. S. Solovieva,* Rousskaya Mysl, Moskva, 1912, Janvar.

TROUBETSKOY, E.: *Mirosozertzanie V. S. Solovieva,* Moskva, 1913, Mamontov.

TROUBETSKOY, E.: *E. L. Radlov o Vl. Solovieve,* Rousskaya Mysl, Moskva, 1913.

TROUBETSKOY, E.: *V. S. Soloviev i L. Lopatin,* Voprossy Filosofii i Psychologii, Moskva, 1914.

TROUBETSKOY, E.: *Zhiznennaia Zadatcha Solovieva i Vsemirnyi Krisis Zhizni Ponimaniia,* Voprossy Filosofii i Psychologii, Moskva, 1912.

TROUBETSKOY, E.: *Smysl Zhizni,* Praga.

TZERTELEV, D. (KNIAZ): *Pamiati Vl. Solovieva,* Voprossy Filosofii i Psychologii, Moskva, 1901.

Vladimirskii Sbornik v Pamiat 950-letia Krestchenia Roussi, '988-1938' Koudakov Institute, Belgrade.

VOLYRSKI, A.: *Smysl Voiny,* Kritika. Severnyi Vestnik, St. Peterburg, 1895.

VVEDENSKI, A.: *O Mistitzizme i Kritizizme v Teorii Poznania V. S. Solovieva,* Voprossy Filosofii i Psychologii, Moskva, 1901.

WESSELING, THEODORE: *Vladimir Soloviev.* The Eastern Churches Quarterly, 1937.

YAROSH, K.: *Inostrannye i Rousskie Kritiki Rossii,* Rousskij Vestnik, St. Peterburg, 1889, T. 200.

YELTZOVA, K.: *Sny Nezdeshniye K 25-Oi Kontchine Solovieva,* Sovremennye Zapiski, Parizh, 1926, Kn. 28.

Z. S.: *Filosofskoe Vozrenie Vl. Solovieva,* Novy Putj, St. Peterburg, 1903.

ZDZINCHOVSKI, M.: *Le Dualisme dans la Pensée Religieuse Russe* Vladimir Soloviev, Cahiers de la Nouvelle Journée, N. 8 L'âme Russe, Paris, 1927.

This book is set in 11-pt. Fournier roman, a letter based on the original design by Pierre Simon Fournier. Fournier was the first of many famous type-designers of the eighteenth century to cut complete families of type. Large- and small-faced romans, condensed, bold, and italic series, are shown in his type specimen book Modèles de caractères, published in 1742. The invention of the point system of type measurement is ascribed to him.

The Monotype version used in this book is based on one of Fournier's medium text types, one of the narrowest book faces available today. The accompanying italic version is a graceful letter differing in its fundamental conception from other italic types.

Typography by Henry Jacob